FRACTURING THE FOUNDING

FRACTURING THE FOUNDING

How the Alt-Right Corrupts the Constitution

John E. Finn

ROWMAN & LITTLEFIELD
Lanham • Boulder • New York • London

Published by Rowman & Littlefield
An imprint of The Rowman & Littlefield Publishing Group, Inc.
4501 Forbes Boulevard, Suite 200, Lanham, Maryland 20706
www.rowman.com

6 Tinworth Street, London SE11 5AL, United Kingdom

British Library Cataloguing in Publication Information Available

Library of Congress Cataloging-in-Publication Data

Finn, John E.
Fracturing the Founding : how the alt-right corrups the constitution
ISBN: 978-1-5381-2367-6 (cloth)
ISBN: 978-1-5381-2368-3 (electronic)

♾ ™ The paper used in this publication meets the minimum requirements of American National Standard for Information Sciences Permanence of Paper for Printed Library Materials, ANSI/NISO Z39.48-1992.

Printed in the United States of America

To Dottie and John

Of all the things which
wisdom provides to make
us entirely happy, much
the greatest is the
possession of friendship.
–Epicurus

CONTENTS

ACKNOWLEDGMENTS

I owe more than a few words of thanks to the many colleagues, friends, and students who helped me with this project, but a few words, and an apology that there is not more, are all I can offer.

Thank you especially to Djuna Schamus, my research assistant in the fall of 2016, and to the students in two iterations of my seminar on alternative constitutionalisms. Thanks as well to George Thomas, of Claremont McKenna College; George Hawley, of the University of Alabama; David Neiwert; Jennifer Tucker of Wesleyan University; Chi-Hoon Kim; Kate McCrery; Jon Golbe; Carter Deane; Bob Osborne; Bob Wipfler; and Rob Wipfler, all of whom who kindly read parts of the manuscript or offered encouragement. A word of thanks also to Angela Miller for her early support and enthusiasm, and to Jon Sisk and the good people at Rowman & Littlefield.

Mary and Judi of BillowHouse merit a warm thank you for a warm stay during a couple of cold months by the beach.

Finally, a sadly inadequate thank you to Linda, who not only read parts of the manuscript, but also had to listen to me talk about it—undoubtedly worse.

All of the errors, and the drinks, are on me.

INTRODUCTION

Some years ago, while I was on sabbatical in a small town in Maine writing a book on the Constitution, an eager reference librarian invited me to a talk at the local library. I don't recall the name of the lecturer or the title of her talk, but I do remember how alarming the event was. The speaker was from a group I had only vaguely heard of—the Patriot Party; or the Constitutionalist Party; or the Tea Party; or some such—and was a self-educated expert on the American Constitution. She called herself a "Constitutional Patriot." Her theme was how politicians and judges, aided and abetted by ill-informed and inattentive citizens, had perverted the meaning of the "True Constitution." The True Constitution, she explained, tolerates no restrictions on speech or on guns or on private property, does not recognize the supremacy of federal law to state and local law, and is built upon the principle of separate but equal (which is to say, but she did not say, "white"). The Miracle at Philadelphia was divinely inspired, she argued, and is certainly Christian. The meaning of every provision in the Constitution is plain and if less than plain, discerned easily by appealing to what the Founders intended it to mean or, failing that, to Holy Scripture, from whence it comes.

The constitution she described bears only a faint resemblance to the Constitution I know and have taught for over three decades.

I had plenty to say, but shamefully I said nothing. There is no excuse for my silence. But I was taken aback. And self-sure in my conviction that intelligent, informed, and engaged citizens would reject her account of the Constitution, not only because it is wrong, but

also because it is a bleak, uninviting way to think about our life
together as Americans. Obviously, I was mistaken. . . .

Although it has been around for a while, the Alt-right achieved a special sort of notoriety in the 2016 presidential election. Condemned by candidate Clinton (in a widely publicized speech that many both in and outside the Alt-right think greatly energized the movement),[1] and tolerated if not applauded by candidate and President Trump,[2] some of us dismiss the Alt-right as a temporary episode of ill humor in the body politic. Even after some in the Alt-right have turned violent and murderous (and celebrate it!),[3] we tell ourselves Charlottesville is a one-off, an aberration.

But Charlottesville has happened before and will happen again. The hateful ideas and the racist violence associated with the radical right and events like Charlottesville long predate the Alt-right and are not unique to it. As the blog *Media Matters* has observed, "In many ways the Alt-right is a rebranding of classic white nationalism for the 21st century."[4]

Indeed, if we define it in terms of what it believes instead of what it names itself, the Alt-right has been a part of American political culture for a very long while.[5] Its origins lay in a protracted history of violence associated with certain elements of right-wing extremism in American politics.[6] The Alt-right is simply the most recent, showiest iteration of a long and ugly tradition, helped along by economic uncertainty and demographic change and shrewdly adapted to the new world of social media.

Most Americans think of the Alt-right as fervent nationalists who "profess an ultra-love of America"[7] as the loudest and most visible part of a resurgent, ultra-conservative right-wing movement in the United States. The Southern Poverty Law Center describes the Alt-right as a set of far-right ideologies, groups, and individuals "whose core belief is that 'white identity' is under attack by multicultural forces using 'political correctness' and 'social justice' to undermine white people and 'their' civilization."[8] As George Hawley observes, the Alt-right is "vulgar, irreverent, ironic, and goofy."[9] And admittedly, avowedly, proudly racist.

Not many of the movement's chief proponents dress themselves or their political program (or is it pogrom?) in the language and ideals of the American Constitution, but in several surprising ways, the Alt-right embraces a comprehensive if unsettling and mistaken understanding about what the Constitution means, where it comes from, and about who and what it protects.

Often when I say the Alt-right has a constitution or a constitutional philosophy, I get looks of puzzlement or incredulity. As George Hawley notes in his insightful book, *Making Sense of the Alt-right* (2017), many of the Alt-right's leading voices appear to have no interest in the Founding Fathers or their handiwork. The Alt-right "does not care at all about limited government per se. It does not even share conservatism's passion for the basic symbols of American patriotism,"[10] including its constitutional heritage. In some ways, the Alt-right's historical disinterest in things constitutional marks a major point of divide between it and other right-wing extremist movements, especially recent ones, such as the Patriot and Militia movements, and the Tea Party.

We can argue about whether Trump's presidency has emboldened if not institutionalized the Alt-right,[11] but long after the Alt-right itself fades central elements of its thinking and ideology will continue to foul American political life. The Alt-right does not exist in isolation. It is just one element in a much larger universe that David Neiwert has called Alt-America.[12] Alt-America "is an alternative universe that has a powerful resemblance to our own, except that it's a completely different America . . . ,"[13] one in which militant racists, emboldened by a powerful right-wing media, have found common ground with the far right, Tea Party conservatives, and Republican activists.

Alt-America isn't simply a rhetorical device—it's both a notional and a physical space, and it has its own constitution, the Alt-constitution. (As we shall see in Chapter 5, some in the radical right even claim to form their own states and their own governments, free of any constitutional or legal restraints except of their own choosing.)[14] Like the Alt-right itself, the Alt-constitution has its origins in a long history of extremist thinking about the Constitution, especially in the Patriot and militia movements, among Christian Identitarians, and in the Tea Party. For that reason alone, it makes more sense to speak of the Alt-constitution than the Alt-right constitution.

To be clear, I don't dispute Hawley's observation about the Alt-right's rhetorical distance from the radical right's constitutional patriotism. What animates the Alt-right is a commitment to white supremacy; its politics are the politics of identity, not a politics grounded in the constitutional ideals of limited government, the separation of powers, federalism, or even individual liberty. Hawley is quite right to conclude that for the Alt-right, "If the Constitution dictates a policy that is inimical to white interests, then the Constitution is the problem."[15]

What this perspective misses is that for many in the larger territory of Alt-America, the Constitution, properly conceived, *is* white. Questions of identity, racial, religious, and cultural, fuel right-wing extremism in the United States. Questions of identity are questions about inclusion and exclusion; about who is entitled to participate in the institutions and rituals of democratic governance; about immigration; education; social welfare; housing; work; and religion. All of these matters turn on who We the People are and who we want to be.[16] Indeed, the most fundamental questions about the American Constitution have always been about identity.[17]

The Alt-right's march in Charlottesville was advertised as an effort to "Unite the Right." The phrasing matters because it reveals both a truth and a blueprint. The truth it lets slip is that the Alt-right differs from other elements of the extreme right wing only by degree, not by kind. The Alt-right is just one of the actors that make up the larger universe of Alt-America, and many of its central precepts and beliefs, though not all, are held in common with those actors. The strategy it reveals— reaching out to those other actors and forming tactical alliances with them—is one that might seem at odds with a movement that sometimes seeks to torch everything and everyone, establishment conservatives (RINOs and "normies") among them. But it is a strategy made possible precisely because key elements of its thinking are common currency in the extremist right.

What unites the radical right?[18] The obvious answer, white racism, is also the correct answer. But the radical right is also united by a shared effort to get the Constitution 'right'—to preach a (true) vision of the Constitution that reflects and sanctifies key elements of militant conservative politics. Even casual observers know the radical right is riddled not only with racists but also with gun nuts and speech freaks—with people who think their right to brandish both guns and words as weapons are absolutely and completely protected by the Second and First Amendments. (I have reversed their order because in many far-right circles the purpose of the Second Amendment is said to be to guarantee the First, as a popular bumper sticker reads: "I Second the First.") As I show in detail in later chapters, however, the Alt-constitution embraces a comprehensive, if not entirely coherent understanding of the American constitutional order writ large—one that reaches past the First and Second amendments, and beyond even the Bill of Rights. The Alt-constitution includes a certain way of thinking about citizenship, about the relationship between the states and the federal government, and about how democracy and elections should work, as well as a way of picturing the role of race, religion, ethnicity, and gender in public affairs.[19] At the center of the Alt-constitution is a vision of American political life that emphasizes absolute rights and unassailable liberties (especially for speech and guns); states' rights and a corresponding suspicion of the federal government; racial classifications recognized and legitimated by law; and privilege for white Christians.[20]

The Alt-constitution also has its own historiography. For many in the far right, the Constitution and several other canonical works, including the Declaration of Independence, are "sacred texts on par with the Christian Bible."[21] Indeed, much of the ideology and thinking of the radical right invokes the Constitution and a few other founding documents as holy text, no less vital to the concerns of men and women than the Bible and, like the Bible, as the revealed word of God. In the radical right, constitution-worship is an article of faith, every bit as fundamental to its worldview as its better known convictions about race, religion, politics, history, and culture.

Continuing with religious comparisons, the Alt-constitution is also an object of missionary zeal. Getting the Constitution 'right,' in both senses of the word, requires an ambitious and comprehensive program of civic education for adults and children alike. As we will see, such programs feature prominently among citizens of the Alt-constitution.

If we don't look too closely, there is much about the Alt-constitution that is familiar, but different. The Alt-constitution seems familiar because it dresses itself up in congenial myths and fairy tales about the Founders and Philadelphia. Its central precepts, however, have less to do with the Founding and James Madison than with Reconstruction and Jim Crow. The Alt-constitution is the antebellum constitution of slavery, states' rights, and nullification. It is the constitution of *Dred Scott v. Sandford* (1857) and *Plessy v. Ferguson* (1896). It sanctifies some provisions (such as the First and Second amendments) as absolute and unalterable, but it also dismisses other parts of the text (such as the Fourteenth Amendment) as fundamentally illegitimate.

I do not aspire in this book to a dispassionate, impartial, or objective account of the Alt-constitution. My purpose instead is to highlight the danger the Alt-constitution poses for the polity. By examining in detail the constitutional beliefs of a number of groups, organizations, and individuals that make up Alt-America (some prominent and some obscure), I hope to show concerned citizens where, how, and why the Alt-constitution threatens the ideals and precepts that truly make up the American constitutional tradition. At the heart of the Alt-constitution is a vision of We the People that is ugly and unappealing, a vision that does not honor but stains the work of the Founders.

Three questions inspire the organization and form the general structure of the book.

1. Who is the Alt-right?
2. What are the core features and principles of the Alt-constitution?
3. Why does it matter?

I. WHO IS THE ALT-RIGHT?

In Chapter 1, I introduce several of the various groups and organizations that comprise the radical right (they come and go and rearrange themselves with maddening frequency), and in the process distill what the radical right believes about the Constitution. Because my objective is to illuminate the principal constitutional tenets of Alt-constitutionalism, I do not attempt to provide a comprehensive overview of either the Alt-right or the radical right as such. Nor is there any need for such a treatment, as there are some very impressive works already in print.[22]

Not even the most prominent of its advocates knows how big the Alt-right really is or even just who it is, precisely. The Alt-right is less a single issue movement than an informal and uncertain alliance of political activists, interest groups, and personalities, organized around a loose and sometimes baffling set of core beliefs.[23] If there is a single issue that defines the Alt-right, it is a belief in white superiority and a commitment to the cause of white nationalism, or to what some call a "white racial project."[24] Again, this commitment is not unique to the Alt-right as such. As Howard Winant argues, "On the far right the cornerstone of white identity is belief in an ineluctable, unalterable racialized difference between whites and nonwhites."[25] The white racial project has a political agenda that starts from the claim that race mixers and race sympathizers control state and society and have abandoned "traditional values." (This notwithstanding, as the *New York Times* has observed, a very pronounced fetish in the Alt-right for Asian women, explained in part by racist tropes about Asians as a model minority and Asian women as subservient and hypersexual.)[26] The agenda is for white nationalists to "recapture" the state and to restore the commitment to traditional values. In some circles this political agenda is the object of peaceful political change through the ordinary channels of democratic participation. In others, though, armed resistance is thought to be a necessity.[27]

Although race infuses every aspect of Alt-right ideology, there is more to the Alt-right than just race, and "given the movement's ideological diversity, it would be a serious mischaracterization to label the Alt-right as exclusively white nationalism."[28] As George Michael, a historian of the far right, has observed, "The movement . . . is more nuanced, encompassing a much broader spectrum of right-wing activists and intellectuals."[29] In the words of Luke O'Brien, "In the broadest sense, the alt right is a populist revolt against the political establishment."[30]

Mapping the Alt-right and its (sometimes unwilling) fellow travelers therefore requires some attention to matters of definition. This may strike some readers as academic and dry. *These* definitions, however, are fundamentally matters of debate and disagreement, sometimes civil, often ugly, not only about who is an authentic member of the Alt-right fraternity, but more importantly about who merits inclusion in We, the American People.

Fraternal disputes about authenticity and identity have consumed the Alt-right since its beginning. Self-identified members of the Alt-right argue about who qualifies as comates, allies, sympathizers, and potential converts, all in a search for ideological purity. (An obsession with purity is hardly a surprise in a movement dedicated to white nationalism and white identity.) On the other hand, there is widespread agreement about who the enemy is. If you don't know, you can't join the club.

The notion of identity also enjoins how the Alt-right locates itself in the larger universe of far-right conservativism. The Alt-right, far from being unique or a fringe element of the conservative universe, is instead an integral part of it. What is the relationship between the Alt-right and a dozen other right-wing organizations? Is the Alt-right an heir to Posse Comitatus? Is it related to the Christian Identity Movement? To the Militia Movement? To the Sovereign Citizen Movement? Is the Tea Party Alt-right? Are neo-Nazis? What is the relationship between the Alt-right and neo-conservatives and paleo-conservatives and Libertarians and Birchers? A key point in Chapter 1 is that there is no bright line we can use to distinguish the Alt-right from the crowd of political groups, associations, civic organizations, and political activists that make up the radical right in American political life.

II. THE ALT-CONSTITUTION

In Chapters 2 through 6, I explore the ideas and precepts that make up the Alt-constitution.[31] My treatment of the key principles of the Alt-constitution draws heavily on the constitutional thought of a wide variety of radical right-wing sources, even though some of those sources and organizations insist they are neither radical nor part of the Alt-right. My objective in these chapters, however, is not classification or taxonomy. Instead, my aim is to construct a composite view of the Alt-constitution and not to describe in great detail the constitutional thinking of any single group or organization. Sorting out who is *really* a member of the Alt-right and who is not is not all that significant. What *is* significant is that several of the central elements of the Alt-constitution are not limited to the Alt-right, but rather are items of faith in the far right generally.

The constitution the extreme right holds as its faith is an odd admixture of the forgotten, the rejected, the racist, and the bizarre. In brief, the Alt-constitution is arranged around several interlocked constitutional principles, prominent among them First Amendment protections for speech and religion; the Second Amendment and gun rights and private militias; the Fifth Amendment and rights to property; the Ninth and

Tenth amendments; and the Fourteenth Amendment and conceptions of citizenship. The Alt-constitution also has a unique take on the separation of powers doctrine and federalism, and the related doctrines of interposition, nullification, and secession. Behind them all is a theory about who made the Constitution and about who gets to decide what it means.

What is distinctive about Alt-constitutional thinking is not its fixation with these constitutional provisions and doctrines. What is distinctive is what it imagines they mean and how they interact with other hallowed texts, including the Bible; the Declaration of Independence; and the Articles of Confederation; and with legal texts and sources they regard as profane, including the Reconstruction Amendments; the Uniform Commercial Code; and admiralty law.

Many in the Alt-right have no use for Christianity in general or the Christian right in particular,[32] so it is almost ironic that the Alt-constitution trades heavily on a type of constitutional fundamentalism. Writing about the Tea Party's deep affection for all things constitutional, Jill Lepore describes Tea Partiers as "historical fundamentalists," or as committed to the belief that "a particular and quite narrowly defined past—'the founding'—is ageless and sacred and to be worshipped; that certain historical texts—'the founding documents'—are to be read in the same spirit with which religious fundamentalists read, for instance, the Ten Commandments, that the Founding Fathers were divinely inspired . . . and that political arguments grounded in appeals to the founding documents, as sacred texts, and to the Founding Fathers, as prophets, are therefore incontrovertible."[33] Michael Barkun similarly notes, "Just as the radical right has embraced religious fundamentalism, so it has been associated with what might be called legal fundamentalism. . . . [L]egal fundamentalism insists on the literal reading of authoritative legal texts and holds that the true meaning of those texts has been lost through distortions allegedly introduced by corrupt interpreters in the past."[34]

Constitutional fundamentalism is not just a Tea Party phenomenon. It is one of the defining features of the Alt-constitution.[35] We will see that constitutional fundamentalism, like religious fundamentalism, is a comprehensive worldview, self-contained, and impervious to other ways of thinking.

The language of fundamentalism is also apropos because the Alt-constitution trades heavily on the "Miracle at Philadelphia."[36] In Chapter 2, we shall see that the language of miracles is more than simply a metaphor. For constitutional fundamentalists, it is way of understanding who the Founders were, what they believed, as well as who we are and what we believe. The divine origins of the Constitution tell us how (and by whom) the Constitution should be interpreted. Its godly provenance requires that we honor the intentions of the Founders. Originalism is not simply about honoring (or idealizing) the constitutional document—it is about "fidelity to a generation of past Americans who, quite simply, knew more about the principles of liberty and power than any generation since."[37] Like the Constitution itself, originalism is an item of faith for the far right. One may be an originalist without being a member of the far right or the Alt-right, but one cannot identify as far right without subscribing to originalism.[38]

Especially in light of current events, it may seem the Alt-constitution has but a single provision, regarding freedom of speech. In Chapter 3, "Speech Freaks," I consider the nature and the meaning of the Alt-first amendment. The Alt-first amendment is a curious creature. It is both more expansive and less ambitious than the First Amendment proper. The Alt-first amendment is absolute and acknowledges no limits on speech. The words "shall make no law" in the Alt-first amendment must be taken literally. The Alt-first amendment thus protects all manner of hateful and bigoted speech, no matter how racist, sexist, or inflammatory. It must likewise be read expansively, to disallow alleged limits on speech that originate not only in the actions of governments but also from private parties and other citizens. On the other hand, these expansive protections protect only certain, favored speakers and only certain, favored points of view. The absolutist approach to the first amendment, for example, does not apply to the establishment and free exercise clauses, which many in the far right argue guarantee religious freedom only to Christians.

In Chapter 4, "Gun Nuts," we see the same constitutional philosophy regarding the Alt-second amendment. Like the Alt-first, the Alt-second amendment is absolute: It guarantees citizens a right to own any and all weapons of their own choosing for any reason, without restriction. The Alt-second amendment is built on the premise that every individual has a God-given right to defend himself, his family, and his property against predations, real and imagined, by governments and by other citizens. The same philosophy means also that the Alt-second amendment protects the rights of citizens to join private militias and to entertain (and to prepare for) the possibility of armed rebellion—a possibility made imminent by the looming threat of gun control and the disarmament of American citizens by their government.

Chapters 5 and 6 take up the most incomprehensible parts of the Alt-constitution—its theories of citizenship and its reliance upon a peculiar understanding of the "common law." In many ways, the common law courts movement and the related "Sovereign Citizens" movement are the logical outgrowth of several Alt-constitutional principles taken to an extreme. As we shall see in Chapter 5, building upon their understanding of social contract theory, federalism, and the First and Second amendments, Sovereign Citizens deny the constitutional authority of the federal and most state governments over their lives and their property. They invoke "the common law" (as they conceive it), to withdraw from the jurisdictional octopus of the federal government and to create their own grand juries and their own courts, staffed by self-taught and self-appointed judges and juries.

In Chapter 6, we consider those parts of the Constitution of the United States the Alt-constitution rejects as inauthentic and illegitimate. First among them are the Reconstruction amendments, and especially the Fourteenth Amendment. The Alt-constitution regards the Fourteenth as improperly ratified and as fundamentally incompatible with the "organic" constitution (which constitutional fundamentalists hold includes only the text of 1787 and the Bill of Rights).[39] Sovereign Citizens in particular view the Fourteenth Amendment with suspicion, seeing in it a conspiracy to deprive (white) citizens of their inalienable rights and replacing their "sovereign" citizenship with a vastly inferior "federal" or "contract" citizenship.

The Alt-constitution also jettisons the Sixteenth Amendment (regarding the income tax), which it sees not only as a violation of property rights, but as instrumental to the unconstitutional expansion of the federal government. Perhaps less obviously, the Alt-constitution also has no room for the Seventeenth Amendment (concerning election of Senators), and some folks have concerns about the Nineteenth Amendment (respecting voting rights for women) as well.

III. WHY THE ALT-CONSTITUTION MATTERS

Some voices in the Alt-right disparage earlier generations of conservative thinkers as "constitutionalists," a term of insult "because it is obvious that the Constitution has not only failed, completely, by its own stated purpose but is being used to restrain the Right. . . . We aren't Conservatives. We aren't philosophers. And we don't care about the Constitution, the Rights of Man, the Enlightenment, the Holocaust, or anything else with capital letters that gets in the way of our success."[40]

The same logic, however, tells us why some in the Alt-right have taken to announcing themselves as constitutional patriots, or at least to invoking constitutional principles (when it suits them). It is no accident that the "Unite the Right" rally in Charlottesville was sold as a defense of freedom of speech. The rally was as much about marketing the right for a popular audience as it was about uniting the right. No matter that it didn't work. It's a long-term strategy. Wrapping one's politics in constitutional paper can be a remarkably effective way of giving noxious ideas mainstream appeal and a patina of legitimacy. This is why Richard Spencer's post-Charlottesville manifesto, "What it Means to be Alt-right," references both the First and Second amendments, if not in name then by principle.[41] This is the stratagem behind branding Alt-right speakers as defenders of freedom of speech. (Is the Alt-right's commitment to freedom of speech sincere? That's not the point.)

Many of us dismiss the Alt-right as bizarre or eccentric. But what the Alt-right thinks about politics, and about the Constitution, cannot be completely separated from right-wing extremism or even mainstream conservative political thought. David Neiwert and George Hawley have both described in detail how several elements of Alt-right political thought trace to earlier right-wing movements.[42] One of the defining elements of the Alt-right is its profound hostility to mainstream conservatism: Hawley notes, "[T]he main target of the Alt-right's wrath, at least for now, is arguably not African Americans, Latinos, or political progressives: it is mainstream conservatives."[43] The Alt-right is thus unlikely to fold into the Republican Party (and would rather destroy it), but political parties often co-opt their ideological critics, and we should not be surprised to find that some of the central elements of Alt-right thinking have made substantial inroads into the conservative movement more broadly. As Greg Johnson, a prominent white nationalist and editor of the webzine *Counter-Currents* has noted, "We cannot remain on the margins. White Nationalism needs to break out and redefine the political mainstream."[44]

Just as scoundrels wrap themselves in the flag,[45] the radical right wraps itself in the Constitution and mythic tales of the Founding. They venerate the Founders and recite solemn vows of constitutional fidelity. Sincere or not, these professions of constitutional devotion serve an important purpose in mainstreaming the radical right's ideological and policy agenda. The extreme right uses its version of the constitution, the Alt-constitution, to legitimate and conceal its racism, bigotry, and sexism, and to appeal to a broader audience.

The Alt-constitution is not the Founders' Constitution. It does not advance the constitutional ideals of due process of law; or of equal protection of the law; or of government based on reason rather than force or chance, to paraphrase *Federalist* #1. The Alt-constitution corrupts those ideals, and in doing so it undermines the very constitutional project it purports to honor. Its vision of government, citizenship, and community, of what it means to pursue a constitutional way of life, is one that all true citizens of the Constitution must denounce.

A NOTE ON STYLE AND USAGE

To distinguish between the Constitution as conventionally understood and the Alt-constitution, I shall capitalize the word Constitution when I mean the former, and I shall use "Alt-constitution" to denote the latter. Similarly, when I refer to specific amendments, I shall use upper case (First Amendment) to refer to the "true" Constitution and lower case (first amendment) when I speak about the Alt-constitutional version of that amendment.

Chapter 1

MAPPING THE ALT-RIGHT AND THE LIKE

Origins, Ideologies, Personalities

Alt-America is populated by a great variety of conservative organizations, associations, obscure political parties, interest groups, civic associations, and churches. These sundry organizations and groups come and go and reorganize and rename themselves with remarkable frequency, though many have been a long-standing part of American political culture. The citizens of Alt-America, like us, are joiners and organizers, drawn to others who share their beliefs and interests. Many of these organizations are small and obscure and nonviolent, but some achieve prominence through inflammatory rhetoric and violence. The Alt-right is just one such group, and arguably not the most significant or influential one. Its recent notoriety and somewhat ambiguous relationship to the other actors and organizations that make up the world of right-wing extremism in the United States make it a good place to begin.

Although it is made up of brash personalities, especially on the Internet, *who* the Alt-right is, like *what* it is, is complicated. Is the Tea Party part of the Alt-right? Is the Militia Movement part of the Alt-right? Are Christian nationalists Alt-right? What about neo-Nazis? What is the difference between the Alt-right, the Alt-Lite, and the Alt-White? Asking such questions helps us to know who the Alt-right is, where it comes from, and why it matters, as well as to understand why and how some of the key elements of its ideology and thinking are part and parcel of right-wing extremism more widely.

WHO IS THE ALT-RIGHT?

Questions of inclusion and exclusion are the heart of the Alt-right movement, if only because so many in the Alt-right are preoccupied with questions of identity and citizenship. German political philosopher Carl Schmitt, a prominent scholar of jurisprudence and public law in Weimar and apologist for the Third Reich, argued that the chief concern of politics is the distinction between "us and them."[1] That same distinction, between *us* (true citizens of the United States) and *them* (everyone else), undergirds right-wing extremism and is especially pronounced in the radical right's understanding of the Fourteenth Amendment to the Constitution, which distinguishes between "Sovereign" citizens and contract or "federal" citizens. Only the former (those who would have been eligible for full citizenship at the time of the Founding) count as full citizens of the American constitutional community. Following this train of thinking, citizenship (and presumably, membership in the Alt-right movement) is restricted to those of us who would have qualified as citizens when the Founders wrote the words, "We the People." We the People, then and now, is limited to whites, males, and Christians,[2] and perhaps to heterosexuals and property owners. (There appears to be some antipathy in the Alt-right to homosexuals and overt hostility to religious minorities, including Jews and Muslims, and many in the Alt-right are skeptical if not contemptuous of Christianity.) Necessarily excluded, not simply from membership in the Alt-right but from full and equal inclusion as citizens in the American constitutional order, are African Americans and others of color, aliens, immigrants (or at least those from "shithole" countries), and anyone who is not full-bodied and gainfully employed. Always implicit and often explicit in such arguments are calls for a return to the doctrine of separate but equal. (Not everyone in the Alt-right subscribes to the "equal" part.) It is a perverse kind of equality, in which only some of us are fully admitted to the great project of democracy and self-governance or entitled to the Blessings of Liberty.

So we can start here: The Alt-right is a perplexing mix of political activists, interest groups, and public personalities, loosely organized around a sometimes self-contradictory set of core beliefs, almost all of which evidence a commitment to white racial superiority, either explicitly or implicitly. A more detailed and insightful inquiry into the Alt-right and its relationship to the larger universe of the radical right requires three things:

1. We need to know how the Alt-right talks about politics.
2. We need to trace its origins, ancestors, and ideology.
3. We need to identify who speaks for the Alt-right.

VOCABULARY AND ICONOGRAPHY.

As with any social movement, one way to recognize the Alt-right is through its vocabulary.[3] The Alt-right likes to deride "cuckservatives" (cuckold + conservative), a term of especial derision it uses to show contempt for mainstream conservatives who have sold out or are too sympathetic to Democrats or liberals.[4] A "cuck" is a milquetoast conservative, and "normies" are people with conventional, mainstream views.[5] Another definition of cuckservative is "a white (non-Jewish) conservative who isn't racially aware."[6] According to *The New Republic*, the term "emerged out of the white supremacist movement as a term of abuse for white conservatives deemed race traitors unwilling to forthrightly defend the interests of white America."[7] This definition tells us that the Alt-right is not equivalent to Republican, conservative, populist, or even right wing. Indeed, the Alt-right ridicules so-called RINOs, or mainstream Republicans who are Republican In Name Only and "who have sold out or are too sympathetic to Democrats or liberals."[8] (Opinions differ, but examples might include Glenn Beck, John McCain, and Jeb Bush.)

Another tag, "Shitlord," lauds true Alt-right believers. The term "DR3" stands for "Dems R Real Racists," a phrase "used by the Alt-right to mock conservatives (e.g., Dinesh D'Souza) who pander to people of color by claiming Democrats are the party of racism and the Ku Klux Klan."[9] Several other entries in the "cucktionary" are little more than racist epithets, such as "Dindu," a slur used to describe African Americans, and "Dindu Nuffin," a racist version of the phrase "'He didn't do nothing,' used to mock the black community's reaction to the arrest or murder of unarmed African-Americans."[10] Slurs abound for Gays (GRID—Gay-related immune deficiency, the antiquated term for

AIDS), Jews (Merchant is one, Shekels is another), and Muslims (Skittles, apparently premised on an infamous tweet by Donald Trump Jr.).

Another common expression in the Alt-right is "red pilling," an allusion to the film *The Matrix*, in which the protagonist Neo (Keanu Reeves) is offered a choice: take a red pill to see the world as it really is, or a blue pill, to remain in a state of ignorant bliss. To red pill, then, is to see the "real" world as the Alt-right sees it (i.e., a world dominated by feminists and racial minorities). "SJW" is a mocking reference to "social justice warriors," used to describe feminists, anti-racists, proponents of LGBTQ rights, and other social progressives. "YWNRU" is shorthand for You Will Not Replace Us, a racist and anti-Semitic chant, first associated with the hate group Identity Evropa and now embraced widely in the Alt-right. (YWNRU was a favorite slogan in Charlottesville.) "ZOG" stands for "Zionist Occupied Government."

Another prominent talking point in the Alt-right movement is the concept of white culture, variously referred to as white culture, white separatism, or white nationalism. Many critics of the Alt-right movement, such as the Anti-Defamation League, argue that terms like culture, heritage, and identity are proxies for "'lightning rod' words such as 'race,' or 'Western Civilization' as a code word for white culture or identity." Most members of the Alt-right "do not make explicit references to white supremacy like the '14 words'" ("We must secure the existence of our people and a future for white children"), a slogan used by neo-Nazis and other hardcore white supremacists,[11] preferring instead to "to talk about preserving European-American identity."[12] In turn, words like diversity and multiculturalism, and policies like affirmative action and community policing, to take just two examples, are designed to promote white genocide. The Alt-right often uses the #whitegenocide hashtag to condemn what they don't like. (The George Lucas film, *Star Wars VII*, for instance, was criticized by the Alt-right for casting African American and female actors in lead roles.)

The Alt-right also has its own iconography.[13] Among these are a confusing assortment of hand signals and tattoos and Internet memes. Of the latter, Pepe the cartoon frog is the best known. Although Pepe was a popular Internet meme for many years,[14] he (I think it's a he) "has been appropriated by white supremacists, particularly those from the 'alt right,' who use it in racist, anti-Semitic or other hateful contexts."[15] Some folks associate Pepe with a parody religion, in which Pepe is actually Kek, an Egyptian deity. Notwithstanding his/her/its innocent origins, Pepe is now on the ADL's list of hate symbols.[16]

Another favorite icon is the "parenthesis meme," in which Jewish names are surrounded by parentheses, typically to target them for abuse on social media: "(((name)))." *The Right Stuff* explains: "The inner parenthesis represent the Jews' subversion of the home [and] destruction of the family through mass-media degeneracy. The next [parenthesis] represents the destruction of the nation through mass immigration, and the outer [parenthesis] represents international Jewry and world Zionism."[17] The Anti-Defamation League includes the echo symbol in its online database of hate symbols. It calls "The echo symbol . . . the online equivalent of tagging a building with anti-Semitic graffiti or taunting someone verbally."[18]

The Alt-right also appropriates the images of various celebrities to spread its message. A favorite is Taylor Swift, whose image it uses as an exemplar of Aryan feminine beauty.[19] Another favorite is Papa John's Pizza, said by *Daily Stormer* to be the "official pizza" of the Alt-right[20] —a claim the company vigorously disavows. Other favorite *Daily Stormer* brands include Wendy's Hamburgers and New Balance tennis shoes.

ORIGINS, ANCESTORS, AND IDEOLOGY

Another way to understand the Alt-right is to ask where it comes from. In part because of its eye-catching reliance on social media and its prominence in the presidential election of 2016, where the Alt-right first entered mainstream public consciousness, the Alt-right may seem like a relatively novel development in United States politics. It's not. According to some accounts, the Alt-right's split with mainstream Republicanism was provoked by President George W. Bush's invasion of Iraq (many in the Alt-right are strict isolationists).[21] The Alt-right has obvious antecedents in several right-wing populist movements, especially in previous right-wing populist campaigns like the Tea Party and the militia movement, but it is distinct from them.

Additional elements of Alt-right ideology include an aversion to political correctness and "opposition to contemporary notions of gender equality and in favor of a more patriarchal society."[22] The latter is typically grounded in a defense of "sex realism," or the proposition that men and women are biologically different and that those differences are properly the foundation for assigning men and women to different roles in society. Some Alt-right members are also adherents of the Men's Rights Movement, which holds that social and legal discrimination against men is a more significant problem than discrimination against women.

As George Hawley has concluded, there is not much else, other than, perhaps, a deep aversion to traditional conservatism, grounded in the conviction that traditional conservatives have been cucked by liberals and have sold out whites, that holds the Alt-right together. What unites the Alt-right, at bottom, is its commitment to white superiority.[23] What distinguishes the Alt-right from several of the other groups and organizations that make up the radical right more generally is its eagerness to say the quiet parts out loud.

THE PATRIOT AND MILITIA MOVEMENTS

Many of the ideas that animate the Alt-right reach very far back in American political history; that is partly why it is foolhardy to dismiss the Alt-right as a fleeting or momentary phenomenon. Its more immediate predecessors, however, are the Patriot and Militia movements of the past two decades. The Patriot movement in particular has grown rapidly in the United States, particularly in Western states.[24] In 2008 there were an estimated 150 groups associated with the movement, and now there are estimated to be over 1,000.[25] The first wave of the Patriot movement originated in a number of violent confrontations between federal agents and armed civilians in the 1990s, most notably in Ruby Ridge, Idaho, and Waco, Texas.[26] Much of the growth of the Patriot movement, however, should be attributed to the election in 2008 of the first African American president, Barack Obama, and to the severe economic recession that started in that year.[27]

Two of the most notable and recent galvanizing events for the Patriot movement were the 2014 standoff at the Bundy Ranch in Clark County, Nevada, and the 2016 occupation of the Malheur Wildlife Refuge in Oregon. The Clark County standoff began when federal agents attempted to arrest Cliven Bundy and clear away his cattle from the land; Bundy had grazed his cattle on federal land for over 20 years without paying for access or obtaining the necessary permits. After hundreds of citizens, many of whom were armed and members of various militia groups, came to support Bundy, federal authorities abandoned their attempt to remove him.[28] Bundy's supporters, including Richard Mack, Wiley Drake (of the Oath Keepers), and Mike Vanderboegh (leader of a militia called the Three Percenters), claimed victory. Vanderboegh wrote on his blog, *Sipsey Street Irregulars*, that "It is impossible to overstate the importance of the victory won in the desert today. . . . . The feds were routed—routed. There is no other word that applies. Courage is contagious, defiance is contagious, victory is contagious."[29]

The Bundy confrontation set the stage for a number of similar showdowns between militia groups and the federal government,[30] including the occupation of the Malheur Wildlife Refuge in early 2016. Ammon Bundy (son of Cliven Bundy) and several other men, many members of private militias and the Sovereign Citizens movement, seized and shut down the federal wildlife refuge in rural Harney County, Oregon. Ammon Bundy is the self-appointed leader of a group he calls "Citizens for Constitutional Freedom." The occupation was meant to protest, among other things, the federal government's extensive ownership and management of large tracts of land in the western United States, which Bundy and many in the radical right believe should be under the control of state and county governments.

As the Bundy and Malheur standoffs reveal, many of the people involved in the Patriot movement are citizens who come together to form private or "citizens" militias. (I discuss the militia movement in detail in Chapter 4.) At a high level of abstraction, the militias and Patriots share a deep-seated distrust of the federal government; they demand "that the federal government adhere to the Constitution and stop what they see as systematic abuse of land rights, gun rights, freedom of speech and other liberties."[31]

One example of such a group is the Central Oregon Constitutional Guard (COCG), an organization of about 30 people who study the Constitution; organize weekly firearms training; practice survival skills; and who broadly define themselves as a "defensive unit" against "all enemies foreign and domestic," with the principal potential enemy being the federal government.[32] After witnessing the Bundy standoff, B.J.

Soper established the COCG "to protect against the government, but partly a way to get back to a simpler America."[33] One of the organization's goals is to teach its members the sorts of skills learned in an organization like the Boy Scouts, such as camping and setting up a shelter; making a fire; and foraging for food and water. However, the underlying mission of the COCG is to be a paramilitary force, trained in using firearms and other "basic infantry" skills.[34]

In addition to support from law enforcement officials, some of whom played an active role in the Malheur occupation, a significant and growing number of elected officials participate in the Patriot movement. Two examples are the Constitutional Sheriffs and Peace Officers Association (CSPOA), and the Oath Keepers. As described on their website, the Oath Keepers are an "association of current and formerly serving military, police, and first responders, who pledge to fulfill the oath all military and police take to 'defend the Constitution against all enemies, foreign and domestic.'"[35] Like the Constitutional Guards of the CSPOA, the Oath Keepers insist their loyalty is to the Constitution, and not to politicians or "unconstitutional" federal commands, "such as orders to disarm the American people, to conduct warrantless searches, or to detain Americans as 'enemy combatants' in violation of their ancient right to jury trial."[36] The full list is in "Ten Orders We Will Not Obey," the first of which (of course) is "We will NOT obey any order to disarm the American people."[37]

Founded in 2009 by Stewart Rhodes (a frequent guest on television shows and especially on Fox News), the Oath Keepers attend Patriot and Tea Party events, conspicuously armed and often warning of imminent threats by the federal government to disarm American citizens. (The brief declaration of martial law in New Orleans after Hurricane Katrina led Rhodes to conclude, "So they disarmed Americans over some bad weather, as though the bad weather suspended the Second Amendment."[38]) The Oath Keepers, Rhodes insists, are not a militia, but they are armed, they frequent militia meetings, and they engage in paramilitary training.[39]

THE IDEOLOGY OF THE ALT-RIGHT

Another way to understand the Alt-right is to ask what it believes and to examine the main tenets of its ideology.[40] This is both more difficult and less useful than it might seem. Like any significant social movement, the Alt-right is not monolithic or uniform, and it has changed over the years. Its adherents do not share an overarching, fully defined political creed or political identity. The Alt-right has many parts and welcomes a wide variety of ideologies, beliefs, and concerns, and often these concerns and ideologies are contradictory or in tension with one another.

"WHAT IT MEANS TO BE ALT-RIGHT"

The Alt-right may not pledge allegiance to a single and shared creed, but there are occasional efforts to compose a Lutheran list of theses, as Alt-right elder Richard Spencer did, not long after the Unite the Right rally at the University of Virginia. Spencer set out a 20-point manifesto of core Alt-right beliefs, entitled "The Charlottesville Statement."[41] Among the central precepts are, unsurprisingly, a commitment to the proposition that "Race is real. Race matters. Race is the foundation of identity," that Jews are different, that America should be a "white ethno-state" because "The founding population of the United States was primarily Anglo-Saxon and Protestant," and that the constitutional liberties of speech and ownership of firearms are absolute and guaranteed to all US citizens (this last proposition is worded in a way, however, to intimate to sympathetic readers that these liberties are guaranteed only to US citizens of European descent).

In addition to a passionate, deep-rooted commitment to white racial supremacy (or, in their parlance, to white equality or white pride), a number of other shared ideas and precepts make up the heart of Alt-right thinking. These include a belief in the sanctity of state and local (county) government, coupled with suspicion if not fear of the federal government; closed borders and strict limits or a complete ban on immigration; and opposition to gun control and the social welfare state.

Another element of the Alt-right are self-described "radical traditionalists," who want to preserve traditional Christian values but from a uniquely white supremacist perspective. One such organization, the Traditionalist Youth Network, espouses a white supremacist form of Christianity and promotes "family and folk" and separation of the races.[42]

Others in the Alt-right see themselves as "neo-reactionaries" who reject liberal democracy and ideas associated with the Enlightenment. (Some neo-reactionaries refer to their theories as the "Dark Enlightenment.") Still others claim to be 'race realists' or alternately 'HBD' advocates, a reference to human biodiversity (those who believe that one's race governs traits such as behavior and intelligence—with non-whites being inferior to whites)."[43]

Finally, some observers, and some folks in the Alt-right itself, like to distinguish between true believers, compatriots, and pretenders. The differences can be difficult to chart, but they provoke anger and sometimes conflict within the Alt-universe,[44] as evidenced by familial squabbles about the differences, if any, between the Alt-right and the Alt-Lite and Alt-White movements.[45] As Luke O'Brien describes them, the "'alt-lite' [is] more casually bigoted mischief-makers, who might bandy about the N-word but are more likely to be upset about PC culture than, say, the Jews. A broader circle still—you could call it the 'alt-white'—encompasses a large number of Trump voters."[46] (It may help to think of these congregations as concentric circles. Or a Venn diagram. Or a family tree. Or something.) One difference is that the Alt-Lite is more Libertarian and, maybe, less passionately devoted to the project of white separatism.[47]

Perhaps the key difference between the Alt-right, the Alt-Lite, and the Alt-White rests in the willingness to openly embrace white racism and the politics of white identity:

> Many of the figures on the New Right reject identity politics entirely, and that means white identity politics too. Rejecting both white nationalism and mainstream Republicanism, individuals associated with this movement espouse a civic nationalism or American nationalism. This is the key distinction; rather than talk about race, those on the alt-lite will talk about protecting Western values against left-wing globalism and multiculturalism.[48]

Some observers think the Alt-coalition is not only fractious but fragile, as evidenced by conflicts between Spencer and Milo Yiannopoulos and

Lauren Southern, the latter both associated with the Alt-Lite, at a "Free Speech Rally" at the Lincoln Memorial in June, 2017.[49] George Hawley, for example, notes that the newcomers have "created a potential problem for the movement's original supporters" and that "Some on the Alt-right want nothing to do with the Alt-Lite. They do not want anyone that is not a hardcore white nationalist to appropriate the term and weaken it," as they think Yiannopoulos and others have done.[50] The conflict underscores the Alt-right's ambiguous standing in the larger universe of right-wing militantism. The Alt-right holds many of its ideological cousins in contempt—a contempt that often runs in both directions—but the fights are among consanguines.

HOW AND WHERE TO FIND THE ALT-RIGHT

Students of the Alt-right like to emphasize the movement's intimacy with social media. The Alt-right is easy to find on Facebook, Twitter, YouTube, podcasts, and an unknown but undoubtedly large number of homepages. Some of these sites are amateurish, if not cartoonish but others are sleek, professional, and sophisticated. Among the latter are sites like *Radix Journal*, founded in 2013, which "publishes original work on culture, race, tradition, meta-politics, and critical theory."[51] In addition to its website, *Radix* publishes a journal and an imprint; all three are funded and operated by the National Policy Institute (NPI), which is "dedicated to the heritage, identity, and future of European people in the United States, and around the world."[52]

Another prominent Alt-right website is Breitbart.com. In its early iterations, *Breitbart* was a mainstream conservative news outlet, but as David Neiwert notes, it "always included the work of a number of far-right figures, particularly those with anti-Muslim preoccupations, and Islamophobia became a steady feature" of its coverage. "In fact, there was often an ugly racial overtone to all of the stories Breitbart promoted."[53]

After Andrew Breitbart's death in 2012 and a period of internecine warfare, *Breitbart* evolved from a very conservative news and political commentary site to "the premier website of the Alt-right," representing "white nationalists and unabashed anti-Semites and racists."[54] In 2016, the Southern Poverty Law Center accused it of embracing ideas on "the extremist fringe of the conservative right" and as promoting racist, anti-Muslim, and anti-immigrant ideas.[55]

Other prominent Alt-right outlets on the Internet include *Vdare, American Renaissance, Vox Populi, The Daily Stormer, The Right Stuff, Political Cesspool*, and *Taki's Magazine*. Some, like *GAB*, are social networking sites for those who might be attracted to Alt-right ideology (*GAB* describes itself as a conservative alternative to Facebook and Twitter). Some, like *Hatreon*, are crowdfunding sites that purport to offer an ultraconservative alternative to Patreon, GoFundMe, and PayPal, which are said to discriminate against conservatives and to be hostile to freedom of speech.[56]

The Alt-right does not simply occupy the Internet—it has weaponized it. It uses the Internet to spread its message to the loyal, to recruit new members, and to campaign against its enemies, institutional and personal alike. It wages war with armies of "trolls" who use Twitter, Facebook, and other social media sites to harass ("trollstorm") SJW's, feminists, liberals, "race traitors," Antifa, and other perceived enemies. Trolls lay siege to the comments sections of online newspapers, blogs, and even retail sites (like Amazon) to bully perceived enemies with derogatory comments, insults, and physical threats. Another favorite weapon is "doxxing," or the practice of hacking to obtain personal information about their targets, such as addresses, phone numbers, social security numbers, and the names of children and the schools they attend, which they then make public.[57] One recent study, by the Institute of Strategic Dialogue, concluded that the tactics used by militant right in Europe and in the United States, are "more reminiscent of state-led psychological operations than that of terrorist groups" and urged policy makers, technology companies, practitioners and activists "to adopt counter-strategies that match the sophistication of the far-right."[58]

In the aftermath of the rally at the University of Virginia, GoDaddy and some other Internet hosting companies denied service to *The Daily Stormer, Vanguard America*, and a few other neo-Nazi groups.[59] *Stormer* has since reappeared (and then disappeared and reappeared again with a new name, *Punished Stormer*).[60] There is something to be said in favor of making the message less accessible, especially since experts seem to think that frequent exposure may help to radicalize some individuals.[61] On the other hand, the sites typically reorganize and reappear elsewhere on the Internet, often on sites well beyond the jurisdiction of US authorities, or on the dark net, as the *Daily Stormer/ Punished Stormer* saga demonstrates. Denying Alt-right groups access to the web also plays into the narrative of the Alt-right as First Amendment/Freedom of Speech martyrs. The assertion that such silencing violates the First Amendment has no merit at all (see Chapter 3), but it has considerable cultural cache.

WHO SPEAKS FOR THE ALT-RIGHT AND THE LIKE?

No one speaks authoritatively for the Alt-right, much less for the radical right writ large, but some voices are louder than others. Not everyone on the following list would consent to being called part of the Alt-right, but all of them are undoubtedly part of the larger, ultraconservative right wing of American politics.

RICHARD B. SPENCER: FATHER OF THE ALT-RIGHT

Richard B. Spencer is sometimes credited with inventing the term "Alt-right,"[62] but he may be better known as the star of an Internet video that went viral in January 2017, in which he was punched in the nose during a presidential inauguration event. Spencer is also often described as the father of the Alt-right,[63] and he is the president and director of the National Policy Institute (NPI), "an independent organization dedicated to the heritage, identity, and future of people of European descent in the United States and around the world."[64] Prior to NPI, Spencer worked for various conservative publications. In 2007, he worked as an editor at *The American Conservative* (TAC) magazine, but was subsequently fired for his radical views;[65] TAC co-founder Scott McConnell noted that Spencer was "a bit extreme for us."[66]

In 2009 Spencer created AlternativeRight.com, "a supremacy-themed webzine aimed at the 'intellectual right wing.'"[67] Unlike many sites at the time, AlternativeRight.com was sleek, professional, and multi-faceted: "Alternative Right differed from other white-nationalist websites . . . in that it was not single-mindedly focused on race. It included many articles on foreign policy, domestic politics, economics, and gender relations . . . . There was also a period when more mainstream writers and academics were willing to provide content."[68] (Spencer sold AlternativeRight.com in 2012, and it shut down that year. Spencer now runs a new site called AltRight.com, which he describes thusly: "Founded on January 16, 2017, AltRight.com brings together the best writers and analysts from Alt Right, in North America, Europe, and around the world."[69]) In addition to his position as president and director of NPI, Spencer oversees the organization's publishing outlets, *Washington Summit Publishers* and *Radix Journal.*

Plainly implicit in Spencer" vision of an ideal society is a critique of the Constitution itself, and he disagrees with other conservatives who advocate for returning to America's "founding principles."[70] Spencer argues that while most contemporary states "are putatively based on the 'rights of man' and 'democracy' our project would be a new kind of political and social order."[71] His society would be "based on very different ideals than, say, the Declaration of Independence." Hence, neither Spencer nor AltRight.com evince much interest in the traditional symbols, institutions, or icons of American conservatism, including the Constitution, the Founding Fathers, or the flag.[72] On the other hand, Spencer's Alt-right manifesto, composed just after Charlottesville, references both the First and Second amendments.

STEVE BANNON: (SOMETIMES) TRUMP ADMINISTRATION INSIDER

On and off again chief executive at Breitbart.com (a position he held before joining and then after leaving the Trump administration and during which *Breitbart* became increasingly and openly a white nationalist organization), Bannon is best known for his prominent association with President Trump. Before his position at *Breitbart*, Bannon worked at Goldman Sachs and was a producer of several conservative documentary films, including an effusive short film on Sarah Palin, called *The Undefeated.* For a time Bannon was an assistant to President Trump and a chief administration strategist; he had a role on the National Security Council, and he was instrumental in helping to draft Executive Order 13769, which restricted US travel and immigration by individuals from seven countries, suspended the United States Refugee Admissions Program (USRAP) for 120 days, and indefinitely suspended entry of

Syrians to the United States. Bannon left (or was dismissed from) the Trump administration shortly after the Unite the Right Rally at the University of Virginia. (It was widely reported that Bannon had helped President Trump to craft a universally criticized statement placing blame on "many sides.")

MILO YIANNOPOULOS: SOCIAL MEDIA CELEBRITY

Milo Yiannopoulos, a British journalist and social media celebrity,[73] is a former Technology Editor at *Breitbart*.[74] He resigned his position at *Breitbart* in February 2017, following a controversy arising from a video in which he said that sexual relationships between 13-year-old boys and adults can be "perfectly consensual" and a positive experience for boys. (Yiannopoulos claims his statements were an attempt to cope with his past.) Yiannopoulos is a vocal critic of feminism, Islam, the Black Lives Matter movement, and other movements and groups that he deems part of, or protected by, "the totalitarian regressive left."[75] Although he is gay, Yiannopoulos is highly critical of other gay individuals, saying "it's a shame that gays who ought to be pushing boundaries have been domesticated and tamed and turned into pets by the progressive left."[76]

Regaling in his status as online provocateur, Yiannopoulos has been suspended from Twitter a number of times,[77] and had his verified account status, reserved for accounts of public interest, repealed for violating Twitter's terms of service.[78] Much of Yiannopoulos's work speaks directly to the current outrage expressed in the Alt-right regarding the apparent attack on free speech coming from the left and "feminism, progressivism, and political correctness."[79] His attraction to these themes, and doubts among some in the Alt-right about his commitment to white nationalism, make Yiannopoulos less a voice for the Alt-right and more a member of the Alt-Lite.[80]

DAVID BARTON: CONSTITUTIONAL HISTORIAN

David Barton is a self-styled constitutional revisionist historian and Christian nationalist. Barton is not a member of the Alt-right, and his devotion to the cause of Christian nationalism might make him an object of contempt in the Alt-right. But Barton is a major voice and influence in the militant right. He is the president and founder of *Wall-Builders*, which is dedicated to "educating the nation concerning the Godly foundation of our country; . . . providing information to federal, state, and local officials as they develop public policies which reflect Biblical values; and encouraging Christians to be involved in the civic arena."[81] In 2005, *Time Magazine* named Barton one of "The 25 Most Influential Evangelicals in America."[82] If he is to be believed, Barton has sold "millions of copies of his books, tapes, and video and it has been reported that his video 'America's Godly Heritage' sold 100,000 copies at $20 a piece in the first three years."[83]

The Christian foundations of the Constitution are a major part of Barton's message. Barton even argues that the Constitution expressly incorporates several biblical prescriptions, and that some key elements of constitutional design and architecture, such as separation of powers, federalism, and the Bill of Rights, are based on specific biblical commands and injunctions, many taken from Leviticus.

Most professional scholars have cast significant doubt (academic speak for "ridicule") on Barton's scholarship. His much publicized book, *The Jefferson Lies: Exposing the Myths You've Always Believed About Thomas Jefferson* (2012) was withdrawn by its publisher, Thomas Nelson (a conservative Christian publishing house), because it "had lost confidence in the book's details" and "learned that there were some historical details included in the book that were not adequately supported."[84] Richard Pierard notes, for example, that that the term "evangelical" didn't even come into use until the end of the nineteenth century and that Barton's attempt to "take a later definition and impose it" on the Founding Fathers is a "historical anachronism."[85] Likewise, "Academic historians, according to the *New York Times*, give Barton's work at best a B minus, noting that while the historical facts he cites are more or less accurate, his biased interpretation of them is not."[86] (B-? Only grade inflation can explain such generosity.) The book has since been re-released by World Net Daily Books, described by Paul Harris, writing for *The Guardian*, as "a niche producer of rightwing conspiracy theories, religious books and 'family values' tracts."[87]

KRIS ANNE HALL: TEA PARTY ACTIVIST AND CONSTITUTIONAL EDUCATOR

Kris Anne Hall is another prominent Christian constitutionalist. Hall travels about the United States, giving lectures about the Constitution and the Founding. She accepts no speaking or travel fees, making money from donations and book and DVD sales.[88] In addition to her speaking tours, Hall has a radio show online and a television show on the Christian Lifestyle Network. Prior to devoting her life to teaching the gospel of the Christian Constitution, Hall worked as a biochemist, served in the army, and practiced as an attorney.[89] Hall claims she was fired in 2010, while working as a state prosecutor for Florida, because she refused to stop giving lectures to Tea Party audiences, reportedly a conflict of interest.[90]

One of Hall's chief assertions is that "The constitution was not invented in 1787, nor was it originally written by anyone in our founder's time. Our Constitution is the product of over 700 years of history."[91] Central to Hall's understanding of the Constitution is the argument that rights are "granted by God, not men."[92] Liberty is "God's gift."[93] Hall's conception of liberty is closely tied to her version of American Exceptionalism: "America is the greatest place of opportunity because we are the only place that believes that liberty is the inherent possession of people and not something that is given by government and by documents, and therefore government and documents cannot take it away."[94] Thus, "Free speech is not GRANTED by the Constitution. The Right to speak freely and voice your conscience is an inherent Right not a gift from government. Government was never delegated the authority to regulate it."[95]

CONSTITUTIONAL SHERIFFS

Established in 2009, the CSPOA believes that sheriffs have "the Constitutional authority to check and balance all levels of government within the jurisdiction of the County" and that within the county unit, the sheriff is the supreme political authority: "The law enforcement powers held by the sheriff supersede those of any agent, officer, elected official or employee from any level of government when in the jurisdiction of the county." They justify this expansive authority by drawing on the historical role of sheriffs, tracing that role from ninth century England to colonial America: "Making its way to America, the Sheriff held his office as the highest law enforcement officer within that county jurisdiction." Furthermore, they ground their understanding of the role of the sheriff in the separation of powers doctrine, explaining, "The vertical separation of powers in the Constitution makes it clear that the power of the sheriff even supersedes the powers of the President."[96] (By "vertical" he means federalism.) Mack explains most of this in his book, *The County Sheriff: America's Last Hope* (2009), where he warns that America's greatest threat is not from terrorism: "It is our own federal government."[97]

Because the CSPOA believes that sheriffs must protect the rights guaranteed to citizens by the Declaration of Independence, the Bill of Rights, and United States Constitution, they must put protection of these rights before federal law, if they think them in conflict. They argue "no agency established by the US Congress can develop its own policies or regulations which supersede the Bill of Rights or the Constitution, nor does the executive branch have the power to make law, overturn law or set aside law."[98] (Some of this argument also traces, as we shall see more fully in Chapter 2, to the precepts of Christian and Mormon constitutionalism, and in particular to the writings of W. Cleon Skousen.) The CSPOA warns that any conduct on the part of the federal government that is contrary to these founding documents, "will be dealt with as criminal activity." Some examples of what the organization defines as an abuse of federal power include the "Registration of personal firearms under any circumstances," and the "Arrest of citizens or seizure of persons or property without first notifying and obtaining the express consent of the local sheriff."[99]

CONCLUSION: DOES THE ALT-RIGHT MATTER?

The America of the near future will be less white, less male, and more racially, ethnically, and culturally diverse. The future of the Alt-right is not as clear. As George Hawley and others have noted, the movement confronts several difficulties, among them questions of how to deal with sectarian conflict between the Alt-right, the Alt-Lite, and the Alt-

White, as well as questions concerning how, if it all, the movement can be institutionalized.[100] In Greg Johnson's estimation (Johnson is a prominent white nationalist based in Seattle, Washington, and editor-in-chief of *Counter Currents Publishing*), "It is now clear that the tendency of the Alt Right since Trump's election has been toward self-marginalization, Right-wing sectarianism, and purity spiraling."[101]

More probable than an ideologically ecumenical Alt-right is the prospect that the Alt-right will eat its own in an ever more strident demand for ideological and identitarian purity. Its definition of who is white, to take one example, is likely to become narrower rather than more expansive, as will its definition and understanding of what is "true" conservativism. (The status of folks like Milo Yiannopoulos and the Alt-Lite may be the first example.)[102] As the movement shrinks into itself, and as the world around it continues to change, the Alt-right is likely to become angrier and more violent. For that reason alone, it is important to know what the Alt-right believes.

The Alt-right also matters because much of what it believes is not confined to it, or even to the Alt-Lite or the Alt-White. Some of it is shared by a considerable number of other right-wing organizations, and even by some who would strongly reject any association with the Alt-right. These include some Christian nationalists, like David Barton, as well as some self-styled defenders of the Constitution, such as the League of the South. The League of the South holds to the proposition that "the Southern People" have and should exercise their constitutional right to secede from the Union and create an independent nation "in the historical, organic, and Biblical sense of the world, namely that they are a distinct people with language, mores and folkways that separate them from the rest of the world."[103] Others include the Constitutional Protection Force, the Constitutional County Project, the preachers of the Constitutional Gospel Movement, the Constitution Party, and the Sovereign Citizens Movement. Not all of these organizations announce themselves as Alt-right, and some vehemently (and perhaps fairly) reject the association, but their ideological projects are undoubtedly similar. Implicit in most of them, including even the Alt-right, is a particular way of thinking about the Constitution.

Chapter 2

UNDERSTANDING THE ALT-CONSTITUTION

Founding and First Principles

In this and subsequent chapters we unwrap the Alt-constitution. The Alt-constitution embodies a comprehensive philosophy about the legitimacy, role, and purposes of government, and concerning the rights and responsibilities of citizens, as well as who qualifies for citizenship. It is shot through with apparent inconsistencies, incongruities, and contradictions.[1] Oftentimes, though, what looks like an inconsistency makes sense, or can at least be explained, by reading the provision in question against the larger background assumptions that inform the text. Back of the Alt-constitution is a vision of the Bill of Rights that emphasizes absolute rights and unassailable liberties (especially for speech and guns and private militias), states' rights and a corresponding suspicion of the federal government, racial classifications recognized and legitimated by law, and privilege for white Christians.[2] If the absolute protection of the speech and religion clauses of the Alt-first amendment does not protect the speech of professional football players, or Black Lives Matter, much less the religious rights of Muslims, the explanation has less to do with constitutional rules than with what the speaker says or who the speaker is.

Calling out these sorts of inconsistencies is not an especially pointed criticism. All constitutions advance philosophies, big and small, about the purposes of government, about the rights and duties of citizenship, and about human nature. Sometimes these philosophies pull in different directions. All constitutions, even utopian constitutions, contain inconsistencies and contradictions. (If it sounds odd to call the Alt-constitution a utopian constitution, the difference between utopian and dystopian depends upon one's point of view. To the radical right, it is our Constitution, not theirs, that is nightmarish.) My point in this chapter is not so much to criticize the Alt-constitution for its inconsistencies and imperfections as to expose them. I hope to show what the Alt-constitution thinks the world should look like and to show how and where that vision differs from the American Constitution. Sometimes, the differences are slight. More often, however, the differences are sobering if not disturbing.

As I indicated in the Introduction, one important component of the Alt-constitution is its account of the religious underpinnings of the Founding, which greatly influences how we understand the Constitution's authority, as well as how it should be interpreted and by whom. Hence, I begin at the beginning, with a familiar story.

FAITH AND FOUNDING: THE MIRACLE AT PHILADELPHIA

> Over Philadelphia the air lay hot and humid; old people said it was the worst summer since 1750. . . . In the Pennsylvania State House, which we call Independence Hall, some fifty-five delegates, named by the legislatures of twelve states (Rhode Island balked, refusing attendance) met in convention, and during a summer of hard work and high feeling wrote out a plan of government which they hoped the states would accept, and which they entitled The Constitution of the United States of America.

First published in 1966, Catherine Drinker Bowen's *Miracle at Philadelphia: The Story of the Constitutional Convention* does not say outright that what happened in Philadelphia that hot and humid summer was a miracle. The language of miracles Bowen takes from the Founders, or at least from George Washington, who opined in a letter to Lafayette that "It appears to me, then, little short of a miracle, that the Delegates from so many different States (which States you know are also different from each other in their manners, circumstances and prejudices) should unite in forming a system of national Government, so little liable to well-founded objections."[3] Madison, too, used the language of divine providence, writing to Jefferson that considering the difficulties involved, "Adding to these considerations the natural diversity of human opinions on all new and complicated subjects, it is impossible to consider the degree of concord which ultimately prevailed as less than a miracle."[4]

If Bowen was careful not to claim the language of miracles as her own, nonetheless she did not dispute it. As Bowen herself admits, she wrote from the perspective of "celebration" and "admiration." Wonderfully written and engaging, Bowen's account of the work of the Founders in the long, hot summer of 1787 straddles if not obscures the fine line between hyperbole and reality. Generations of students have learned from Bowen that the events that produced the American Constitution were truly miraculous, and we all know that men (they were all men) don't do miracles—gods and saints do. No less a student than Chief Justice Warren Burger blurs the line Bowen draws, writing in his Foreword for the book that the "miracle" at Philadelphia was "a boon to the cause of freedom everywhere."[5]

At least the Chief Justice put the word in quotation marks, perhaps indicating he appreciated the hyperbolic nature of the description. Others have been less careful and more literal in their reading, both of Bowen and of history. In some quarters, and especially in the radical right, divine inspiration at the Founding is not simply a literary device or an excess of enthusiasm. It is not a metaphorical truth but a literal one. It is a claim about the Constitution's authority, what the Constitution means, and how to interpret it. As I argued in the Introduction, talk of miracles engenders a kind of constitutional fundamentalism, in which certain truths are incontrovertible and unassailable. It leads to Constitution worship.[6]

The Institute on the Constitution, for example, a right-wing think-tank founded and funded by Michael Peroutka (once the presidential nominee of the Constitution Party), offers multi-part courses and other instructional materials that outline the biblical basis of the Constitution and the Founding.[7] The best-known proponents of the religious character of the Founding and the Constitution, however, are probably David Barton and Kris Anne Hall. As you will recall from Chapter 1, Barton is a Christian nationalist and a revisionist historian and the author of several books on the Founding and the Constitution; his work has been exceptionally influential in far-right religious circles. In 2005, *Time Magazine* called Barton "a major voice in the debate over church-state separation [and] a hero to millions, including some powerful politicians."[8] Barton is associated with the Christian Identity movement and has spoken at white supremacy events. (Barton denies both charges.)[9]

Part entrepreneur and part provocateur, Barton's constitutional expertise is a matter of question. He holds no advanced degrees in history or in law, and most of his "scholarship" has been dismissed by academics, even Christian academics, as spurious if not scandalous. For example, Barton's most recent book, *The Jefferson Lies* (2012), was widely criticized by scholars and especially by other Christian scholars (see Chapter 1) as inadequately researched, incomplete, and misleading, especially concerning Jefferson's manumission of his slaves at Monticello.

Barton is currently the Founder and President of *WallBuilders*, an organization "dedicated to presenting America's forgotten history and heroes, with an emphasis on the moral, religious, and constitutional foundation on which America was built—a foundation which, in recent years, has been seriously attacked and undermined."[10] Among *WallBuilders'* undertakings is an ambitious project of civic education and constitutional literacy:

> Constitution ALIVE! is an 8 hour course that covers the key principles that make the US Constitution the most remarkable political document of all time. We will skip the boredom, the confusion and all the rest of the mind-numbing horror you would expect to get from a college lecture. We've extracted all the bad and pumped in a whole lot of good! The end result is that we did something that most thought was impossible; we made learning about the Constitution not just fun . . . but fun AND exciting![11]

The promotional materials for Barton's course underplay the point, but all of Barton's work on the Founding and the Constitution has been to show that America is a Christian nation, founded on and dedicated to the advancement of biblical law. The choice at Philadelphia was, as Ronald Mann writes, "Christ or Chaos."[12]

For Christian supremacists and many in the extreme right, talk of constitutional miracles is not casual or inadvertent. It is also a claim about constitutional history, about the origins of rights, and about the influence of theology in the evolution of Western constitutional thought. Barton, and other far-right commentators, such as Glenn Beck, even argues that the Constitution traces directly to the Bible. Barton has argued, for instance, that fully 94 percent of the quotations that appear in the writings of the Founders are taken from the Bible and that several key constitutional principles, including the separation of powers, derive directly from biblical injunctions.[13]

Invoking Founders' intent, Barton argues that read properly, the religion clauses in the First Amendment reveal the true purpose of the First Amendment: to prevent the "establishment of a particular form of Christianity" by Episcopalians, Congregationalists, or any other denomination. So, for example, in *The Myth of Separation* (1989), Barton argues that the Founders anticipated that only Christians could hold public office (an exceptionally narrow reading of Article VI of the Constitution, which prohibits religious oaths as a condition of office).

Barton's work borrows from a long tradition of conservative writing that is often called Christian revisionism or Christian nationalism. Media personality Glenn Beck is a prominent voice in the Christian nationalism movement. He cites Barton's works frequently to make the argument that the Constitution and other Founding documents are based on the Bible and in particular (but not only) on the Book of Deuteronomy.[14] Much of the sentiment behind these arguments traces to the influential writings of W. Cleon Skousen. A prominent anti-communist, Skousen was a prolific speaker in far-right circles (he died in 2008). In 1971, Skousen founded the Freeman Center, which in 1982 rebranded as the National Center for Constitutional Studies (NCCS), a private think tank associated with the Mormon Church and "nestled securely in the metropolis of Malta, Idaho (2000 Census population 177: white population 174)."[15] Skousen's most important work is *The Five Thousand Year Leap* (1981). *The Five Thousand Year Leap* enjoyed a resurgence in popularity when heavily promoted by Beck, who called it "divinely inspired" and written by someone "much more intelligent than myself."[16]

The NCCS offers a wide variety of civic education courses conducted by sanctioned volunteer lecturers who teach/preach from materials that NCCS itself produces or approves. The chief text of course, is *The Five Thousand Year Leap*, also available in a condensed form, with a slightly more pointed version of the miracle message and condemnations of the twentieth century social welfare state, called *The Making of America*. (Anticipating the Alt-right in some ways, early editions were astonishingly blunt in their racism: Newer editions of *The Making of America* "lack the glaring racism of Skousen's original version. But the current NCCS president, Earl Taylor, is not unknown to echo some of Skousen's controversial views. At a Mesa, Arizona, seminar earlier this year, a *Washington Post* reporter heard Taylor argue that Thomas Jefferson hesitated to free his own slaves because of his 'benevolence.'"[17]) There is a distinct element of Mormonism in both Skousen's writings and in the work of the NCCS, but not so much as to be off-putting to religious fundamentalists and conservatives. The essential message is a familiar and, for its target audience, a comforting one: The United States is a religious nation, founded on religious principles that are easily comprehended by consulting the sacred text—the Constitution.

Conversely, America's problems stem chiefly from abandoning fundamental and divinely inspired constitutional truths. Our salvation (the word should be taken literally) lies in a return to fundamental constitutional principles and in repudiating "the tyrannical, implicitly sinful, nature of the modern federal government. . . . America's return to extremely limited government, as they think God intended, is destined to happen, NCCS lecturers teach, because God has already shown an interventionist role in American history."[18]

Read carefully, Skousen does not claim that the United Sates is a theocracy. But the point is hard to miss when he writes:

> I see the wisdom of our Founding Fathers in making this a Republic rather than a Theocracy. Not one of the Founder's comments concluded that the government of this nation is Christian. Some did say and others agreed that our form of government would be inadequate to govern citizens who do not embody the moral, legal, ethical and brotherly love principles that are espoused in Biblical teachings. . . . What our Founding fathers said was not that our government should be based upon religion, but that the citizens of our Republic must be subject to allowing the principles of moral turpitude and human relationships taught by the Ten Commandments to govern their behavior so that our government would be capable of governing them.[19]

If there is any substance to the distinction between theocracy and encouraging human relationships to be governed by the Ten Commandments, it is too fine to matter to constitutional fundamentalists.

Like Barton's work, Skousen's scholarly reputation is completely at odds with his influence in the extreme right. Bluntly speaking, the academic community has nothing but contempt for Skousen's work. Jack N. Rakove, to take one example, a highly respected professor of American constitutional history and winner of a Pulitzer Prize, has described *The Five Thousand Year Leap* as "a joke that no self-respecting scholar would think is worth a warm pitcher of spit."[20]

Why do these works appeal to the far right? It is tempting to dismiss their appeal on grounds of self-interest (White conservative Christians think the Constitution is White, conservative, and Christian. Who would have thought it?), or to dismiss it as conspiracy-based thinking (embedded in the DNA of much of the extreme right), or to the paranoid style in American political culture,[21] or to identity politics. All of these explanations have some merit. But it is also important to remember that claims about the Christian origins and character of the Founding are not just fantasy. The assertion that human rights are divine or come from God or natural law or are "pre-constitutional" in origin draws upon a long tradition of Western constitutional thinking, a tradition grounded not only in a particular political worldview, but in a long theological one as well.[22]

ON CONSTITUTIONAL THEOLOGY

Most historians of constitutionalism locate the idea that limits on the powers of government are conducive to human happiness and responsible government in Western theological traditions.[23] In the twentieth century, noted constitutional scholar Edward S. Corwin wrote extensively about the "higher law" background of the American Constitution. Corwin's seminal article shows how the concept of a higher law was understood by the leading thinkers of the American Revolutionary period, as well as how the ideal of the higher law influenced the creation of the Constitution.[24]

The idea that human rights trace their origins to a divine source, therefore, is very much a part of American constitutionalism. Similarly, the language of inalienable rights courses throughout the canonical texts of American constitutional history. Its most famous iteration is in the Declaration of Independence:

> We hold these truths to be self-evident, that all men are created equal, that they are endowed by their Creator with certain unalienable Rights, that among these are Life, Liberty and the pursuit of Happiness—That to secure these rights, Governments are instituted among Men, deriving their just powers from the consent of the governed. . . .

Comparable language appears earlier in "A Summary View of the Rights of British America" in 1774, which Jefferson penned for Virginia's delegates to the First Continental Congress. There, Jefferson wrote "that these are our grievances which we have thus laid before his majesty, with that freedom of language and sentiment which becomes a free people claiming their rights, as derived from the laws of nature, and not as the gift of their chief magistrate." None of the Founders would have regarded such language as odd or extreme. Similar references appear in the Virginia Declaration of Rights (1776), initially drafted by George Mason, and in the New London Resolution opposing the Stamp Act in 1765.

What does the phrase "unalienable rights" mean? In the strictest sense, it means that rights may not be forfeited or withdrawn from us, even if we consent to it. But the concept is better approached as a proposition about where human or constitutional rights come from. Jefferson answered that question of provenance in the Declaration when he observed that we are "endowed" with certain unalienable rights by our Creator. We possess such rights because we are human creatures, not because we are members of an enlightened political community or by dint of a social contract or by virtue of a beneficent state. Neither the Declaration of Independence nor the Constitution create or give us rights; rather, rights predate both texts and are independent of human invention. Constitutional instruments simply recognize and acknowledge that unalienable rights are inherent in what it means to be a person. Such claims were so obvious to Jefferson and to most of the Founders that they needed no justification and very little elaboration.

I alluded to the religious provenance of the constitutional document in the Introduction. It is one thing to claim that the historical origins of human rights lay in Christian theology,[25] or in a Higher Law,[26] or that unalienable rights come from a divine source. It is something else to jump from that observation to claiming that the Constitution is Christian or that the United States is a Christian nation. It is also something else to insist, as does the Alt-constitution, that the Founders' handiwork is divinely inspired, the revealed word of God in the same way that scripture is said to be God's work. Think about the implications of this proposition. One must be that what God has done humans must not undo. The implication, plainly, is that human authority to repeal, modify, or alter what has been divinely ordained is profoundly limited. Such a constitution implies a "hierarchy of authority: God, people, the Constitution."[27] A related implication is that the original (it is often called the "organic") Constitution is perfect and has no need of change. What was is what must be. Implicit in such thinking is a claim about the perfection of the original constitution; changes made to it, especially after the demise of the Founding generation, are less entitled to our respect, if not open to outright suspicion. It is only a slight step from there to suggest that a wide array of constitutional changes in the 19th and 20th centuries, including the Fourteenth, Sixteenth, Seventeenth, and Nineteenth amendments, are fundamentally unwise if not literally unconstitutional. This helps to explain the far right's dismissive posture toward several constitutional amendments, including the Reconstruction amendments, that have no direct lineage to the Founding or to the Founders (see Chapter 6).

What are the unalienable rights that every person possesses by virtue of being human (and, building upon Blackstone and Jefferson, by virtue of having been created in God's image)? In the Declaration, Jefferson identified life, liberty, and the pursuit of happiness, but these are not the only such rights. Also included must be the right to property and freedom of religious conscience. In campaigning directly for a bill of rights, for example, Jefferson stated that, "By a declaration of rights, I mean one which shall stipulate freedom of religion, freedom of the press, freedom of commerce against monopolies, trial by juries in all cases, no suspensions of the habeas corpus, no standing armies. These are fetters against doing evil which no honest government should decline."[28]

In the Alt-constitution, unalienable rights include all of those and certainly the Second Amendment as well. An essay on Brietbart.com, for example, argues that "The 'unalienable rights' explicitly protected by the Bill of Rights include, but are not limited to, the rights of free speech and religion, the right to keep and bear arms, self-determination with regard to one's own property, the right to be secure in one's own property, the right to a trial by a jury of one's peers, protection from cruel and unusual punishment, and so forth."[29]

The Constitution's divine providence is more than just an historical fact and a claim about where rights come from. It is also a claim about the limits of governmental authority to restrict or limit rights. In some circles of the far right, for example, the divinely ordained right of self-defense and to bear arms is wholly beyond governmental control. In the Alt-right in particular, the inherent right to freedom of speech likewise means that governmental efforts to shutter or censor speech are necessarily and always improper and illegitimate.

The divinely inspired origins of the Alt-constitution thus also tell us something about what individual provisions in the Bill of Rights mean. I will discuss this more fully in Chapter 3, but it is plainly not much of a step from thinking that the Constitution is divinely inspired to concluding that freedom of religion means freedom to worship the Christian god of that inspiration but no other, or to thinking that the separation of church and state is not what the Founders really had in mind.

CONSTITUTIONAL ORIGINALISM

The Christian nature of the Constitution also serves an important purpose when we take up questions about how it should be interpreted and by whom it should be interpreted: We must approach the Constitution as a believer approaches any sacred text. The key concept is fidelity, or faithfulness, which one demonstrates by making an effort to discern what the author of the text intended it to mean. Hence the appeal of "Framers intent" and its close relative, originalism, as the only legitimate methods of constitutional interpretation. Originalism and Framers' intent promise us the true meaning of the Constitution. A commitment to originalism, to put it simply, is a visible sign that one is a true constitutional patriot. The same logic explains the pronounced tendency to Constitution and Founder-worship in the far right, and especially why originalism and a fascination with all things constitutional was (and is) a central preoccupation of the Tea Party.[30]

Like all methods of constitutional interpretation (and there are dozens if not hundreds of methods, depending upon how one counts and who does the counting)[31] originalism and Framers' intent are simply tools we use to determine what the Constitution means when the plain words fail us. And although devotees of the Alt-constitution like to insist that the meaning of the Constitution is plain, they know better. As James Madison observed in *Federalist* #37:

> When the Almighty himself condescends to address mankind in their own language, his meaning, luminous as it must be, is rendered dim and doubtful by the cloudy medium through which it is communicated. Here, then, are three sources of vague and incorrect definitions: indistinctness of the object, imperfection of the organ of conception, inadequateness of the vehicle of ideas. Any one of these must produce a certain degree of obscurity.

Originalism holds that constitutional interpretation must have a single, overriding purpose: to determine what the provision in question meant "originally," or when it was propounded. The project is not as easy as it seems, or even possible in most cases, as a great number of scholars from different academic standpoints have demonstrated,[32] but it has an obvious cultural and political appeal. Originalism promises to preserve the faith of the Founders and to guard against efforts to change or update or "improve" the Constitution, especially by liberal activist judges and social justice warriors. By way of contrast, interpretive devices that seek to bring the Constitution into the twenty-first century, or methods of interpretation that find implicit rights in the Constitution or which admit that constitutional provisions might be ambiguous and their meaning subject to dispute, are akin to abandoning the Constitution, or worse.

It is important to understand why originalism appeals to the right and what work it does in constitutional fundamentalism. Any serious student of originalism will admit that it seldom tells anyone what the "right" answer is to any open constitutional question. Even true believers in originalism sometimes sharply disagree about what it requires in any particular case. Several of Justice Thomas's former law clerks have created a website, called JusticeThomas.com, to highlight the differences between Justice Thomas's originalist jurisprudence and Justice Scalia's: "Former Thomas law clerk Neomi Rao says Thomas, in some ways, is 'a more thoroughgoing originalist' than Scalia was. Thomas 'is more willing to go back and overturn precedents, to go back and find the original meaning of the Constitution.'"[33] What do believers make of these disagreements? As Robert Brent Toplin has observed, familial disagreements among fundamentalists fade in the face of a common enemy[34]—in this case, liberals and judicial activists.

If the point of originalism is to give clear guidance about what one or another of the vague clauses of the Constitution really means, then it fails us. But asking whether originalism elicits a single, clear, indisputable answer to hard constitutional questions is the wrong question. That is not its purpose. Originalism (and its related companions, "plain words" and Founders' intent) are a kind of virtue signaling on the right. Calling one's self an originalist tells others who you are and what you believe, simultaneously a show of faith and an act of devotion. It venerates the Founders and demands that we be faithful to their work. The point of originalist constitutional interpretation is not to adapt the Constitution to our world and certainly not to fix it or make it better. The point, rather, is to discern what its unchangeable meaning requires of the faithful. As Cass Sunstein has observed, "Strict construction of the Constitution finds a parallel in literal interpretation of the Koran or the Bible. Some 'judicial' fundamentalists seem to approach the Constitution as if it were inspired directly by God."[35] For constitutional fundamentalists, the qualifier "as if" understates things.

One of my mentors liked to distinguish *how* to interpret the Constitution (by appealing to the plain words? by invoking framers' intent? by appealing to moral philosophy?) from the question of *who* should interpret the Constitution.[36] Holding that the Constitution is divinely inspired affects how we approach that question as well. The far right believes that the meaning of the Constitution is open to all citizens willing to make a modest effort to learn. Importantly, that learning can be had without formal training in the law and without relying upon the expertise of judges, lawyers, and professors. Many in the radical right approach the Constitution as "evangelical Christians who have transferred the skills and approaches of Bible study directly to the Constitution."[37]

Some faith traditions, mostly Protestant in denomination, hold closely to the idea that God's Word is accessible to any and every one who
seeks it; no special training in theology or cosmology and no ministerial
education is required to know and understand the Bible. Some other
religions, in contrast, believe that God should be approached only
through chosen intermediaries and that access to and understanding
the Word requires the tutelage if not the translation of authorities. In
these religious communities, saints, priests, and rabbis hold a special,
almost private knowledge, and our access to that knowledge must be
mediated and indirect.

Building on these different understandings and traditions, Sanford
Levinson distinguishes between Protestant and Catholic approaches to
constitutional interpretation. In Levinson's schema, "Protestant" interpreters of the Constitution start from a position that the constitutional
document is accessible to anyone who makes an effort, whereas "Catholic" interpreters start from the necessity of mediation, or the position
that understanding the Constitution is the work of judges and others
schooled in the law. In this framework, constitutional fundamentalists
are protestant-like in their devotion to the sacred text; they do not
believe that understanding the Constitution requires the tutelage of
expert judges or academics. Indeed, a prominent theme in the far right
is a deep distrust of judges and academics, but not all judges are the
object of suspicion. Those who preach the faith of originalism, such as
the late Justice Scalia and Justice Thomas, are lauded for their fidelity
and their courage, while those who embrace other interpretive methods, such as Justice Ginsburg, are ridiculed as judicial activists who
believe in a living constitution.

The conviction that the meaning of the fundamental texts that comprise the American constitutional canon is accessible to all citizens is a
long-standing feature of many populist and fundamentalist movements.[38] In like fashion, the belief that the meaning of the Alt-constitution is there to anyone who wants to know it and is willing to do a little
studying is one of the central pillars of Alt-constitutionalism and of the
far-right community. Just as evangelicals study the Word in Bible study
groups, by purchasing and listening to courses on tape and by attending
services conducted by itinerant ministers, constitutional patriots form
study groups, purchase materials designed to teach themselves and
their children constitutional fundamentals and attend lectures and talks

that are part instructional and part preachy-devotional. In addition to
David Barton and Kris Anne Hall (see Chapter 1) there are dozens of
itinerant minister/speaker/scholars who hawk constitution-study materials on the Internet and who travel the lecture circuit. For one list of
speakers (and contact information), consult the "Camp Constitution
Speakers Bureau," available on the "Camp Constitution" website.[39]

Not all of the speakers are obscure or self-educated experts on the
Constitution. Justice Antonin Scalia, the best-known prophet of the
gospel of originalism, famously accepted an invitation from Representative Michelle Bachmann to speak to the Tea Party Caucus in Congress.
(In fairness to Justice Scalia, he spoke at a wide variety of venues, not all
of them predisposed to welcome his message. Indeed, Justice Scalia
spoke to my classes at Wesleyan University, not known as a far-right
retreat.)

Many if not most of the websites associated with Alt-constitutional
patriotism offer a wide variety of self-help, instructional materials on
the Founders and the Constitution. A quick review reveals several preferred if not formally sanctioned texts and authors. Foremost among
them is Barton, notwithstanding, or more likely because his work has
been so thoroughly discredited by "mainstream" secular historians,[40]
and Skousen's *The Five Thousand Year Leap* (1981).

Another favored study guide to the Alt-constitution is, unsurprisingly, the Constitution itself. A much-beloved activity in study groups is
reading the text aloud, and not just in study groups. In 2011, House
Republicans proposed to read the document from start to finish on the
House floor, halting occasionally to note not only what the text says, but
what it does not say. But the emphasis, as it is in some religious traditions, is on the written word and not on the unwritten constitution. As
Dahlia Lithwick observes, "no matter how many times you read the
document on the House floor, cite it in your bill, or how many copies
you can stuff into your breast pocket without looking fat, the Constitution is always going to raise more questions than it answers and con-
found more readers than it comforts. And that isn't because any one
American is too stupid to understand the Constitution. It's because the
Constitution wasn't written to reflect the views of any one American."[41]

I should probably confess that I too have cashed in on the Constitution, having produced two courses, one on Civil Liberties and the Bill of
Rights, and one on the First Amendment, for The Great Courses Com-

pany (check the note for information on how to order them).[42] I occasionally receive emails from admiring and more frequently from deeply critical consumer/students; much to my astonishment, a routine complaint is that I am a sycophant of Justice Scalia. Equally astonishing is how many folks tell me they use my courses as sympathetic texts in their study of the Alt-constitution.

❖ ❖ ❖

In sum, the claim of divine inspiration (or is it intervention?) opens up questions about who owns the Constitution and who its (chosen) people are. It tells us how to identify both the delivered and the forsaken. It speaks to our responsibility to the past and to the future and about the importance of fidelity. It encourages a culture of worship and veneration, rather than a culture of dialogue and engagement.

In some hands, insistence that America has a Christian constitution is also a claim about the *limits* of the Constitution's authority. Several years ago I took about 10 college seniors on a field trip from Hartford, Connecticut, to Montgomery, Alabama. Our plan (plan might be too strong a word) was to take a look at the (in)famous Ten Commandments monument that the Chief Justice of the Alabama Supreme Court had installed in the Court's beautiful rotunda. The 5,280-pound granite monument depicted the tablet Moses brought down from the mountain and several other ancient texts, designed to convey a message of . . . well, the message was plain, and Chief Justice Roy Moore made no effort to obscure or dilute it: God's Law is the Highest Law, the only legitimate source of man-made law, and superior to any other law, Constitution included. In any case where the Constitution appears at odds with God's Law (I say "appears" because in such instances, the supposed conflict is almost always a consequence of failing to interpret the Constitution properly), concerning, for example, abortion or same-sex marriage, then God's Law must govern. This claim is more than just hyperbole. In such cases, Moore preaches, Christian civil disobedience may be justified.

Flanked by two very large, muscular men in dark, ill-fitting suits, the Chief Justice was exceptionally gracious with his time, meeting, talking, and answering questions and arguing with us for well over an hour in the center courtroom. (Our pointed questions caught him by surprise. In asking the Chief Justice to grant us an audience, we may have hinted that our small university was of the John Wesley(an) tradition—not

Wesleyan University, of Yankee New England, famous for its liberal orthodoxy. I sort of almost feel just a little bit bad about that.)

Asked by my students if state-sponsored religious displays in public spaces violate the establishment clause of the First Amendment, Judge Moore waxed eloquently about the evils of the wall of separation and how the Founders had actually intended to enshrine protections for the Christian faith. Asked how the Constitution could evolve if hitched permanently to the past by Founders' intent, Judge Moore became animated and agitated. I was so mesmerized by his presentation that I lost track of the argument itself. Before I knew it, the Chief Justice was talking about evolution and Adam and Eve and the differences between male and female or some thing or other. (I don't think he said anything about the age of consent.)

Whatever one thinks of Judge Moore's principles, he is a man of principle, albeit one the true Constitution rejects. Ordered by a federal court to remove the statue, he refused on principle and ultimately was booted from the Alabama Supreme Court. Later, "When the high court, in *Obergefell v. Hodges*, discovered a constitutional right to same-sex marriage, Moore, back on the Alabama court, defied the decision, was suspended again and resigned."[43] In both instances, Moore believed that the Constitution (interpreted incorrectly) was in violation of (his) Christian faith and its own Christian pedigree. *Obergefell* and *Roe* both embraced principles that contradict the moral law, and so must be resisted. Moreover, both cases turned on a second fundamental maxim of the Alt-constitution by extending federal influence into areas of concern that the Founders had intended to leave with state governments.

FOUNDATIONAL PRECEPTS: SEPARATION OF POWERS, FEDERALISM, AND STATES' RIGHTS

I wrote in the Introduction that much of the Alt-constitution looks familiar. The Alt-constitution is organized around recognizable principles and precepts like the separation of powers, judicial review, federalism, and enumerated, limited powers. What those principles mean, however, is hitched not to twenty-first century jurisprudence (or, for that matter, to 1787), but rather to the constitution of the mid-nineteenth century. The antebellum constitution was a constitution of limited federal powers and equally of robust and far-reaching understandings of states' rights. It included such powerful tools as interposition and nullification. It was a constitution that gave a very narrow reading to the necessary and proper clause in Article I, Section 8 (a reading the Court famously rejected in *McCulloch v. Maryland* [1819]) and to Article VI (the supremacy clause), but an expansive reading to the Tenth Amendment. Lastly, it was a constitution in which the guarantees of the Bill of Rights ran only against the federal government, not the states; consequently, federal courts had very little authority to enforce the Bill of Rights against state governments.

SEPARATION OF POWERS

The separation of powers doctrine is an essential piece of the Constitution. Madison's description in the *Federalist Papers* is the best account. Writing in *Federalist* #51, Madison explained that ambition must be made to counteract ambition, thus indicating that the separation of powers doctrine is a mechanism for coping with human nature and the concentration of power in a single institution. We all know that many of the Founders feared a too powerful Congress, but the device is meant to guard against the concentration of power in any of the three branches of the federal government.

Most constitutional historians trace the doctrine to the French political theorist Charles-Louis de Secondat, baron de La Brède et de Montesquieu, an eighteenth-century French social and political philosopher. In *Spirit of the Laws* (1748) Montesquieu described the *trias politica*, a system of governance comprised of separate branches (executive, legislative, and judicial) with distinct but equal powers. The Founders had more than just political theory to guide them in Philadelphia, having before them the varied experiences of the American colonies, which had adopted several different variations of the doctrine. The Founders, therefore, had to make a choice about how to structure and implement the separation of powers of doctrine. They chose a model we know as "checks and balances," in which the powers and responsibilities of the three branches are not watertight, but instead overlap. As the great constitutional scholar Edward Corwin wrote, the separation of powers doctrine is not a principle set in stone, much less a set of clear, unambiguous paper rules, but rather "an invitation to a struggle."[44] Nothing in the text of the Constitution or in constitutional history foreordains the proper result of that struggle.

The Alt-constitution has a built-in bias in favor of a strong executive branch. The radical right's conception of the separation of powers movement reads Article II of the Constitution liberally, emphasizing broad, capacious interpretations of the President's oath to support the Constitution, to faithfully execute the laws, and of his powers as commander-in-chief. This seems predictable when one thinks about the Alt-right's affinity for strong leaders and its admitted if not proud historical association with neo-Fascist political movements. It is important to remember, though, that expansive understandings of executive power are common on the right generally, and certainly predate both the Alt-right and the Trump presidency.[45] Consider, for example, the concept of the unitary executive, which found its foremost expression in the second Bush presidency. The theory of the unitary executive, especially as advanced by academics like John Yoo and several prominent Republican politicians, including Dick Cheney, holds that the separation of powers doctrine imposes very few direct constraints on the power of the executive.[46] Because in Article II the Constitution assigns to the president "the executive power," the President can set aside laws that limit his power over national security.[47] In the Bush and Obama administrations, the unitary executive theory was proffered as a constitutional justification for unchecked presidential power over the use of military force, the detention and interrogation of prisoners, extraordinary rendition, and intelligence gathering.[48] In the Trump administration, it has so far manifested, without the terminology, in Trump's overt hostility to the federal judiciary (and especially respecting his comments on the travel ban) and in his assertion that "I have absolute right to do what I want to do with the Justice Department."[49]

The unitary executive is tailor made to the Alt-constitution, at least as long as the President is of the correct political persuasion. To no one's surprise, many of the proponents of the unitary presidency rediscovered limits on the executive when Obama was elected to office.[50] Conservative aversion to Obama led many on the right at the time to emphasize the limits on presidential power, and is likely to do so again when a Democrat or a RINO or a cuckservative is elected to office. This dissimulation is hardly unique to the right; indeed, one's understanding about the reach and limits of presidential (or congressional, or judicial) power almost always is hitched to which party holds office, and has been since 1796.

It is probably a mistake, therefore, to conclude that the Alt-constitution's conception of the separation of powers doctrine is driven only by political opportunism or that the radical right's conception of presidential power owes only to its admiration of strong(man) leaders. Some in the far right trace the doctrine of separation of powers not to American colonial experience, or even to Montesquieu, but to the Bible. The separation of powers doctrine, David Barton argues, comes "from the Book of Isaiah, because Isaiah 33:22 says, For the Lord is our judge, the Lord is our lawgiver, and the Lord is our king."[51] I suppose one can read Isaiah to say that power takes three forms—judicial, legislative, and executive—but I read it as concentrating all three of those powers in a single person (Being? Deity?). To my mind, concentrating power and separating power is not quite the same thing.

FEDERALISM AND STATES' RIGHTS

The separation of powers doctrine divides power on a horizontal axis. Federalism, in contrast, separates power on a vertical axis. No precept is more central to the Constitution, and likewise to the Alt-constitution, than federalism and the related notion of states' rights. The Civil War is evidence enough of the importance of federalism in United States history. But the centrality of federalism to the American constitutional order is best captured by the simple fact that federalism, alone among the several principles that make up the Constitution, is the only one that cannot be amended. The Constitution provides for federalism in perpetuity.[52]

Like the separation of powers doctrine, the Founders were less interested in the theory of federalism than in its practice. Unlike the separation of powers doctrine, though, discussions of federalism provoked intense political conflict and excited local and regional jealousies, to use the admittedly somewhat biased language of the *Federalist Papers*. The intense (and continuing) controversy involved in creating a single nation of several states should be no surprise. Creating a Union required the states to surrender part of their sovereignty both to other states and to a new sovereign, an unknown and potential leviathan. No topic generated more discussion in Philadelphia, or in the ratification debates that followed, especially between the Federalists and the anti-Federalists, than the question of how to allocate power between the national government and the states.

In contest in those debates were, and are, two different visions of America. One (it is only a little misleading to call it anti-Federalist) is a vision in which state and local governments, because closest and most accountable to their citizens, should be the primary instrumentalities of governance. In these smaller communities, citizens would govern themselves and their neighbors in the spirit of civic virtue. Strong state governments were juxtaposed against a weaker, distant federal government entrusted with only a few enumerated powers essential to the collective interests and needs of the several states acting in unison, such as the power to conduct war or to facilitate interstate commerce. A stronger national government, anti-Federalists feared, was vulnerable to corruption and a first step to tyranny.

The other (it is only a little misleading to call it Federalist) is a vision of the states united by a common government, limited in the powers entrusted to it but supreme regarding the reach of those powers. Unlike the Articles of Confederation and Perpetual Union, Federalists foresaw a central government possessed of the "energy and dispatch" necessary to govern in the public interest, an interest that transcended the interest of any single state.

It is tempting to think that debates between the Federalists and the anti-Federalists are safely confined to history or to academia. But as with the separation of powers, the federalism provisions in the Constitution are less a set of formal rules than an invitation to a struggle. The constitutional text tells us that the terms of the federal bargain are always subject to interpretation if not negotiation (except, of course, regarding the states' equal suffrage in the Senate). The tension is reflected, among other places, in the many contests between the commerce clause and the Tenth Amendment, and less obviously in the pull and push of Article VI and Article VII. Or consider the oft-forgotten Preamble to the Bill of Rights (PBR), which recalls the jealousy and fears of state governments. The PBR begins by announcing a desire on the part of the states to "prevent misconstruction or abuse" of the powers delegated by the Constitution to the new national government.

Federalism hides behind nearly every provision of the constitutional document. Consider, for example, the establishment clause of the First Amendment. In *Everson v. Board of Education* (1947), the Supreme Court ruled that the establishment clause applies to the states as well as to the federal government, and thus imposes significant restrictions on the ability of states to enact legislation that might tend to "establish" or to grant preferential aid to religion over irreligion. *Everson* is an open insult for many in the Christian right, and we'll take it up more completely in Chapter 3. The important point here is that the establishment clause, once incorporated, significantly impinges on areas of public life that were once the prerogative of the states alone. The Court's decision in *Everson*, in other words, has a direct impact on how federalism actually works. Some folks even think that the establishment clause is more concerned with federalism than with an individual religious liberty. In a dissent in the case of *Elk Grove United School District v. Newdow* (2004), Justice Thomas wrote, "The text and history of the Establishment Clause strongly suggest that it is a federalism provision intended to prevent Congress from interfering with state establishments. . . . Quite simply, the Establishment Clause is best understood as a federalism provision—it protects state establishments from federal interference but does not protect any individual right."

It is not much of a stretch to see *all* of American constitutional history through the lens of federalism. The history of federalism is the history of slavery, the Civil War, the commerce clause and the New Deal, and the civil rights movement of the 1960s. The history of federalism is the history of prohibition, the war on drugs, welfare reform, immigration, the women's movement, same-sex marriage, and the gay and trans-rights movements. It is the history of gerrymandering, environmentalism, and gun control. In each of these policy areas, invocations of federalism are almost always claims about what public policy should be regarding X, Y, or Z, but also and equally important, about *who* decides what it should be.

In other words, under the mantle of federalism, the who and the what of constitutional decision-making coincide. They have done so since the Civil War, if not since the Founding or even the Declaration of Independence, when the cause of federalism became the cause of slavery and vice versa. The marriage between states' rights and racism is the single most durable feature of the American constitutional order. Not every claim on behalf of federalism, or even states' rights, is grounded in racism (far from it), but history entitles us to ask of the champions of states' rights and federalism if their advocacy is driven by an elevated commitment to the honorable cause of local self-governance or something less salutary.

To be clear, federalism can serve good purposes as well as evil ones. Long before John Calhoun and others pressed states' rights in the run up to the Civil War, New England Federalists met in Hartford in the winter of 1815–1816 to discuss, among other things, their opposition to the War of 1812, removing the three-fifths clause from the Constitution, and their concerns about the Louisiana Purchase. Secession was among the topics broached, although many historians doubt the seriousness of those discussions, and the final report did not press the cause. Two centuries later some towns in Vermont and other New England states have invoked federalism to resist Bush and Obama-era security legislation and to advance the sanctuary movement in opposition to President Trump's immigration policies. Some scholars (myself among them) have argued that a reinvigorated form of federalism might be utilized to advance other liberal political causes as easily as conservative ones.[53] But its history and association with racism, whether overt or veiled, tells us why federalism features so prominently in the Alt-constitution.

THE TENTH AMENDMENT

Federalism in the Alt-constitution starts with the Tenth Amendment, which provides that "The powers not delegated to the United States by the Constitution, nor prohibited by it to the States, are reserved to the States respectively, or to the people." It is commonly held among us constitutional law types that the Tenth Amendment is but a truism. The Supreme Court said precisely this in *United States v. Darby* (1941), writing:

> The amendment states but a truism that all is retained which has not been surrendered. There is nothing in the history of its adoption to

suggest that it was more than declaratory of the relationship between the national and state governments as it had been established by the Constitution before the amendment or that its purpose was other than to allay fears that the new national government might seek to exercise powers not granted, and that the states might not be able to exercise fully their reserved powers.

The amendment is a truism because the entire Constitution, as Madison explained, is a grant of powers, and powers not granted to the federal government by the constitutional instrument, or fairly implied by it (this qualification, we shall see, is deeply contested and not a part of the Alt-constitution), by definition were reserved to the states or to the people, who held them originally in their sovereign capacity. Madison advanced a similar logic as a reason why the original constitutional document did not need a Bill of Rights, referring to drafting them as that "nauseous project of amendments."[54] On this rationale, the Tenth Amendment is indeed just a truism, a simple declaration of a constitutional fact and not, obviously, an independent grant of powers to the states, much less a grant of power that would undermine the powers the Constitution does give to the general government or one that would defeat the supremacy clause in Article VI.

It makes more sense to think of the Tenth Amendment not as a grant of power to the states, or even as a qualification on the powers granted to the federal government, but rather as a set of instructions. The Tenth Amendment (like the obscure Preamble to the Bill of Rights) doesn't tell us what the Constitution means; it tells us how to read the Constitution. It tells us the federal government possesses only those powers that it possesses and no more. It is an interpretive tool, a declarative provision, not an independent grant of power.

In the Alt-constitution, by way of contrast, the tenth amendment *is* an act of investiture and a significant source of state power. Far from a truism, the Alt-tenth amendment describes a far-reaching power that states can use to defend their sovereignty from the national government. It does so first by acting as a reservation on powers that are granted by the Constitution to the national government, such as the commerce clause (a matter of recurrent constitutional controversy since the early 1800s and a fertile ground for Supreme Court decisions) and the taxing power, and secondly by leaving to the states certain other matters of governance, including voting, intrastate commerce, and criminal procedure, among several others.

The best-known Supreme Court case involving the conflict between federal and state authority, although not the most significant, is *McCulloch v. Maryland* (1819). In *McCulloch*, the Court waded into one of the most politically charged matters of the era—the creation of a national bank. Maryland argued that nothing in Article I, Section 8 of the Constitution gives Congress express or implied authority to create a bank, and that therefore the power to create banks must reside with state governments. The national government argued that several explicit grants of power, such as the powers to coin money, to establish tariffs and to tax, and especially the power to regulate interstate commerce, did imply a power to create a bank, as well as to do other things that would facilitate the exercise of the powers explicitly granted. Crucial to the national government's argument, and to the Court's decision in *McCulloch*, was the necessary and proper clause of Article I. The clause provides that "The Congress shall have Power . . . [t]o make all Laws which shall be necessary and proper for carrying into Execution the foregoing Powers, and all other Powers vested by this Constitution in the Government of the United States, or in any Department or Officer thereof." Both the wording of the clause and its advisability were a matter of considerable debate in Philadelphia and during ratification. Anti-Federalists argued that the necessary and proper clause would defeat the Constitution's claim of enumerated and limited powers. Patrick Henry argued just this point at the Virginia Ratifying Convention, claiming that "If you grant them these powers, you destroy every degree of responsibility."[55] James Madison, in turn, argued that the sweeping clause could be used only in service of enumerated powers, and in *Federalist* #44 he noted that "Few parts of the Constitution have been assailed with more intemperance than this; yet on a fair investigation of it, no part can appear more completely invulnerable. Without the SUBSTANCE of this power, the whole Constitution would be a dead letter."[56]

Writing for the Court in *McCulloch*, Chief Justice Marshall held that the necessary and proper clause, although not an independent grant of power to the federal government, indicates that the powers that are delegated to the federal government must be read generously:

> We admit, as all must admit, that the powers of the Government are limited, and that its limits are not to be transcended. But we think the sound construction of the Constitution must allow to the national legislature that discretion with respect to the means by which the powers it confers are to be carried into execution which will enable that body to perform the high duties assigned to it in the manner most beneficial to the people. Let the end be legitimate, let it be within the scope of the Constitution, and all means which are appropriate, which are plainly adapted to that end, which are not prohibited, but consist with the letter and spirit of the Constitution, are Constitutional.

Maryland's reading of the necessary and proper clause was quite different. It argued that if the clause anticipated the existence of any implied powers at all, it would be only those "strictly" necessary to the achievement of powers explicitly granted. In other words, the necessary and proper clause was not meant to facilitate the exercise of federal power but rather to limit it, and this reading should be preferred because it is the only one consistent with the Tenth Amendment's reservation of powers to the states.

The Alt-tenth embraces the reading the Court rejected in *McCulloch* by insisting that the Tenth Amendment adopts a substantive vision of federalism in which the states are immune from federal authority in a number of different policy arenas, including criminal law and procedure, race relations, internal (or intrastate) commerce, and several others. It advances this broad interpretation of the Tenth Amendment by simultaneously adopting an exceptionally narrow interpretation of each of the powers granted to Congress in Article I, Section 8, and similarly of the necessary and proper clause. It does not deny the claim of federal supremacy set out in Article VI and pressed in *McCulloch*, but it does insist that the federal government is supreme only in those few areas the Constitution entrusts unambiguously to the national government.

WHO DECIDES? INTERPOSITION AND NULLIFICATION

The Alt-tenth amendment is at its most ambitious in its understanding not of which powers are granted to which level of government, but in its understanding of *who* gets to decide where authority falls when the subject matter is in dispute. The question of who decides is at the center of the doctrines of interposition and nullification. Both doctrines hold that states, acting in concert or individually, have the constitutional authority to resist federal power when they determine for themselves that the federal exercise is unconstitutional.

Although they are closely related, there are some important differences between interposition and nullification. As advanced by Madison, interposition holds that unconstitutional actions undertaken by the federal government can be opposed by the people, acting in concert with state legislatures or independent of them. Opposition might take several forms, including formal declarations, public protest, petitions to Congress, or constitutional amendment. Madison described these as "the several constitutional modes of interposition by the States against abuses of powers."[57] Nullification, in contrast, ordinarily involves a formal declaration by a state legislature that it will not comply with the federal law at issue (to which Madison fervently objected). In most treatments, these distinctions are of no interest. The most famous expositor of nullification, John C. Calhoun, used the terms interchangeably, and I have yet to find anyone on the far right who favors interposition, strictly speaking, over nullification, or even anyone who knows or cares about the differences.

Interposition and nullification have long and checkered histories. James Madison invoked interposition in the Virginia Resolution of 1798, and Thomas Jefferson advanced a theory of nullification in the Kentucky Resolution of 1799. The Resolutions were a response to the infamous Alien and Sedition Acts of 1798, which most of us know were a grave affront to freedom of speech. The Resolutions, however, were provoked more by concerns about federal overreach and states' rights than with freedom of expression. (The Alien and Sedition Acts were also racist, but the objection to them had little to with that; see Chapter 6.)

In the run up to the Civil War, "nullificationist tactics were adopted by both southerners seeking to protect slavery, and northerners trying to resist the federal Fugitive Slave Act."[58] This tells us that interposition and nullification can be used to advance constitutional ideals as well as to injure them. The logic behind a claim of nullification is the same whether one employs it in the service of Sanctuary cities or an all-white Aryan compound; or a safe space community for white conservatives, such as the Christian Covenant communities established in Kamiah, Idaho, by Bo Gritz; or the Justus Township, established in Montana by the Montana Freemen.

Most commentators have seen immediately that nullification and interposition raise questions that go not only to the nature of our constitutional union, but also to its survival. George Washington made just that point in a letter to Patrick Henry, warning that if "systematically and pertinaciously pursued, 'they would' dissolve the union or produce coercion."[59] Washington's comments foreshadow, of course, the important role nullification would play in the run up to the Civil War. John C. Calhoun, unsurprisingly, cited the Virginia and Kentucky Resolutions favorably in making the argument for secession. Equally unsurprising, President Jackson opposed them.

In addition to its obvious association with the cause of slavery, nullification is best known as a weapon of the states' rights movement against desegregation and the civil rights movement of the 1950s and 1960s. Calls for nullification followed a series of Supreme Court decisions that meant to dismantle racial segregation and Jim Crow. *Brown v. Board of Education* (1954) is the best known of these cases, but in some ways, a later case, *Cooper v. Aaron* (1958), is more instructive on nullification. In *Cooper*, the Court declared the efforts of Little Rock, Arkansas, to resist *Brown* a violation of the Constitution and an assault on the Court's authority to interpret it, as established in *Marbury v. Madison* (1803). Arkansas took the position that *Brown* was wrongly decided and that it had the constitutional authority to resist federally mandated desegregation. Arkansas was hardly alone in its opposition to *Brown*. In March, 1956, 10 of the 11 Southern states sent to Congress a "Declaration of Constitutional Principles" (the *Southern Manifesto*), signed by Senator Throm Sturmond and 100 other politicians (overwhelmingly Southern Democrats). The *Manifesto* begins by calling the Court's decision in *Brown* "a clear abuse of judicial power" that encroaches "upon the reserved rights of the States and the people." Elsewhere it describes the decision as "contrary to the Constitution," and calls upon the states "to resist forced integration by any lawful means."

The Court's response in *Cooper* was unambiguous:

> We should answer the premise of the actions of the Governor and Legislature that they are not bound by our holding in the Brown

case. It is necessary only to recall some basic constitutional propositions which are settled doctrine. . . . Article VI of the Constitution
makes the Constitution the 'supreme Law of the Land.' "In 1803,
Chief Justice Marshall, speaking for a unanimous Court, referring to
the Constitution as 'the fundamental and paramount law of the nation,' declared in the notable case of Marbury v. Madison, that 'It is
emphatically the province and duty of the judicial department to say
what the law is.' This decision declared the basic principle that the
federal judiciary is supreme in the exposition of the law of the Constitution, and that principle has ever since been respected by this
Court and the Country as a permanent and indispensable feature of
our constitutional system. . . . No state legislator or executive or
judicial officer can war against the Constitution without violating his
undertaking to support it."

The Court rejected these arguments in *Cooper*, but as with the Civil
War, or with South Carolina's attempted nullification of federal tariffs
in 1828 and 1832, force, or at least the threat of force, was required.[60]

Desegregation also provoked attempts at interposition. Louisiana,
for example, attempted to interpose federal efforts to desegregate its
elementary schools, including a formal legislative resolution of interposition. In *Bush v. Orleans Parish School Board* (1960), a United States
District Court in Louisiana squashed that effort, ruling that "The conclusion is clear that interposition is not a constitutional doctrine. If
taken seriously, it is illegal defiance of constitutional authority. Otherwise, 'it amounted to no more than a protest, an escape valve through
which the legislators blew off steam to relieve their tensions.' . . . However solemn or spirited, interposition resolutions have no legal efficacy."

"TENTHERS"

Nullification and interposition live in the Alt-tenth amendment and are
frequent topics of conversation in the "Tenther" movement. As explained at TheTenthAmendmentCenter.com,[61] Tenthers seek to restore the original meaning of the Tenth Amendment as a way of resisting the mounting power of the federal government: "While the establishment left and right continue to expand federal power, our goal is
straightforward. The Constitution: Every issue, every time. No excep-

tions, no excuses." Among the policy areas Tenthers seek to influence through nullification are Obamacare (it has even written proposed legislation, the "Federal Health Care Nullification Act"), gun control, asset forfeiture, immigration, local control of education/common core, school prayer, right-to-try, industrial hemp, and several others. The Tenth Amendment Center's definition of nullification, however, is so expansive that it robs it of any real meaning: "[W]e define nullification like this: Any act or set of acts which renders a law null, void or unenforceable."[62] "Nullification is not something that requires any decision, statement, or action by any branch of the federal government. . . . Nullification does not require permission from any person or institution outside of one's own State."[63]

The Tenther movement is not a fringe crusade. In the spring of 2017, Texas considered adopting the "Texas Sovereignty Act," which would allow it to override federal laws through the same process as passing an ordinary bill.[64] Several states have passed or tried to pass nullification statutes, among them Missouri (resisting federal gun control legislation) and Arizona and Montana. In 2009, for example, Montana passed the Firearms Freedom Act (later struck by a federal court), which provided that firearms manufactured in the state of Montana after October 1, 2009, and which remained in the state, were exempt from United States federal firearms regulations, provided that these items were clearly stamped 'Made in Montana' on a central metallic part.[65] The Montana statute prompted similar legislation in about six other states. In 2013, the Missouri legislature passed a statute that claimed to nullify in the state *all* federal gun control legislation. The Missouri bill was unique in also making it a crime for federal officers to enforce federal gun legislation. Governor Nixon vetoed that bill, but efforts continue to nullify federal gun control legislation, not only in Missouri, but also in Montana and Kansas. In April, 2013, for example, "Kansas passed a law asserting that federal gun regulations do not apply to guns made and owned in Kansas." Under the law, Kansans could manufacture and sell semi-automatic weapons in state without a federal license or any federal oversight. Kansas' 'Second Amendment Protection Act' backs up its states' rights claims with a penalty aimed at federal agents: when dealing with 'Made in Kansas' guns, any attempt to enforce federal law is now a felony. Bills similar to Kansas' law have been introduced in at least 37 other states."[66] Another popular target for nullification proposals are "right-to-try" statutes, which would permit some terminally ill patients to have access to some investigational drugs, biological products, or devices that the FDA has proscribed. Colorado, Louisiana, Michigan, Missouri, Oregon, Connecticut, and several additional states have all passed or are considering right-to-try statutes.

The constitutional objections states advance to nullify federal legislation will differ depending on the nature of the legislation at issue. In Montana, for example, federal gun legislation was decried as a violation of the commerce clause, whereas in Missouri the offense was said to be to the Second Amendment. Health care nullification efforts seem squarely to rest on commerce clause and Tenth Amendment claims, as did efforts in the 1990s by several states to nullify federal marijuana laws and efforts by some states, including Texas and North Carolina, to nullify the Court's same-sex marriage decision in *Obergefell v. Hodges* (2015). In North Carolina, for example, several Republican state legislators introduced the "Uphold Historical Marriage Act," which states, "Marriages, whether created by common law, contracted, or performed outside of North Carolina, between individuals of the same gender are not valid in North Carolina."

I want to reiterate that nullification, although a central component of the Alt-constitution, is neither inherently conservative nor liberal. Nullification talk has flourished in several states and cities in the form of sanctuary cities that vow to resist President Trump's immigration policies. Officials in Denver and Aurora, Colorado, for example, have pledged that "they will not enforce federal immigration laws," and John Hickenlooper, the governor of Colorado, has "hinted he would block any federal agents from coming in."[67]

SECESSION AND THE ALT-CONSTITUTION

Over the past two decades, several candidates for the Republican nomination for the presidency have advocated for nullification and even for the right of states to secede. Again, such efforts are usually associated with the right, but they need not be, as evidenced by ballot initiatives in some states to secede (such as #Calexit and the proposed "Oregon Secession Act," later withdrawn by its sponsors after it generated intensive negative reaction), immediately following President Trump's election.[68] Perhaps the most widely reported example is Governor Rick Perry's comment in 2009, in which he expressed sympathy for the idea that Texas might secede (again) from the Union. On several occasions since, Governor Perry has stated clearly that he does not favor secession as a live possibility, but he also has stated that "There's a lot of different scenarios. . . . . We've got a great union. There's absolutely no reason to dissolve it. But if Washington continues to thumb their nose at the American people, you know, who knows what might come out of that. But Texas is a very unique place, and we're a pretty independent lot to boot."[69] Perry's remarks should be read against the backdrop of a small but vocal nationalist movement called the Texas Nationalist movement, which in turn follows upon the Republic of Texas movement of the 1990s. The Texas Nationalist group claims its membership soared both after Perry's comments and around the 2012 election (it now claims over 250,000 members), and its political presence was affirmed at the start of the 2013 legislative session, when the group secured a meeting with Lt. Governor David Dewhurst.[70]

Secession movements also simmer in Alaska (Alaska Independent Party), Colorado (the 51st State Movement), California, Oregon, Maryland (A New State Initiative), New Hampshire (NHexit), Vermont (Vexit), Hawaii (Hawexit), and South Carolina, and are likely inchoate in others.[71] There are regional secession movements afoot or adream in New England, the Pacific Northwest (such as the proposed State of Jefferson, comprised of several counties in Northern California and Southern Oregon), and in some US territories. In addition, there are several (no one knows exactly how many) private groups and associations that seek to secede from the United States by establishing de jure and de facto independent communities and compounds. Some of the better known examples include "townships" created (or taken over by moving in members) by militia movements and Christian Identitarians, such as Tigerton Dells in Wisconsin, Almost Heaven in Idaho, and the Justus Township, Montana.

We should not dismiss these movements because they are small or because they are at the very far edge of American politics or because they contravene accepted constitutional theory, especially in a world with Brexit and serious campaigns for separation in Scotland, Catalonia, and elsewhere. James Poulos notes that, "As modern social and cultural forces continue to make most of us more interchangeable, interest in leaving the Union has spread out from coast to coast with remarkable regularity."[72] A Reuter's poll from 2014 indicated that at least 19 percent of respondents in America's eight major regions supported the idea of their state "peacefully withdrawing from the United States of America and the federal government."[73] "In the Great Lakes, Mid-Atlantic, Plains, and Far West, secession sympathizers top out at 22 percent of the population. In the Southeast, the group counts 1 of every 4 respondents. In the Rockies, the number climbs to 26 percent, and in the Southwest, fully a third are on board."[74] Perhaps predictably, support in the Reuter's poll ran stronger among Republicans than Democrats, and especially among Tea Party respondents, where support for secession hit 53 percent. Nevertheless, Reuters concluded that secession talk "was neither red nor blue but a polychromatic riot."[75]

The unconstitutionality of secession has been plain since the South lost the Civil War and the Supreme Court's decision immediately thereafter in *Texas v. White* (1869). In *Texas v. White*, the Court ruled that:

> The Constitution, in all its provisions, looks to an indestructible Union composed of indestructible States. . . . When, therefore, Texas became one of the United States, she entered into an indissoluble relation. All the obligations of perpetual union, and all the guaranties of republican government in the Union, attached at once to the State. The act which consummated her admission into the Union was something more than a compact; it was the incorporation of a new member into the political body. And it was final. The union between Texas and the other States was as complete, as perpetual, and as indissoluble as the union between the original States. There was no place for reconsideration or revocation, except through revolution or through consent of the States.

The Court's decision built on a foundation laid by President Lincoln. By the time of his first inaugural address on March 4, 1861, the topic of secession was no longer just a talking point. Jefferson Davis had assumed the presidency of the Confederacy just two weeks earlier. Lincoln went to great length to assure the South that he had no intention of interfering with the slave trade, saying plainly and directly, "I have no purpose, directly or indirectly, to interfere with the institution of slavery in the States where it exists. I believe I have no lawful right to do so, and I have no inclination to do so."

Some might think it odd, but the Confederate constitution was unclear on the question of secession from the Confederacy, especially because one might logically anticipate that the Confederate constitution would be predisposed to a strong conception of states' rights. Moreover, the Preamble to the Confederate constitution can be read to support that assumption. Unlike the US Constitution, which begins with the familiar "We the People," the Confederate constitution reads:, "We, the people of the Confederate States, each state acting in its sovereign and independent character. . . ." In fact, however, the relative position of the Confederate states to the Confederate national government was more complex. In several respects, including, for example, the power to regulate commerce and regarding taxes and tariffs, the confederate states retained considerable autonomy. And the Confederate constitution included no grant of power to the central government to act for the general welfare. But the same preamble that waxes elegantly about the sovereign character of its states also announces a purpose "to form a permanent federal government." And like the US Constitution, the Confederate text was silent on secession. David Currie notes that "It was proposed that the new [Confederate] Constitution explicitly recognize the right of secession, but the idea was dropped after others suggested that 'its inclusion would discredit the claim that the right had been inherent under the old government.'"[76]

All of which begs the question: does the Alt-constitution include the right of a state to secede? Not everyone in the radical right thinks secession is unconstitutional. An editorial at *American Renaissance* (you will recall from Chapter 1 that *American Renaissance* is a white supremacist online magazine) argues that "Some people have argued that secession is unconstitutional, but there's absolutely nothing in the Constitution that prohibits it. What stops secession is the prospect of brute force by a mighty federal government, as witnessed by the costly War of 1861."[77] Most of the argument in favor of a right to secede hinges upon proposals made just months before several states seceded in 1861 that would have amended the Constitution to make secession explicitly illegal: "Would there have been any point to offering these amendments if secession were already unconstitutional?"[78] As is ordinarily the case with rhetorical questions, the answer is not obvious.

The real influence of secession talk, however, lays less in the possibility of secession as a fact than in rhetoric. Rhetoric influences what the radical right thinks about the limits of federal power and of states' rights. The more radical talk of secession makes expansive if historically repudiated understandings of the Tenth Amendment, like the doctrine of neo-nullification, seem like a moderate alternative to the nuclear option of withdrawing from the Union. Unlike classical examples of nullification, which typically involve both a declaration by a state that it believes a federal law is unconstitutional and an effort to subvert or obstruct that law, neo-nullification typically involves simple noncompliance with federal mandates and policies, or a refusal to enforce them. The latter strategy is a consequence of Supreme Court decisions like *New York v. United States* (1992) and *Printz v. United States* (1997), where the Court held that the federal government cannot commandeer state officials or state legislatures to enforce federal law. This counts as nullification in the loose sense identified by the Tenth Amendment Center, and it is as much a part of the US Constitution as of the Alt-constitution.

Secession talk also matters because it speaks directly to questions of identity and to the literal and figurative question of who we are. One example of this is the idea of "cultural secession," prominent in some Southern intellectual circles in the 1990s. In a "Declaration of Southern Cultural Independence," the League of the South, founded in 1994 by academics Thomas Fleming, Clyde Wilkson, and Michael Hill, declared that southerners are "a separate and distinct people, with an honorable heritage and culture worthy of protection and preservation," and vowing to "cooperate economically to build and sustain our separate educational and cultural institutions."[79]

Legal claims of interposition, nullification, and secession, in contrast to cultural claims, involve arguments of dubious constitutionality and raise fundamental questions about the meaning and purpose of the Tenth Amendment. Does the Tenth Amendment offer up any sort of a remedy to the states if the states think the federal government has encroached upon their powers? What might a remedy look like? Such questions return us to questions of interpretive authority (Who interprets?) and back of that, to one of the most rudimentary of all constitutional questions: Who made the Constitution? The answer to this question tells us a lot about who should interpret the Constitution and about the limits of the Constitution's authority.

THE COMPACT THEORY OF THE CONSTITUTION

The compact theory holds that the Union, and the Constitution that cements it, is a "compact" made by the states in their sovereign capacity as independent nation-states. (Recall the preamble to the Confederate constitution.) This understanding of who made the Constitution reaches at least as far back in American constitutional history as the Virginia and Kentucky Resolutions.

The purpose of the compact between the states is to mediate conflicts between the states and to secure collective cooperation in those few areas of concern that the individual states chose to delegate to the federal government. There are three key points to understand about this delegation of power. First, the delegation is by the states as sovereign entities, not by the "We the People" acting in some collective or shared sovereign capacity. Parenthetically, although the Preamble to the Constitution seems to embrace the latter account of who made the Constitution, the compact theory finds some support in Article VII. Article VII provides that "the Ratification of the Conventions of nine States shall be sufficient for the Establishment of this Constitution between the States so ratifying the Same. DONE in Convention by the Unanimous Consent of the States present the Seventeenth Day of September in the Year of our Lord one thousand seven hundred and eighty-seven and of the Independence of the United States of America the Twelfth." Clearly, the argument runs, the actors in Article VII are the States, not the "People."

Second, the delegation of power from the states to the federal government is limited. It includes only those areas of governance the constitutional text identifies and no more. Interestingly, the plain words of the Tenth Amendment, one of the cornerstones of compact theory, seem to undermine this claim. It provides "The powers not delegated to the United States by the Constitution, nor prohibited by it to the States, are reserved to the States respectively, or to the people." For states' rights activists, however, what it *means* is this: "The powers not *expressly* delegated to the United States by the Constitution, nor prohibited by it to the States, are reserved to the States respectively, or to the people." This meaning seems so obvious, in fact, that on occasion even the Supreme Court has misquoted the Tenth to reflect it.[80] It is a significant, if not momentous mistake, for the Alt-tenth, with the addition of the word "expressly," denies the federal government any implicit or implied powers, as well as forces a constricted reading of the necessary and proper clause in Article I. Put another way, the states are sovereign actors, free to run their own affairs as they see fit, free of federal parenting except in those few areas where the states have expressly ceded a part of their sovereign powers through the compact. (Some versions of compact theory go further in arguing that even the grants the states made to the federal government do not constitute diminutions in their authority because "federal power to settle disputes between the states is different from sovereignty and jurisdiction.")[81]

Third, a state's consent to join the Union may be revoked at any time and for almost any reason a state elects. Obviously federal overreach would suffice as a reason for any state to revoke its consent to the compact. Upon revocation, the state would no longer be subject to the terms of the compact/constitution, or presumably even a part of the Union, although as Lincoln noted, the Union is older than the Constitution.

Under the compact theory, then, not "We the People," but rather the states made the Constitution, and the states can unmake it if they choose. The compact theory is the wrong answer to an important question, and it has been wrong since President Lincoln's first inaugural address, since the North won the Civil War, and since the Supreme Court's response in *Texas v. White* (1869). Lincoln's rejection of the compact theory is worth quoting at length:

> I hold that in contemplation of universal law and of the Constitution the Union of these States is perpetual. Perpetuity is implied, if not expressed, in the fundamental law of all national governments. It is safe to assert that no government proper ever had a provision in its organic law for its own termination. Continue to execute all the express provisions of our National Constitution, and the Union will endure forever, it being impossible to destroy it except by some action not provided for in the instrument itself.

> Again: If the United States be not a government proper, but an association of States in the nature of contract merely, can it, as a contract, be peaceably unmade by less than all the parties who made it? One party to a contract may violate it—break it, so to speak—but does it not require all to lawfully rescind it?

Descending from these general principles, we find the proposition that in legal contemplation the Union is perpetual, confirmed by the history of the Union itself. The Union is much older than the Constitution. It was formed, in fact, by the Articles of Association in 1774. It was matured and continued by the Declaration of Independence in 1776. It was further matured, and the faith of all the then thirteen States expressly plighted and engaged that it should be perpetual, by the Articles of Confederation in 1778. And finally, in 1787, one of the declared objects for ordaining and establishing the Constitution was ' to form a more perfect Union.'

But if destruction of the Union by one or by a part only of the States be lawfully possible, the Union is less perfect than before the Constitution, having lost the vital element of perpetuity. It follows from these views that no State upon its own mere motion can lawfully get out of the Union; that resolves and ordinances to that effect are legally void, and that acts of violence within any State or States against the authority of the United States are insurrectionary or revolutionary, according to circumstances.

Lincoln's logic is compelling but not irrefutable; it is simply an *interpretation* of the Constitution. Like the Confederate constitution, the text of our Constitution itself says nothing at all, at least directly, about the right of a state to secede.

In the Alt-constitution, built on the compact theory, the power to adjudge whether federal action encroaches on powers reserved to the states is held by the states themselves. As the actual language of the Tenth Amendment makes clear, however, powers not delegated to the federal government are not reserved to the states alone, but rather "are reserved to the States respectively, or to the people." Implicit in the language is a reminder that it is not the states that are sovereign but the people. And the logic that reads the Tenth as permitting states to nullify federal law, notwithstanding Article VI, would seem to authorize the sovereign people to nullify federal acts as well. How might the people act in their collective sovereign capacity to nullify legislation? Elections are the first possibility, and as we saw earlier, Madison suggested a couple of others, all of which fell substantially short of secession and even of nullification in the strong sense.

Do we want individuals to be able to nullify laws? As we will see in Chapter 5, something very much like an individual right to secede from the Union is one of the central claims of the Sovereign Citizen Movement (SCM). In brief, Sovereign Citizens claim a right to withdraw (secede) or to be beyond the reach of the lawful authority of the federal government, which they believe to have overstepped the limits of its constitutional authority—a determination they make for themselves. It is difficult to see how any government could function under such a rule, least of all one committed to the broad purposes outlined in the Preamble. Surely if there is a right to secede it requires the people to act in their collective capacity and not as individual sovereigns.

Arguments about secession and nullification are arguments about the nature of the constitutional union and about the distribution of political power, as well as about what the Constitution means, how to interpret it, and who has (final) authority to interpret it. Some arguments for nullification, or for various versions of it, are perfectly respectable and plausible interpretations of the commerce clause, the necessary and proper clause, the supremacy clause in Article VI, and the Tenth Amendment. What cannot be defended is a conception of nullification that authorizes its use only when marshaled for conservative (or liberal) causes, or in ways that subvert the Union or that undermine the Founders' undoubted purpose to create a vibrant and robust central government, equal to the task of governing where it is authorized to govern, as set out in the Preamble and Article I.

CONCLUSION

The religious (Christian and Evangelical) bent of the Alt-constitution tells us what the Constitution is, what it means, how it should be interpreted, and by whom. It is the single most important key to understanding what the Alt-constitution means, not only as a matter of constitutional law but also, and just as importantly, as a cultural artifact. It is also the single most important threat to the Constitution and to the secular, democratic, inclusive, and egalitarian community it envisions, not only because it advances distorted and self-defeating interpretations of individual provisions, such as the necessary and proper clause and the First, Second, and Tenth Amendments, but also because it rejects as unsound and as illegitimate the Reconstruction Amendments, the Sixteenth and Seventeenth Amendments, and perhaps others.

The religious character of the Alt-constitution encourages citizens to revere the Constitution rather than engage it. It encourages a kind of constitutional fundamentalism that asks citizens to memorize the Constitution, but not to think about it critically. In its devotion to the Founders it misses what the Founders *really* intended for us—not to venerate what they did, but to continue their work.

Chapter 3

SPEECH FREAKS

The Alt-First Amendment

It is sometimes tempting to think the Alt-constitution has just a single provision. So-called speech crises at several respected academic institutions, including at Claremont McKenna College; University of Missouri; Evergreen State; University of Florida; Brown University; and the University of Connecticut, agitate the radical right until another controversy comes along. The appearance of Charles Murray at Middlebury College; canceled or contentious talks by Milo Yiannopoulos and Ann Coulter at Berkeley; Richard Spencer at the University of Georgia; and of course the violence at the University of Virginia (triggered by an Alt-right demonstration peddled in part as a Free Speech rally) seem to suggest that the First Amendment, if not the sum of the radical right's concern with the Constitution, is certainly the most important. For all their mocking talk about SJW's and Snowflakes, the Alt-right has eagerly assumed the mantle of victim.

Many in the Alt-right see themselves, and more importantly, want us to see them, as Free Speech Warriors. Indeed, the "official line" on AltRight.com concerning Charlottesville is that:

> Anyone who still thinks free speech and freedom to assembly still exists anywhere in the White world can clearly see for themselves what happens when White people try to peacefully assemble and advocate for their interests. The state disregards our rights, we are physically assaulted in the streets by non-Whites and political oppo-

nents, and the lying media runs propaganda campaigns to smear us. As of now, they are blaming the three deaths in Charlottesville on us.[1]

The Alt-right's account of what happened—to them—at Charlottesville is a fairy tale of victimization by Antifa, George Soros, and the extreme left.[2] According to the Alt-right, "the white nationalist protesters were thrust defenseless into crowds of armed thugs, beaten, and forced to defend themselves to the extent that one of their ranks killed in self-defense."[3]

The complaint that *their* speech is the target of censorship, especially in universities and on Twitter, is a familiar trope in the Alt-right. Making an effort to understand why they think this (assuming for the moment they really believe it) does not lend legitimacy or substance to the claim, much less constitute any sympathy for it (just to be clear, I have none). We need to understand it because it reveals what and how the Alt-right thinks about freedom of speech in particular and about constitutional liberties as a general proposition. Moreover, the Alt-right's effort to gain legitimacy by portraying themselves as free-speech martyrs has "quickly migrated to more mainstream conservative sites that also cater to alt-right audiences."[4]

The claim that conservative speech is a frequent target of censorship, whether on college campuses or social media, is not just talk. As Keith Whittington (and several others) has observed, threats to campus speech are a familiar and long-standing concern in American higher education, and it also true that "Free speech on college campuses is perhaps under as great a threat today as it has been in quite some time."[5] There should be little doubt that on many college campuses there are real and substantial threats to freedom of speech, or that these threats have taken a great variety of forms, some obvious (such as banning some controversial speakers) and some less obvious (such as charging exorbitant if not punitive "security" fees to "protect" speakers and students). But more often than not, supposed threats to the campus speech of conservatives are imagined, trumped up, and manufactured.

Several conservative speakers at several compuses have had events disrupted, rescheduled, or canceled. On a few occasions, confrontations between the Alt-right and counter protesters, like Antifa, have become violent, as was the case at Cal-Berkeley. One person was shot during a talk by Milo Yiannopoulos at the University of Washington. Richard Spencer's much publicized talk at the University of Florida in October, 2017, was accompanied by at least three men shouting "Heil Hitler," who were arrested for attempted murder upon reports that they had shot at a crowd of protestors.[6]

The Alt-right likes to portray itself as the lamb in these confrontations, hence the alleged need for splinter "defensive" groups like the Poor Boys and the Alt-Knights to maintain an armed presence at these events. Positioning themselves as beleaguered constitutional purists has the effect of putting those who condemn racist or hate speech on the "wrong" side of the argument by making them look intolerant of freedom of speech.

Andrew Anglin makes a good example of this sort of disingenuous branding. Anglin is the founder of *The Daily Stormer*, a notorious neo-Nazi website. Anglin and the *Stormer* are especially well known for "troll storming," or the practice of encouraging followers to harass and intimidate others with comments and postings on social media. One of Anglin's targets, realtor Tanya Gersh, who is Jewish, has sued Anglin in a federal court in Montana for invasion of privacy, intentional infliction of emotional distress, and violations of Montana's Anti-Intimidation act. Gersh told CNN that her family endured weeks of harassment and anti-Semitic slurs, including edited images of her face on the gates of Auschwitz, a voicemail with the sound of gunshots, and threats on social media to her and her children. Anglin claims it is all protected by the First Amendment. In their motion to dismiss the case, Anglin's attorneys argue that "Even Nazi expression, no matter the psychic harm on Jewish residents, is nonetheless protected speech. . . . Every word uttered by Mr. Anglin in this public dispute is protected by the First Amendment, no matter how many people find those views intolerable."[7]

In the aftermath of the Unite the Right rally at the University of Virginia, GoDaddy and some other Internet hosting companies denied service to *The Daily Stormer*, *Vanguard America*, and a few other neo-Nazi groups.[8] The *Stormer* has since reappeared (and then disappeared and reappeared again with a new name, *Punished Stormer*).[9] There is something to be said in favor of making the message less accessible, especially since experts seem to think that frequent exposure may help to radicalize some individuals.[10] On the other hand, the sites typically reorganize and reappear elsewhere on the Internet, often on sites well beyond the jurisdiction of US authorities, or on the dark net, as the Daily *Stormer/Punished Stormer* saga demonstrates. Denying Alt-right groups access to the web also plays into the narrative of the Alt-right as First Amendment/Freedom of Speech martyrs. The assertion that such silencing violates the First Amendment has no merit at all, but it has considerable cultural cache.

Posing as free speech warriors is the culmination of a long strategy on the right. The strategy has its origins in conservative opposition in the 1980s and 1990s to campus speech codes, which were said to threaten academic freedom and the First Amendment rights of conservative students and professors on overwhelmingly liberal college campuses. One of its most recent iterations has been a campaign to get state legislatures to pass "freedom of speech" legislation that purports to protect speech on college campuses. In Louisiana, for example, Governor Edwards signed Senate Bill 364, which, among other things, provides that public universities must include "a statement that it is not the proper role of an institution to shield individuals from speech protected by the First Amendment of the Constitution . . . including without limitation ideas and opinions they find unwelcome, disagreeable, or even deeply offensive."[11]

Behind such efforts is an intricate and complex history. Movement conservatives have not always been free speech patriots, and for many years conservatives held differing views about the purpose and the reach of the First Amendment.[12] Wayne Batchis, for example, distinguishes between two distinct conservative approaches to the First Amendment. "Moralistic conservatism" allows considerable regulation of speech to promote virtue or a particular moral agenda, and is often associated with Christian conservatives. A second approach, "libertarian conservatism," draws upon free market understandings to advance a more latitudinarian approach to freedom of expression.[13] Over time, Batchis argues, and in large measure in response to changes in political culture, including but not only the rise of political correctness on college campuses, a significant part of the conservative movement began to coalesce around the libertarian and free market approaches to speech.[14]

That college campuses make a concerted effort to exclude conservatives and conservative viewpoints is by now an incontrovertible truth in much of the conservative movement. Several websites (Campusreform.org, TheCollegeFix.com, ProfessorWatchlist.org) and watchdog organizations (Foundation for Individual Rights in Education/FIRE.org, Charles Koch Institute, American Center for Law and Justice/ACLJ.org), and media outlets (Fox News) routinely play up examples of liberal intolerance and the Left's zeal to trample speech rights. Very few campus speech codes actually punished speech simply for its political content, but some did (and do) permit university officials to censure and to punish speech that was discriminatory, or which amounted to harassment based on race, gender, religion, sexual identity, class, and ethnicity. Whether speech codes violate the First Amendment is a complex question and depends, in part, upon how narrowly or expansively the code in question is drafted and how it is enforced. Several federal courts have found constitutional flaws in some speech codes.[15] In some cases the codes were vague or failed to distinguish between protected and unprotected speech. In a few other cases, the codes discriminated on the basis of viewpoint, or otherwise prohibited speech that should clearly be protected.[16]

Arguably the most important of these decisions, both in terms of legal doctrine and in its effect on galvanizing opposition to speech codes, was *Doe v. University of Michigan* (1989), in which a United States District Court judge struck Michigan's code as unconstitutionally vague and overbroad.[17] *Doe* also acknowledged, however, that there might be ways to draft speech codes that do conform to constitutional rules.

There is room for a serious argument about how far we should protect speech rights in colleges and universities.[18] Speech freaks think the First Amendment begins and ends any discussion about campus speech codes, relying either implicitly or explicitly on the assumption that the First Amendment is absolute. But it is not enough simply to invoke the First Amendment. Whatever its simplistic rhetorical appeal, the claim that anyone can say anything anywhere anytime is not a convincing proposition in any community. Once we acknowledge that some limitations on some speech will sometimes be appropriate (as all courts do, including the District Court in *Doe*), we can't avoid talking about what specific limits are advisable, when, and why. If the question at hand concerns campus speech codes, some of the discussion will have to address the reasons why speech and academic freedom are important to university communities. So, for example, if (the conditional is deliberate) the reason we value academic freedom is to facilitate the search for knowledge, then we might plausibly limit speech that impedes that search. If (again, deliberate) the reason educational communities exist is to educate students, then we might plausibly think about limits on speech that impede the ability of (some) students to learn. I'm not trying to fully develop or defend these sorts of arguments here, and I recognize that there are good arguments one can make to the contrary. I point to them only to demonstrate that simplistic exhortations about speech rights obscure complex questions about the nature and purposes of the community and membership in it. Moreover, this is not a problem limited to academic communities. Implicit in the claim that the First Amendment is absolute is a rank-ordering of constitutional norms and values, about the weight of speech relative to public order or the common defense or the general welfare, or about the relative weight and standing of our commitments to speech and to equality, human dignity, or some other important constitutional value. Speech freaks and First Amendment absolutists simply assume what must instead be demonstrated—that the First Amendment is always more important than our pursuit of other constitutional ideals.

A FIRST AMENDMENT PRIMER

The First Amendment is a fairly recent invention. Almost all of the rules and doctrines that make up the complicated jurisprudence of the First Amendment are a post-World War II development. The reason is because the Bill of Rights did not apply to state governments until well into the twentieth century, when the Supreme Court began to develop the doctrine of "incorporation."

Incorporation is a fascinating story in its own right. The story begins at the Philadelphia Convention when, against the advice of George Mason, Charles Pinckney, and others, the Founders decided not to include a bill of rights in the document they submitted to the states for ratification. The absence of a bill of rights was a major point of divide in the ratification debates. Several colonies conditioned their ratification on the promise of a Bill of Rights, and Madison, at least, was influenced by Jefferson's observation in a letter that a bill of rights might be a useful reminder to officials and citizens about the importance of liberty, as well as provide a check in the hands of the judiciary.

In the important case of *Barron v. Baltimore* (1833), the Court was asked for the first time to hold a provision of the Bill of Rights (in this case, the Fifth Amendment's takings clause) applicable to the states. The Court refused, noting that the purpose of the Bill of Rights was to restrain the powers of the newly created federal government. As Chief Justice Marshall noted in *Barron*, for protections against state governments, citizens must turn to their state constitutions. (Barron was reaffirmed in the controversial *Slaughterhouse Cases* [1873], which held wrongly that the recently ratified privileges and communities clause of the Fourteenth Amendment had not, as many assumed, overruled *Barron v. Baltimore*. I take up that catastrophe in Chapter 6.)

By virtue of the Supreme Court's decision in *Barron*, the speech and religion clauses of the First Amendment did not apply to the states until well into the twentieth century, when the Court began to "incorporate" the individual provisions of the Bill of Rights into the due process clause of the Fourteenth Amendment. Among the first provisions of the Bill of Rights to be incorporated, or made applicable against the states, was the First Amendment.

The First Amendment is far from a simple matter. Its 45 words have given rise to a convoluted body of rules and doctrines, the consistency and clarity of which elude most judges, scholars, and citizens. Moreover, the rules constantly change and evolve. If one steps back, however, there is a single and simple overriding principle of free speech jurisprudence that cannot be denied, except by Speech Freaks: the First Amendment does not protect all manner of speech or expression. Depending upon what kind of speech is involved, where it occurs, and sometimes even upon who the speaker is, the state can regulate and sometimes even prohibit speech altogether, provided it advances a good reason for doing so. What counts as a good reason, and how weighty the reason must be, depends on the circumstances and the sort of speech involved. The state's authority to proscribe political speech, for instance, is ordinarily quite narrow. The state cannot prohibit political speech simply because it disagrees with it or because it thinks it is wrong or false. Proscriptions on political speech must advance a compelling state interest (such as national security, or physical harm to another person), which means the state's interest in proscribing political speech must be very serious, and the limitations must reach no farther than necessary to effectuate the state's compelling interest.[19] On the other hand, some kinds of expression, such as symbolic speech and commercial speech, get less protection, and some, like pornography and (maybe) so-called fighting words, get no protection at all.[20] In these latter instances the state may proscribe or regulate speech so long as it has a rational basis for doing so; and, in judicial hands, the rational basis requirement is exceptionally easy to satisfy.[21]

We call the idea that different kinds (categories) of speech merit different degrees of protection the "categorical" approach to the First Amendment. It may not be easy to locate the categorical approach in the absolutist language of the First Amendment ("Congress shall make no law"), but it is not difficult to see why the idea appeals to so many judges and scholars. The clearest alternative to it (although not the only one), the absolutist approach, has one obvious advantage and one obvious flaw. The advantage to absolutism is that it seems straightforward and simple to apply. The disadvantage is that it is completely unworkable: no community could long survive, much less flourish, under such a rule.

There is one other foundational principle of First Amendment jurisprudence, a principle that many citizens do not fully comprehend. The state action doctrine provides that all of the liberties guaranteed in the Bill of Rights, speech and religion included, are protected only against the actions of governmental officials. The category of public official is quite broad; it includes, for example, public employees, including teachers in public schools, but it is also limited. An example will help: If you work for a private employer, say as a *chef de tournant* at Finn's House of Omelet Perfection (FHOP),[22] your employer (me) is under no First Amendment obligation to protect your speech while you are at work. The First Amendment does not protect freedom of expression from private parties, including employers, private schools, and citizens who disagree with or subject you to scorn and ridicule. Simply said, the First Amendment does not shield you from the criticism of other citizens who take issue with what you say. You are not the target of censorship and no one has violated your First Amendment rights if someone calls you a racist when you talk about white heritage, or if your employer refuses to let you speak to other employees about Christian Identity. All one can say in such a circumstance is that someone else does not like your speech and has it within their (legal) power to act on their dislike, perhaps by disciplining you at work or at school, or by firing you, or by shaming you—and even, ironically, by doxxing you.[23] You have no right to speak anywhere or everywhere, no right to say whatever you want, and certainly no First Amendment right to compel others to listen to you. The disjuncture between the Alt-first amendment and the "real" First Amendment on this point has proved to be a real shock to some folks in the Alt-right, who complain loudly when they lose their jobs after *they* are outed by social media, and yet have no use for NFL quarterbacks whose speech gets them boycotted. There is an explanation for the inconsistency: The Alt-first amendment applies wherever and whenever its proponents want to speak and it shields whatever *they* want to say. When other citizens refuse to listen or won't give them a platform, they cry censorship. The Alt-right are not Free Speech Warriors; they are Free Speech Snowflakes.

Under the Alt-first amendment, in contrast, vocal criticism from an angry crowd (one you sought to provoke for just this reason), or an angry Twitter storm, or termination by your employer, violates the sacred guarantee of freedom of speech, which protects you not only from the state, but also from liberals, feminists, SJW's, Antifa, George Soros, and uppity teenagers, like David Hogg, who have the temerity to respond to bullying by such First Amendment stalwarts like Laura Ingraham.

Trading on this widespread misunderstanding about what the First Amendment means, Alt-righters position themselves as victims of intolerance and as First Amendment patriots. First Amendment absolutists and Speech Freaks assume that the First Amendment's reach is not burdened by the distinction between public and private. It is a curious if not convenient mistake for a movement that warns constantly of the dangers of tyranny. At least as regards speech rights, the Alt-right appears to think all of civil society should be constitutionalized. That too is a discussion worth entertaining, but I doubt that very many in the extreme right are genuinely committed to the idea that the Constitution, in its entirety, should apply to private life. To some ways of thinking, that would be the sort of totalizing tyranny the radical right purports to fear.

PRIVATE SPEECH AND CAMPUS CENSORSHIP

The state action doctrine means that in many of the free speech controversies on college campuses an absolute commitment to free speech should not simply be assumed, not because some institutions are intolerant, but because private institutions are under no constitutional obligation to respect formal First Amendment rules. Put another way, speech codes at public universities are subject to First Amendment requirements and those requirements, as *Doe v. University of Michigan* demonstrates, do impose limits on how (public) colleges and universities can regulate expression. In contrast, speech codes adopted at private colleges and universities, strictly speaking, cannot violate the First Amendment because the First Amendment simply does not apply to them. The First Amendment does not guarantee you a right to speak at Middlebury College or Brown University; or on the campus of Google, Microsoft, or at the local convenience store. These are all private institutions, free of First Amendment strictures and promises. They have no constitutional obligation to invite you to speak, nor any constitutional obligation to listen quietly and politely to your speech, or to let you speak without interruption. Whether social, cultural, or academic norms counsel this kind of civility is an interesting and important question (and if you think the answer is obvious, I'd urge you to think about it some more, no matter which side you lean to), but it is not strictly a First Amendment issue.

AN ALT-FIRST AMENDMENT PRIMER

In contrast to the many complications of the real First Amendment, the Alt-first amendment is a simple matter. Its jurisprudence is certainly easier to learn: The Alt-first amendment means what it says. It admits no limitations on freedom of speech. The Alt-first amendment does not distinguish between different categories of speech or balance speech against any countervailing state interest in limiting speech.

Some readers may think my description of the Alt-first amendment sounds like a version of the First Amendment often attributed to Justice Hugo Black—no law means no law. In fact, Justice Black did not hold to such a view, at least not consistently, and his apparent affinity for protecting speech was limited by his surprisingly narrow definition of "speech." Indeed, Justice Black dissented in one of the Court's best known and most important freedom of speech cases, *Tinker v. Des Moines* (1968). In *Tinker*, the Court ruled that public school students who wore black arm bands to protest the Vietnam War were engaged in an act "akin to pure speech." Justice Black dissented, writing, "It is a myth to say that any person has a constitutional right to say what he pleases, where he pleases, and when he pleases. Our Court has decided precisely the opposite."

HATE SPEECH AND THE ALT-FIRST AMENDMENT

What Justice Black calls a myth is one of the central pillars of the Alt-first amendment. Any number of perfectly constitutional restrictions on freedom of speech must be rejected as unconstitutional under the Alt-first amendment. First Amendment rules that prohibit slander and libel, to take one example, must fall under the Alt-first amendment, as would limitations on speech that originate from concerns about privacy, or criminal procedure, or national security.

The differences between the Alt-first amendment and the real First Amendment are not always so stark. The Supreme Court sometimes does protect speech that many of us find uncivil, offensive, inflammatory, or hateful, and sometimes at considerable social cost. Recall, for example, *Texas v. Johnson* (1989), the flag burning case. In that case the Court asserted: "If there is a bedrock principle underlying the First Amendment, it is that government may not prohibit the expression of an idea simply because society finds the idea itself offensive or disagreeable." A conception of speech that allows the state to silence what others find disagreeable, just because they find it disagreeable, is no guarantee of freedom of expression at all.

Some scholars and judges argue that fighting words or hate speech may be banned not because they are disagreeable, but because they harm other people or dent our commitment to other, equally important constitutional norms and values, such as respect for others, including racial and other minorities, and a commitment to human equality.[24] We routinely tolerate restrictions on speech because we think the expression in question contributes nothing to the marketplace of ideas, or to self-government, and sometimes because we place a higher value on other interests, such as preventing threats to democracy itself or harm to the community or to individuals.[25] Words matter and words have consequences. That is why we protect them and why sometimes we don't, and why sometimes we shouldn't.

Because the right to say anything to anyone, no matter how offensive or hateful, is an essential first principle for the Alt-right, it is useful to compare and contrast how the First Amendment and the Alt-first amendment treat hate speech. Hate speech demeans, degrades, or insults others on the basis of an attribute or a characteristic of that person's identity, such as their race, gender, ethnicity, religion, disability, or sexuality.[26] Prohibitions on hate speech typically start from the assumption that speech *can* harm those who are its object, either by reinforcing negative social stereotypes about some groups or by directly causing emotional distress and sometimes even physical harm. Some scholars further hold that hate speech both causes and reinforces the subordination of some minorities and liminal groups, and in so doing undermines our commitment to equality.[27] Hence there is said to be an overriding public interest (a compelling state interest) in circumscribing hateful speech that might otherwise qualify for protection under the First Amendment.

Contrary to popular belief, laws that punish hateful speech have a long history in the United States, especially if one uses a relaxed definition both of hate and of speech. The idea made its first appearance in a case called *Chaplinsky v. New Hampshire*, decided in 1942. One Saturday afternoon, Walter Chaplinsky, a Jehovah's Witness, offended passersby and a crowd of people in the small city of Rochester, New Hampshire, with a speech/rant littered with disparaging references to organized religion as a "racket." Fearing an agitated crowd, a police officer escorted Chaplinsky to the police station, where Chaplinsky confronted a town official he had met earlier, calling him "a God-damned racketeer"" and "a damned Fascist." Chaplinsky was charged and convicted under a New Hampshire statute that made it illegal for anyone to address "any offensive, derisive or annoying word to anyone who is lawfully in any street or public place . . . or to call him by an offensive or derisive name."[28]

If the New Hampshire statute appears breathtakingly broad (it made it illegal to address an *annoying* word to another person), the Court had no difficulty upholding it. In a unanimous opinion by Justice Frank Murphy, the Court noted that "it is well understood that the right of free speech is not absolute at all times and under all circumstances."

Justice Murphy next insisted that:

> There are certain well defined and narrowly limited classes of speech, the prevention and punishment of which have never been thought to raise any Constitutional problem. These include the lewd and obscene, the profane, the libelous, and the insulting or "fighting" words—those which, by their very utterance, inflict injury or tend to incite an immediate breach of the peace. . . . Such utterances are no essential part of any exposition of ideas, and are of such slight social value as a step to truth...that any benefit that may be derived from them is clearly outweighed by the social interest in order and morality.

The *Chaplinsky* rule is straightforward: There are certain well-defined and narrowly limited classes of speech, including the lewd, the obscene, the profane, the libelous, and fighting words that the state may regulate with little constitutional problem. The state may punish these categories of expression because they are not an essential part of any exposition of ideas and are of little social value.

Many scholars think *Chaplinsky* is obsolete, and the Court has rarely if ever upheld a conviction under the fighting words doctrine since *Chaplinsky*. But in the case of *Beauharnais v. Illinois* (1952), the Supreme Court did uphold a state statute that made it a crime "to exhibit in any public place any publication which 'portrays depravity, criminality, unchastity, or lack of virtue of a class of citizens, of any race, color, creed or religion' which 'exposes the citizens of any race, color, creed or religion to contempt, derision, or obloquy.'" Writing for a majority, Justice Frankfurter said:

> Illinois did not have to look beyond her own borders or await the tragic experience of the last three decades to conclude that willful purveyors of falsehood concerning racial and religious groups promote strife and tend powerfully to obstruct the manifold adjustments required for free, ordered life in a metropolitan, polyglot community. . . .
>
> There are limits to the exercise of these liberties [of speech and of the press]. The danger in these times from the coercive activities

of those who in the delusion of racial or religious conceit would incite violence and breaches of the peace in order to deprive others of their equal right to the exercise of their liberties, is emphasized by events familiar to all. These and other transgressions of those limits the states appropriately may punish.

Frankfurter did not speak for a unanimous Court. In dissent, Justice Black, joined by Justice Douglas, wrote that:

No rationalization on a purely legal level can conceal the fact that state laws like this one present a constant overhanging threat to freedom of speech, press and religion. . . . [T]he same kind of state law that makes Beauharnais a criminal for advocating segregation in Illinois can be utilized to send people to jail in other states for advocating equality and nonsegregation.

Justice Black's dissent has come to be regarded as more persuasive by a majority of Supreme Court justices.

A more reliable guide to the current state of the law on hate speech is the case of *RAV v. City of St. Paul* (1992). The case arose from a classic hate crime: In the predawn hours of June 21, 1990, several teenagers allegedly made a cross by taping together broken chair legs. They then burned the cross inside the fenced yard of an African American family. They were charged under a city ordinance that made it a misdemeanor to place "on public or private property a symbol, object, appellation, characterization or graffiti, including, but not limited to, a burning cross or Nazi swastika, which one knows or has reasonable grounds to know arouses anger, alarm or resentment in others on the basis of race, color, creed, religion or gender." Relying on *Chaplinsky*, Minnesota courts had construed the modifying phrase "arouses anger, alarm or resentment in others" to limit the ordinance to fighting words or to "conduct that itself inflicts injury or tends to incite immediate violence."

In his opinion for a majority of the Court, Justice Scalia struck the ordinance as a violation of the First Amendment, observing that:

Displays containing abusive invective, no matter how vicious or severe, are permissible unless they are addressed to one of the specified disfavored topics. Those who wish to use 'fighting words' in connection with other ideas—to express hostility, for example, on the

basis of political affiliation, union membership, or homosexuality—
are not covered. The First Amendment does not permit St. Paul to
impose special prohibitions on those speakers who express views on
disfavored subjects.

RAV is a complicated if not confusing decision in its particulars, but its
general disposition is clear: hate speech prohibitions are not per se
(automatically or by definition or always) a violation of the First
Amendment, but they must be drawn very narrowly to pass constitutional muster.

Under *RAV*, there may be occasions when the state can penalize
hate speech, provided the statute is drafted in ways that do not favor or
disapprove of some points of view, and provided the state can advance a
sufficiently important (compelling) interest. In *Virginia v. Black* (2003),
the Court upheld a state law that prohibited cross burning. Black was
arrested for burning a cross at a KKK rally. He argued that his conviction should be set aside because he had burned the cross not to intimidate (as the Virginia law proscribed), but rather to inspire his fellow
Klan members.

Writing for the majority (including Justice Scalia), Justice O'Connor
held that a state may enact a statute banning the act of cross burning
with the intent to intimidate because the First Amendment permits
content-based restriction of "true threats." In this case, however, the
Virginia statute was unconstitutional because it further required the
trial court to instruct jurors that any cross burning is prima facie evidence of an intent to intimidate. In dissent, Justice Thomas argued that
cross-burning should fall entirely outside the First Amendment. The
decisions in *RAV* and *Black* reveal some disagreement among judicial
conservatives about the constitutionality of limitations on speech that
derive from concerns about human dignity or morality.[29]

The Alt-first amendment rejects the nuances of the *Black* and *RAV*
decisions, not simply because they leave some space for regulating hateful speech, but because they allow the state to silence the speech of
whites. A number of articles on the prominent Alt-right website
VDARE, for example, complain bitterly about state laws that violate
their freedom of speech. For example, on June 17, 2015, the day after
Dylan Roof murdered nine people at a Charlestown, South Carolina
Church, hoping to provoke a race war, police in Rocky Mount, Virginia
arrested Jack Turner (a 51-year-old white man), for hanging a life-sized

dummy wearing a black ski mask from a tree in his yard. Turner told investigators the dummy was a scarecrow, but he later admitted the figure was meant to scare people and that he is racist. Turner was prosecuted under a law that made it a crime to display a noose with the intent to intimidate.

Of course, *VDARE* believes that such displays must be protected by the First Amendment. Just as importantly, however, *VDARE* cites the case as just one of many that amount to a deliberate campaign to lynch white males for exercising what should be protected speech: "Ever since VDARE.com was founded at Christmas 1999, it has chronicled the war on whites' First Amendment and other constitutional and legal rights. It has been an ugly, one-sided history, in which the government has encroached ever more on American whites' rights, while increasingly suspending legal sanctions against non-whites or other protected groups. . . . "[30] A long list of examples follows. Included are the cases of two college students arrested for "making fun" of Black History Month, a high school student who burned a cross at school, and several white police officers who were "fired for criticizing racist, black thugs." *VDARE* concedes that such speech is cruel and offensive, if not "as racist" as some other acts (such as displaying a swastika in Skokie):

> But the issue is not whether they should have found a more polite way of expressing their grievances. It's about whether whites have constitutional rights—not just First Amendment rights, but Fourteenth Amendment rights (remember equality before the law?) and Eighth Amendment rights (protection against cruel and unusual punishment), as authorities use draconian sentencing to coerce whites into pleading guilty, implicating others, and to crush white resistance. Increasingly, the answer appears to be no.[31]

Another article on *VDARE* complains that "mocking blacks has been transformed into a felony."[32] Worse, "While whites are illegally arrested and prosecuted, blacks are given carte blanche not only to spew racial epithets against whites, but to do so while committing felonies against them. Thus, whites endure hyper-policing, while blacks enjoy de-policing."[33]

One supposed example of this reverse bias is the so-called "Jena Hoax," in which four to six African American high school students in Jena, Louisiana, are alleged to have tried to murder a white schoolmate.

The incident began when several white students hung a noose from a tree at the school to frighten black students from sitting under it. A fight ensued, and several black students were arrested. As *VDARE* describes it:

> On September 20, 2007, some 30,000 blacks converged on Jena for a Nuremberg-style rally in support of the black attackers—"The Jena 6." While black ralliers waited at a bus stop in Alexandria, LA on their way home, a drunken white 18-year-old called Jeremiah Munsen, along with and a 17-year-old friend, pulled a practical joke: They tied electrical cords to look like nooses from the back of Munsen's pickup truck. Munsen then drove 'round and 'round the bus stop, in view of hundreds of outraged, black activists. Federal prosecutors threatened Munsen, via unconstitutional and duplicative charges, with 11 years in the federal pen—in effect, a death penalty for a scrawny, white, teenager—and coerced him into pleading guilty to a "hate crime."[34]

In the racist right, the Jena Hoax is not simply a story about the suppression of speech. It is a story in which political correctness, liberals, and the media elite all conspire to deprive whites of their constitutional rights and liberties to advance a liberal agenda of racial equality. The Alt-right's account of what happened at Charlottesville continues this narrative of white victimization.

The affront to alt-freedom of speech in such cases takes two forms. First, speech values are slighted or diminished in importance to the social pursuit of equality. Alt-right complaints about liberal censorship in favor of racial equality begin with the claim that anti-bias laws and hate speech prohibitions have made freedom of speech constitutionally inferior to racial equality and equal protection; the First Amendment is emasculated by the Fourteenth, an obvious (to the far right) inversion of the correct relationship between these two constitutional provisions. Significantly, in this narrative, the right to equality makes almost no appearance in the organic constitution and the Bill of Rights. (The Founders' constitution included no ringing declaration about the equality of men and indeed, in several places ratifies the greatest affront to equality we can imagine.) Equality's status as a constitutional precept, because it traces to the Fourteenth Amendment, cannot draw on the legitimacy or the sanctity of the Founding or the Founders. Instead it is deeply suspect and illegitimate, as are the Reconstruction amendments writ large (more on that in Chapter 6).

As amended, the Constitution enjoins us to protect speech *and* to guarantee equal protection of the laws. Sadly, it doesn't give us much guidance about what to do when these commands pull us in different directions. One resolution starts with a common talking point, that freedom of speech is our most cherished liberty as evidenced by its inclusion in the very *first* amendment A simple thought experiment ought to demonstrate how specious the logic is behind this way of thinking: Is the Third Amendment obviously more significant than the Fourth, Fifth, or Seventh? One might as easily appeal to the well-known principle of statutory construction that privileges not what is first but what is last in time—(i.e., the maxim of *Leges posteriores priores contrarias abrogant*)—and thus conclude that the Fourteenth Amendment must be more important than any and all of the thirteen amendments that precede it in constitutional time. Additionally, any attentive history of the drafting of the Bill of Rights will reveal that their ordering is not a function of their putative importance, but is instead mostly an accident of history.

The second affront to the Alt-first amendment is that the state, in the opinion of the Alt-right, has taken a side in a cultural if not an existential war about the meaning of America and the makeup of American identity. To be more precise, the complaint is not that the state has taken *a* side, in contravention of some implicit rule about impartiality or about viewpoint neutrality. (Recall Justice Scalia's observation in *RAV* that "The First Amendment does not permit St. Paul to impose special prohibitions on those speakers who express views on disfavored subjects.") Rather, the objection is that the state has taken the *wrong* side, to wit—favoring equality over speech, and minorities over whites. This reveals another fundamental truth about the Alt-first amendment: the Alt-first amendment is white. Its absolutist protections for freedom of speech protect what *white* people have to say (with perhaps two notables exceptions I will discuss later, one regarding religion, and one regarding guns).

I want to be very clear about this. The Alt-constitution protects hate speech, racist and bigoted speech, fighting words, slurs, slights, and insults, whenever and wherever a brave Free Speech Warrior dares to say what the Left says should not be said. Who gets this protection? The question is only rhetorical. The obvious answer is that freedom of speech protects white males, first if not only, but it is rare to find the qualification put so bluntly. Notice how Richard Spencer makes the point *indirectly* in the Charlottesville Statement: "American citizens should enjoy freedom of speech as guaranteed by the Constitution; we endorse this value for all European peoples."[35] The restriction is couched in euphemisms: full access to constitutional liberties, speech among them, is confined to those of "European" heritage, or to those who share a certain racial or cultural identity. As Michael Harriot noted in a perceptive essay in *The Root,* "When you hear white supremacist asswipes like Richard Spencer, the Ku Klux Klan and Bill Maher conjure white tears when their freedom of speech has been infringed upon, remember that they don't care about the universal right of free speech; they care about their own free speech."[36]

THE FINE PRINT AND FOOTNOTES

Freedom of speech is so important to the Alt-right that it sometimes trumps our commitment to democracy itself. Writing on Altright.com, Vincent Law complains that "Authoritarian states tend to be freer in many ways. When the people's political opinion doesn't matter, their opinions don't have to be so closely monitored and controlled. Centuries ago in the West, you got only punished when you spoke against the king or the church, but now everything is self-regulated, every thing [sic] we do, say and believe, therefore potentially every word we say can bring social ostracization upon us."[37]

In this telling, it is not primarily government that threatens freedom of speech, notwithstanding its power to fine or even jail you, but rather civil society by using the weapons of shame, ridicule, and condemnation. This version of the first amendment protects you not only against the state, but also against those who have the gall to disagree with you and to say so. It rejects the second principle of First Amendment jurisprudence that we identified earlier in this Chapter—namely, that First Amendment guarantees run only against state action and not against private actors.

Hence, it would be ironic if it were not intentional, but Speech Freaks have no hesitation in silencing the speech of their critics or of speakers who reject their worldview. One example should make this point clear. Very few in the Alt-right appear to argue that the Alt-first amendment protects the speech of activists in the Black Lives Matter movement. Likewise, to my knowledge, no one prominent in the Alt-right has come forward to defend the First Amendment right of players in the NFL to kneel during the national anthem. Again, the (real) First Amendment likely does not protect this speech either. The National Football League is a private organization, and team owners, acting individually or as an association, are under no compulsion to respect the constitutional rights and liberties of its players/employees. But as we have seen, the Alt-first amendment takes no account of the state action doctrine or of the distinction between public and private. Where are the voices in the extreme right that complain loudly about censorship and campaign for the right to say what is unpopular or unwelcome? Is their silence a consequence of the message, which no one can doubt is anathema to the far right? Or is it less a function of the message than of the presumed identity of the speaker?

This hypocrisy is especially evident on college campuses. The Alt-right complains bitterly about how liberal students and administrators silence their speech, but "free speech warriors are nowhere to be found when faculty of color, or those speaking out against racism, are the targets."[38] As Steven W. Thrasher notes, "The Jonathan Chaits and Frank Brunis and Sean Hannitys of the world are not lacking in a freedom to speak, nor are the white conservatives on college campuses they seem so worried about. It's women and people of color who struggle the most finding a platform—but there is a conspicuous lack of concern about that by free speech crusaders."[39] Indeed, the radical right has for years waged a coordinated campaign, now prominently on the Internet and social media, to punish the speech of liberal academics and especially persons of color and white "race traitors." There is an entire cottage industry dedicated to the project, including websites like CampusReform, TheCollegeFix, and ProfessorWatch.[40] Some professors have been fired or forced to resign their positions, and some have received death threats.[41]

My point is not to call into question the integrity of the radical right's commitment to an absolutist conception of freedom of speech, but rather to make clear that it comes with fine print and footnotes. The most important qualification is that the freedoms guaranteed by the Alt-first amendment, unlike the First Amendment generally, depend upon who the speaker is—and especially depending upon their race and their political views; that is precisely the kind of viewpoint discrimination Justice Scalia condemned in *RAV*. A principled account of the First Amendment cannot protect only the speech rights of one race or gender or class and not all others. That was one of the arguments Justice Kennedy used in *Citizens United v. FEC* (2010), to strike as unconstitutional certain limits on corporate spending in political campaigns. As Justice Kennedy wrote for the Court, "Speech restrictions based on the identity of the speaker are all too often simply a means to control content. The First Amendment protects speech and speaker, and the ideas that flow from each." First Amendment jurisprudence holds closely to the proposition that what matters is speech, not the identity of the speaker. It is a wise rule, although it can sometimes lead to undesirable results if improperly applied, as it did in *Citizens United*. A state that guarantees the speech of only some speakers and not of others defeats almost every purpose we can assign to protecting speech in the first place. It restricts instead of expands the marketplace of ideas; it impedes the search for truth; it excludes from public conversation certain points of view and ideas and thus obstructs the self-governance conception of freedom of speech.

But perhaps most importantly, there is an obvious inequality involved in allowing some of us to speak and silencing others simply because of who we (and they) are. A rule that requires us to focus on speech and not speaker is counseled by our constitutional commitment to equality. Many scholars and Supreme Court justices will be skittish around the language of human dignity, but few political theorists will deny that the development of human personality demands a robust freedom to speak one's mind.

The absolute Alt-first amendment also makes room for restrictions on speech that challenge what the extreme right regards as unassailable truths. The Dickey amendment, for example, (a provision first inserted as a rider into the 1996 federal government omnibus spending bill), mandates that "none of the funds made available for injury prevention and control at the Centers for Disease Control and Prevention (CDC) may be used to advocate or promote gun control." In 2011, Governor Rick Scott of Florida signed legislation that prohibited physicians from seeking information from their patients about their ownership of weap-

ons and ammunition. Florida offered no medical rationale for this limi-
tation on the speech and association rights of physicians and patients.
Instead, Scott characterized the provision in question as a protection of
Second Amendment rights.[42]

In 2013, Louisiana amended its concealed handgun statute to include a provision that makes it unlawful for "any person" to "intentionally release, disseminate, or make public in any manner any information
contained in an application for a concealed handgun permit or any
information regarding the identity of any person who applied for or
received a concealed handgun permit." The practical effect of the
amendment was to "criminalize speech on gun permits. . . ."[43] The
Second Amendment is necessary to guarantee the First Amendment,
but only if the First doesn't interfere with the Second. The NRA made
just this argument following the Santa Fe school shootings in May 2018.
Colion Noir, host of an NRA-television show, tweeted that "It's time for
Congress to step up and pass legislation putting commonsense limitations on #MSM's [Mainstream Media] ability to report on these school
shootings."[44]

FREEDOM OF RELIGION

The Alt-first amendment's ambitious protections for speech stand
alongside considerably less generous protections for religious freedom.
The Alt-establishment clause does not prohibit government from extending privileges and protections that favor Christians, including state
sponsored prayer in public schools and at other public events. Similarly,
the Alt-free exercise clause fully protects the free exercise rights of
Christians, but welcomes restrictions on the religious practices of Muslims, Jews, and secular humanists, to say nothing of Buddhists, Hindus,
Santerians, and Native Americans. The contrast between the Alt-first
amendment's speech and religion clauses may seem odd, but it has a
certain coherence when read against the Alt-constitution as a whole,
and especially when we recall the miracle at Philadelphia.

The First Amendment contains two provisions that speak to the role
of religion in public affairs. The establishment clause provides that
"Congress shall make no law respecting an establishment of religion"
and the free exercise clause provides that Congress shall not prohibit

the free exercise of religion. The meaning of both has been a matter of deep divide at least since the Supreme Court's decision in *Everson v. Board of Education* (1947), when the Court first ruled that the establishment clause applies to the states as well as to the federal government, and thus imposes significant restrictions on the authority of states to enact legislation that might tend to "establish" or to grant preferential aid to one religion over another or religion to irreligion. The aid in *Everson* involved state benefits to parochial schools in the form of reimbursement to parents of children who took public transportation to school, which the Court upheld.

Notwithstanding the result, in *Everson* the Court insisted upon a wall of separation between church and state, writing, "In the words of Jefferson, the clause against establishment of religion by law was intended to erect a 'wall of separation between church and State.'" *Everson* is an object of derision and scorn in much of the radical right, and especially among those who preach the gospel of Philadelphia. The chief objection to *Everson* is its uncritical embrace of the wall of separation metaphor. For Christian constitutionalists, *Everson* is no less detestable than the School Prayer decisions of the early 1960s, *Roe v. Wade* (1973) (abortion), and *Obergefell v. Hodges* (2015) (same-sex marriage), all of which are said to be hostile to people of faith.

Everson established (bad pun) a way of thinking about the establishment clause that we call strict separationism. Strict separationism holds the state to a position of neutrality with respect to religion—the state can neither aid nor penalize religion. The Court seemed to equate the phrase with a very strict, if not complete, division between the state and religion. David Barton argues that the doctrine of separation of church and state is a myth if not a calculated misreading of Thomas Jefferson's well-known *Letter to the Danbury Baptists*. Rather than intending a wall of separation between church and state, Barton claims that:

> Jefferson believed that God, not government, was the Author and Source of our rights and that the government, therefore, was to be prevented from interference with those rights. Very simply, the "fence" of the Webster letter and the "wall" of the Danbury letter were not to limit religious activities in public; rather they were to limit the power of the government to prohibit or interfere with those expressions. [45]

Invoking Founders' intent, Barton argues that read properly, the religion clauses tell us the true purpose of the First Amendment is "to prevent the 'establishment of a particular form of Christianity' by the Episcopalians, Congregationalists, or any other denomination." On this reading, the establishment clause was designed to keep the state from choosing sides in a familial disagreement among Christians. It has nothing to do with the religious rights of non-Christians or non-believers. In *The Myth of Separation* (1989), Barton further argues that the Founders anticipated that only Christians could hold public office (an exceptionally narrow reading of Article VI of the Constitution, which prohibits religious oaths as a condition of office).

The Christian right's objection to the establishment clause goes well beyond its obvious distaste for Jefferson's "wall of separation" metaphor, although that is its favorite target. For many Christian conservatives, what the Court calls strict separation they see as overt hostility to religion and especially to conservative Protestants and Evangelicals. In their view, liberals and secular humanists use the establishment clause as a weapon to purge the public square of people of faith.[46] Jay Sekulow, a legal adviser to President Trump and Chief Counsel for the American Center for Law & Justice (ACLJ), called the doctrine "a mere 'guise' to take away the rights of Christians."[47]

In the past thirty years or so, some members of the Court have rejected the wall of separation imagery. In *Wallace v. Jaffree* (1985), the Court considered whether an Alabama law that authorized teachers to set aside one minute at the start of each day for a moment of "meditation or voluntary prayer" violated the establishment clause. Writing for the Court, Justice Stevens concluded that it did. In an important dissent, Justice Rehnquist urged the Court to reject the strict separationist approach to the establishment clause. "There is," Rehnquist wrote, "simply no historical foundation for the proposition that the Framers intended to build a wall of separation that was constitutionalized in *Everson*." Rehnquist argued that the establishment clause does not require government neutrality between religion and irreligion; "nor does it prohibit the government from providing nondiscriminatory aid to religion."

This approach is often called the "accommodationist" understanding of the establishment clause. It starts from the premise that the wall of separation approach to the establishment clause is a wrong understanding of history and should be abandoned. In Rehnquist's view, a view shared by Justices O'Connor and Scalia, and others, governmental accommodations of religious displays of faith do not always violate the establishment clause but instead simply recognize that religion has long played an important role in American culture and history. A wide variety of public acknowledgements of religion that would be unconstitutional under the strict separation approach, such as prayer in schools or nativity scenes in public parks, would likely survive the accommodationist perspective.

For Christian constitutionalists, the accommodationist perspective is a clear improvement over the *Everson* test. But there is another, even more attractive option. Justice Clarence Thomas argues that the original meaning of the establishment clause tells us that it is not a "civil liberties" provision at all, but rather a federalism provision. In a dissent in the case of *Elk Grove United School District v. Newdow* (2004), in which a majority of the Court determined that Michael Newdow did not have standing to challenge the constitutionality of the phrase "under God" in the pledge of allegiance, Thomas wrote, "The text and history of the Establishment Clause strongly suggest that it is a federalism provision intended to prevent Congress from interfering with state establishment. . . . [T]he Establishment Clause is best understood as a federalism provision—it protects state establishments from federal interference but does not protect any individual right."

Justice Thomas's opinion about the meaning of the establishment clause is a cornerstone of the Alt-constitution's conception of freedom of religion. It frees up states to establish—in other words, to give aid to—religion in all sorts of ways, although they would still have to respect the free exercise rights of citizens.

Why might this reading be an attractive feature to the Alt-constitution? Justice Thomas's establishment clause allows Christians to use the power of the state to advance (their) religion and a form of Christian supremacy. It does not reach quite as far, but neither is it too far removed from David Barton's insistence that freedom of religion means freedom of religion only for Christians. You can imagine who it does not protect. Bryan Fisher, host of the popular "Focal Point" radio program produced by the American Family Association, argues that "Islam has no fundamental First Amendment claims, for the simple reason that it was not written to protect the religion of Islam. Islam is entitled only to the religious liberty we extend to it out of courtesy. While there certainly ought to be a presumption of religious liberty for non-Christian religious traditions in America, the Founders were not writing a suicide pact when they wrote the First Amendment."[48] "I believe Muslims can and should be excluded from Congress," Fischer added, "for the same reason that Communists can and should be and legally are, because they believe in a totalitarian system, a totalitarian ideology."[49] In short, the free speech provisions of the Alt-first amendment are white, and the religion clauses are Christian.

THE ALT-FREE EXERCISE CLAUSE

In like fashion, the free exercise clause protects the free exercise of religion by Christians and possibly of religions that are consonant with or do not aggressively contravene Christian theology. Other belief systems, however, fall outside its reach.

In some ways, the Alt-free exercise clause resembles the free exercise clause as interpreted by the Supreme Court in one of its earliest religion cases. In *Davis v. Beason* (1890), a unanimous Court upheld a federal law that prohibited polygamy in the Idaho territory. Two aspects of the decision are important. First, the Court appeared to deny that Mormonism was a religion for First Amendment purposes, saying that "The term 'religion' has reference to one's views of his relations to his Creator, and to the obligations they impose of reverence for his being and character, and of obedience to his will. . . . To call [Mormon] advocacy a tenet of religion is to offend the common sense of mankind." The Court has long since adopted a more ecumenical definition of religion, one that is neither Christian nor tied to the notion of a Creator.[50]

Another principle from *Davis*, however, remains part of the Court's freedom of religion jurisprudence. *Davis* introduced the belief-conduct distinction, or the principle that the religion clauses guarantee one's right to *believe* anything or nothing, without restriction, but: "However free the exercise of religion may be, it must be subordinate to the criminal laws of the country, passed with reference to actions regarded by general consent as properly the subjects of punitive legislation." What you believe is beyond the government's reach, but how you act—

your conduct—is another matter. Some of us think the distinction between religious faith and religious conduct itself reflects a Protestant
theology that is difficult to reconcile with some other religious traditions, such as Judaism and Roman Catholicism, but the distinction is a
staple of the Court's free exercise jurisprudence.

The application of the principle can be seen in another Supreme
Court case, *Church of the Lukumi Babalu Aye, Inc. v. Hialeah* (1993).
In *Hialeah*, the Court struck down a city ordinance designed for the
express purpose of prohibiting the Santeria Church from conducting
animal sacrifice within city limits. In astonishingly frank language, the
Court observed that "The principle that government may not enact laws
that suppress religious belief or practice is so well understood that few
violations are recorded in our opinions. . . . Our review confirms that
the laws in question were enacted by officials who did not understand,
failed to perceive, or chose to ignore the fact that their official actions
violated the Nation's essential commitment to religious freedom."[51] It
seemed incredible to the Court that city officials would purposefully
discriminate against the free exercise rights of Santerians.

But what looks like a remarkable ignorance of elementary principles
of religious freedom, as the Court seemed to think was the case in
Hialeah, can be explained under the Alt-constitution and once one
understands that the free exercise clause is Christian. What looks like
deliberate discrimination against a (seemingly) non-Christian religion is
in fact a fair application of a radically different principle, a principle that
simply excludes non-Christian faiths from the protection of the religion
clauses. (Just for the record, Santerians incorporate elements of Roman
Catholicism in their theology.) I am not saying the Alt-right was responsible for the city ordinance in the *Hialeah* case—the Alt-right as such
did not exist then. I mean only that the Alt-free exercise clause would
justify religious discrimination directed against non-Christians.

The Alt-constitution thus yields a complex jurisprudence of religion,
in which the state is at liberty (in some quarters, obligated) to account
for religious beliefs in public life generally, as in erecting Christmas
crèches or by requiring students to pray in public schools. On the other
hand, any effort by the state to "accommodate" the religious practices
and beliefs of atheists and non-Christians is said to be an unholy affront
to the alt-free exercise right of Christians. Prayer in school and at public
meetings offers a good example.

In the case of *Good News Club v. Milford Central School* (2001), the Court ruled that public schools may not prohibit student groups and clubs from holding after school hour meetings in school facilities simply because those groups are religious—in this case, the group, the Good News Club, was an evangelical Christian club for children. Conservatives praised the decision as a defense of religious liberty.

In 2016, *The Washington Post* reported that the Satanic Temple, cofounded in 2014 by Lucien Greaves, planned to create "After-School Satan Clubs" that would meet in public school buildings.[52] Good News Club, Satan Club—what's the difference? Unsurprisingly, not many Evangelicals rallied to protect the free exercise rights of Satanists. As the *Christian Science Monitor* reported, "A group of Christians in Tacoma, Washington, are fighting against a proposal to form an after-school Satan Club in a local elementary school. 'We don't know who's teaching it, their motives behind it, it's not pure. You know children are innocent,' Tacoma School District parent Kiana Simpson, told the local KPCQ-TV Fox News station."[53] Again, what looks like rank hypocrisy to others is simply a logical extension of the principles of Christian supremacy.

What animates those principles is a vision of civic and public life in America in which Christianity has a guaranteed seat at the head of the table, a guarantee issued by the Founders. It is simultaneously a vision of the future and of a lost, idyllic past in which America was a better, more wholesome, safer, and Godlier place.

CONCLUSION

Speech Freaks think they can say anything they want, anywhere, anytime, to anyone, without consequence or reproach by governmental authorities or even by their fellow citizens, much less by the targets of their provocations. Speech Freaks like to talk, and when others choose not to listen, they claim they have been silenced.

Speech Freaks present themselves as First Amendment loyalists not to advance but to deflect discussions about their noxious ideas. The Alt-first amendment is simply a tool they utilize for political advantage and discard when it causes inconvenience. That duplicity is not a good reason to silence the Alt-right, or skinheads, or neo-Nazis, or militia members; an inquiry into the motives behind Speech Freaks would itself raise significant First Amendment objections. But it is relevant to a civic discussion about the meaning of the First Amendment, especially in conjunction with our commitment to other important constitutional principles, such as liberty, equality, and human dignity.

Not all of us will agree that freedom of speech is always more important than equality, or security, or the general welfare, but the right to make the argument, as well as the argument against it, must be protected. It is important, therefore, not to censor the radical right because we think their devotion to the First Amendment is impure or simply a matter of convenience. But it is just as important not to accept as gospel the simplistic view that the First Amendment necessarily protects any and all sorts of racist speech, no matter what. The Alt-first amendment may hold that speech is beyond circumscription, but whether the real First Amendment should embody that principle is an open question.

Prioritizing the First Amendment is a choice we don't have to make. Whether it is a choice we *should* make requires an argument (as do claims that we ought to limit speech to advance equal protection). The Alt-constitution simply assumes that freedom of speech is absolute, and to call it absolute is simply to assert that it is always more important than any other constitutional value. Paradoxically, the Alt-constitution reflects a certainty and rigidity about political life (and philosophy) that the Founders rejected for themselves and for us when they wrote the First Amendment.

Chapter 4

GUN NUTS

The Alt-Second Amendment

There is more to the Alt-constitution than just the first amendment and Speech Freaks. In the Alt-constitution, the second amendment is at least if not more crucial to the preservation of liberty than freedom of speech or religion. For most folks in the radical right, the two go hand in hand. Here is a representative example: "A well-armed society is a safe society. Our Founding Father's [sic] knew this. That's why they wrote the 2nd Amendment. And it is the 1st Amendment: freedom of religion, speech, assembly and the press, which is protected by the 2nd."[1] Here is another, from the Michigan Militia: "The Second Amendment is really the First in our country . . . because without guns for protection from tyrants, we would have no free speech."[2]

One graphic illustration of the conjunction is the Fraternal Order of the Alt-Knights (FOAK). Like similar organizations, such as the "Proud Boys," "DIY Division," and the Oath Keepers, the Alt-Knights are a loosely organized if not irregular clutch of young white nationalists prepared to use violence to "protect themselves" and Alt-right protesters at public demonstrations. According to the *New York Times*, the Alt-Knights are "Part fight club, part Western-pride fraternity" made up mostly of young white males. "Some have initiation rituals that include violent hazing and an oath of fealty to Western culture. Their followers thrive on hyper-masculinity and celebrate when one of their brethren hits a leftist agitator. They mock Islam and purport to be soldiers against a 'war on Whites.'"[3] Although the Knights seem cartoonish, especially given their association with the Proud Boys (a white nationalist and men's rights group well-known for its bizarre rites of initiation, which include a pledge not to masturbate more than once a month), FOAK "is for those that possess the Warrior Spirit. The weak or timid need not apply."[4]

The Alt-Knights are the self-appointed paramilitary wing of the Proud Boys, and some say of the Alt-right movement generally. Their founder, Kyle Chapman (he calls himself Based StickMan, an allusion to Chapman's attack on an Antifa protester at a Cal-Berkeley demonstration with a stick) is a repeat felon who sometimes wears a baseball helmet, shin guards, ski goggles, and a gas mask. Chapman claims that "Our emphasis will be on street activism, preparation, defense and confrontation. . . . We will protect and defend our right wing brethren when the police and government fail to do so."[5] The language of self-defense (against liberals and "thugs," code words for minorities) neatly marries the self-defense and freedom of speech claims.[6] Given the violence at Berkeley and a few other demonstrations, it is a mistake to dismiss the Alt-Knights and similar groups as just free speech poseurs. For the Alt-Knights, the battle is rhetorical *and* real.

GUN NUTS AND THE GOSPEL OF GUNS

Like Speech Freaks, Gun Nuts are constitutional absolutists. And like the Alt-first amendment, the Alt-second amendment is as much a cultural coat of arms as a constitutional prescription. As David C. Williams noted some years ago, "the Second Amendment [is] a primary cultural text in an ongoing *Kulturkamp*. So considered, the Amendment is not a culturally neutral rule but the central provision for a special consistency—the so-called gun culture."[7] The jurisprudence of the Second Amendment has changed significantly since Williams wrote, but nothing has changed. Gun Nuts are still fighting the *Kulturkamp*, in which there are "two alternative views of what America is and ought to be."[8] One view is dismissed (by the right) as cosmopolitan, urban, elite, and most of all, alien; the other is rural, small town, and most of all, American.[9]

The belief in the right to own guns is an article of faith, and the Second Amendment a gospel in its own right. As with Holy Scripture, the Second Amendment must be read literally and must not be altered by human touch. Hence the Alt-second amendment is an especially apt candidate for an originalist interpretation, which will (presumably) protect it against liberal elites and effetes, who would regulate firearms in ways the Founders would have rejected. Holding the Second Amendment to its original meaning (whatever that is, and it is not quite as clear as Gun Nuts suppose) is thus required if we are to honor the faith of our Fathers. But "Gospel and Guns" has another meaning, too, more sociological or ethnographic in nature. Many of the most passionate defenders of the right to own firearms are conservative Christians, Christian nationalists, and Identitarians.[10] Their second amendment fundamentalism mirrors their religious fundamentalism, especially in its devotion to the sacristy of the text. Second Amendment fundamentalists hold that the Constitution does not grant but instead simply recognizes a (preexisting or natural) God-given right to own a firearm in the service of self-defense,[11] and that right is absolute.

This is a major point of divide between the true Second Amendment and the Alt version of the second amendment. Although a majority of justices on the United States Supreme Court have agreed that the Second Amendment must be interpreted to elicit its original meaning (again, whatever that is), it has not agreed that the right to own firearms is absolute. The absolutist nature of the Alt-second amendment is thus significantly different than the real Second Amendment, at least according to the High Court.

In *DC v. Heller* (2008) the Court ruled that the Second Amendment does protect an individual right to own certain types of weapons. There is much in Justice Scalia's homiletic that should comfort Gun Nuts. Justice Scalia begins with a valiant effort to take the plain words of the Second Amendment seriously. One immediate difficulty is that the plain words of the Second Amendment, unencumbered by an appeal to colonial history, Founder's intent, original meaning, or any other plausible source of constitutional meaning, don't have an obvious or undisputed meaning, much less the one Justice Scalia favors. Arguably, the most sensible reading of the words standing alone is that the right to keep and bear a firearm is limited to membership in a well-regulated militia, as the Court's earlier jurisprudence seemed to suggest.[12] In other words, the prefatory clause (about the militia) tells us something about what the operative clause (to own a firearm) means.

In contrast to the reading I just outlined, Justice Scalia concluded that the prefatory clause does not delimit the right alluded to in the operative clause. In Justice Scalia's framework, the right of the people to keep and bear arms (the operative clause) is independent of membership in a state militia (the prefatory clause). In other words, the Second Amendment creates (recognizes) an individual right to self-defense, no matter the militia clause.

Justice Scalia's bafflegab about the relationship between prefatory and operative clauses (he devotes over thirty paragraphs to the issue) is simply an effort, familiar to lawyers and academics but puzzling to any sensible person, to wrestle with the obvious difficulty that the plain words of the Second Amendment do not easily support his conclusion. Hence, Justice Scalia supplements the argument from plain words and text with appeals to colonial history (appeals that are mostly an exercise in Founder/Founding worship) and originalism. Both of these interpretive techniques ought to comfort constitutional fundamentalists and Gun Nuts, except here the methods yield a conclusion they don't like.

It is not necessary to explore in detail Justice Scalia's use of originalism to find that the Second Amendment guarantees an individual right to own a firearm. It is worth noting, though, that originalism does not provide the sort of interpretive clarity its devotees want. One of the most striking features of *DC v. Heller* is Justice Stevens' dissent. Criticizing the majority, Stevens wrote that "The right the Court announces was not 'enshrined' in the Second Amendment by the Framers." Rather, "it is the product of today's law-changing decision." The remarkable thing about Stevens' dissent is not that it is a dissent, but rather that it reaches its position by calling upon originalism to do so.[13]

Both opinions are vulnerable, but the contrast between them is a wonderful example of what everyone who is not an originalist (and what most honest originalists) already know: As a method of constitutional interpretation, originalism is surprisingly forgiving. Rarely is there a single originalist answer to a complicated question. Originalism is just fine as one way of asking what the Constitution means, but it fails spectacularly at telling judges what the "right" answer is, not because there is no right answer, but precisely because there are too many right answers, even in an originalist framework.[14] What originalism *does* do in

Justice Scalia's majority opinion, however, is what its supporters expect it to do and why it is favored as a method of interpretation in the Alt-constitution: It appropriates the symbolic legitimacy of the Founders and the Founding to dress partisan, political decisions in ostensibly neutral constitutional clothing.

Insofar as *Heller* found (or invented) an individual right to own a firearm, the case is of monumental importance. In a literal sense, however, *Heller* was also a very narrow decision. Its ruling applied only to the regulation of firearms in the District of Columbia, which is under the jurisdiction of the federal government. In *McDonald v. City of Chicago* (2010), the Court addressed a more important question: Did the due process clause of the Fourteenth Amendment "incorporate" the Second Amendment and thus make the individual right applicable against state and local governments as well as the federal government? At issue in *McDonald* were several firearm regulations in Chicago; critics alleged that in toto, they amounted to a near absolute ban on private ownership of guns in the city. Writing for a five to four majority, Justice Alito concluded that "It is clear that the Framers and ratifiers of the Fourteenth Amendment counted the right to keep and bear arms among those fundamental rights necessary to our system of ordered liberty." The dissents in *McDonald* reiterated their belief that *Heller* was wrongly decided. They also argued, however, that such a right, if it does exist, is not fundamental and so not protected against state and local governments.

Heller and *McDonald* were wrongly decided. But neither makes my "Ten Worst Supreme Court Decisions" list. (The list is already full, but it's my list, so there is room for more than just ten decisions.) One reason why *Heller* and *McDonald* don't make the list is because they don't amount to much. Yes, they wrongly adopt an individual rights interpretation of the Second Amendment. (Having done so, though, it is not obvious to me that the majority was wrong to incorporate the right in *McDonald*.) Just as importantly, though, "The right to keep and bear arms," according to Scalia in *Heller*, is "not a right to keep and carry any weapon whatsoever in any manner whatsoever and for whatever purpose." Indeed, he adds, "nothing in our opinion should be taken to cast doubt on a wide range of gun restrictions, including such categories as 'laws imposing conditions and qualifications on the commercial sale of firearms,' 'prohibitions on carrying concealed weapons,' and prohibitions on 'dangerous and unusual weapons,' a listing of 'pre-sumptively lawful regulatory measures' that 'does not purport to be exhaustive.'"[15] Put simply, *Heller* and *McDonald* leave the right to own a firearm subject to a considerable degree of governmental regulation.

As interpreted by the Court, then, there is some space in the Second Amendment—as there cannot be in the Alt-second amendment—for regulating firearms. Lower courts have found several federal gun stat-utes consistent with the Second Amendment, including statutes prohib-iting firearm possession (1) by people convicted of felonies and domes-tic violence misdemeanors, (2) while committing another crime, (3) in violation of a court order, or (4) in a prohibited location.[16]

That concession marks a bright line between the Second Amend-ment and the Alt-second amendment. For many folks in the radical right, *any* proposal to regulate or restrict (and for some, even to regis-ter) firearms is obviously the first step toward the abolition of the Sec-ond Amendment (and, in some quarters, the first step to secession, as evidenced by a measure introduced by some Republican state legisla-tors in South Carolina that would authorize the state to secede from the United States if the federal government began to seize legally pur-chased firearms in the state).[17] Thus, for many in the radical right, *Heller* and *McDonald* are a direct threat to the God-given right to self-defense and to own a weapon. The irony here is delicious: One of the two judicial decisions affirming an individual right to own a firearm was decided by the originalist-in-chief, using originalism, and yet still held that governments may regulate guns in a wide variety of instances.

There will be another gun tragedy (estimates vary, but according to the *New York Times*, there is on average a mass shooting, defined as an incident in which four or more people are shot, nearly every day[18]). It too will arouse calls for gun control legislation, likely something fairly modest. It won't matter to Gun Nuts—every call for regulation is a transparent effort to repeal the Second Amendment by indirection.[19]

Repealing the Second Amendment won't solve gun violence, but it is a good idea—we *should* repeal the Second Amendment. For just a moment, imagine a world where such talk could be taken seriously. (I know it cannot, but I am heartened by Justice Stevens' recent re-marks.[20]) As a matter of constitutional theory, repealing a constitutional amendment is not out of bounds. Indeed, we have done it at least once before: The Twenty-First Amendment repealed the Eighteenth. And in

a larger sense, the Constitution of 1787 amounted to a repeal of the
Articles of Confederation and Perpetual Union. So if we could get
around the impossible politics of it, the idea of repealing the Second
Amendment should not be categorically out of order.

I raise this improbable example to illustrate a larger principle behind
the Alt-second amendment in particular and the Alt-constitution in
general. Any talk about repealing the Second Amendment is certain to
encounter the objection that the right to self-defense, or to own a weapon, is God-given and cannot be taken away or repealed by human agency. Consequently, any effort to repeal the Second Amendment, even if
the processes and procedures of doing so fully complied with the requirements of Article V, would be "unconstitutional." Not because the
Second Amendment (or any other provision in) the Constitution prohibits it, but because, as we saw in Chapter 2, the Constitution does not
create fundamental rights—it *acknowledges* them. Such rights are "pre-
constitutional" and "unalienable," literally (and constitutionally) beyond
human dominion. Here is a representative example from a group called
the Gun Owners of America:

> The first problem with the "Second Amendment is my gun permit"
> mantra lies in the fact that it implies the amendment creates a right.
> It doesn't.
>
> It does not "give you" the right to keep and bear arms. It merely
> prohibits the federal government from infringing on a right you al-
> ready had.
>
> The right to keep and bear arms flows from a more basic right—
> the right to self-defense. This falls within the umbrella of "natural
> rights." You have them "naturally" simply because you exist. The
> right to defend yourself and your property makes up part of what it
> means to be human. In other words, it's natural to human existence.
>
> No government can bestow natural rights—and no government
> can take them away. But governments can "infringe" on natural
> rights. Or to put it another way, interfere with them.[21]

A similar publication, "Our Right to Bear Arms Is a God Given
Individual Right," appears on the homepage of the Sherriff Brigades of
Pennsylvania.[22] The Brigades takes Justice Scalia to task for *Heller*,
saying, "Disappointedly, Justice Scalia is wrong to consider that there
are any limitations of this constitutionally secured, protected and guar-

anteed right. For example, Citizens can lawfully have a tank in their driveway, ready to fire, in order to repel an invader/trespasser on their property."[23] It concludes with the claim that "We all have a God given, individual right to bear arms, any arms!"[24]

I can find no evidence that this last claim is not serious. Here the absolute nature of Alt-second amendment rights is almost comically (or is tragically?) clear, as is the difference between the Alt-second and the Court's pro-gun decisions in *Heller* and *McDonald*. The Alt-second amendment does not simply protect your right to own a gun—it protects your right to own a weapon. Any weapon. If the Alt-second Amendment protects your right to own a tank, then it must protect my right to own a fighter plane or an aircraft carrier. Or a Death Star.

The argument that a repealing amendment would be unconstitutional thus starts from an interesting premise: Some parts of the Constitution are inferior to God's law or so essential to what the Constitution means that they cannot be repealed, removed, or denied. An amendment that repealed the Second Amendment would thus be unconstitutional.[25]

The claim that a constitutional amendment, especially one that complies with all of the rules concerning how the process works, could nevertheless be unconstitutional, is not entirely novel. In a fascinating but fairly obscure case from early in the twentieth century, *Leser v. Garnett* (1922), the State of Maryland asked the Supreme Court to declare the Nineteenth Amendment (extending the vote to women) unconstitutional because "so great an addition to the electorate, if made without the state's consent, destroys its autonomy as a political body." Justice Brandeis casually dismissed the argument, saying simply, "This amendment [the Nineteenth] is in character and phraseology precisely similar to the Fifteenth. For each, the same method of adoption was pursued. One cannot be valid and the other invalid. That the Fifteenth is valid, although rejected by six states, including Maryland, has been recognized and acted on for half a century." The Court's response was politically astute, but on the merits it leaves something to be desired.

The notion of an unconstitutional constitutional amendment suggests still another question: Can parts of the Constitution be unconstitutional? Is there a way to argue that even without a repealing amendment, the Second Amendment is unconstitutional, no matter what it says or how we interpret it? We might appeal to the idea that some parts of the Constitution are so central to what the Constitution is or means or hopes to do, to suggest that the Second Amendment is unconstitutional because it defeats those fundamental purposes. Whatever it meant and whatever its necessity at the Founding, we might say, in *our* time the Second Amendment does not advance constitutional ideals—it sabotages them. A culture of guns is an immediate and dire threat to the life and constitutional liberties of all citizens, the argument would run. Instead of advancing the great and noble purposes of the Constitution that the Preamble identifies, the Second Amendment makes our efforts to secure the Blessings of Liberty more difficult and perhaps impossible. The argument is not unlike those advanced by some abolitionists about the unconstitutionality of slavery even before the Constitution included the Thirteenth Amendment. In *The Unconstitutionality of Slavery* (1845), Lysander Spooner argued that the Constitution prohibited slavery notwithstanding several provisions in the text that seemed to protect it, because slavery contravened principles that were fundamental to the very purpose of the Constitution.

Arguments like those made by Spooner and in *Leser*, if untenable in most contemporary scholarship, are perfectly compatible with the Alt-constitution. Of course, the extreme right doesn't hold every constitutional principle or provision in the same high regard. As we shall see in Chapter 6, efforts to repeal the Reconstruction, Sixteenth, and Seventeenth Amendments are a staple in the constitutional talk of the far right because, unlike the Second Amendment, they are not part of the "organic" constitution or suitable objects of veneration.

THE MILITIA MOVEMENT

Another bedrock principle of the Alt-second amendment is that it protects the right of citizens to form private militias, as well as the right of militia members to own firearms. The militia movement is not coextensive with the Alt-right, but there are some similarities in demography and ideology—both tilt male, white, and ultra-conservative. Militia members see themselves as the last, true American patriots, "the modern defenders of the United States Constitution in general and the Second Amendment in particular."[26]

Although militias have been the object of intense journalistic, scholarly, and even congressional investigation since the early to mid-1990s, no one knows precisely how many militias there are, where they are all located, or how many people have joined them. In part this is because many militias are by design both small and secretive. On the other hand, but equally a problem for estimates, some are more like weekend recreational clubs and subject to gross variations in interest and commitment. Another impediment is that militias come and go like summer weeds, highly responsive to political weather and in particular to forecasts that warn of impending gun control.

THE ORIGINS OF THE MILITIA MOVEMENT

Some treatments put the origins of the modern militia movement in the 1950s and 1960s, and some locate it in the Sagebrush rebellion of the 1970s. Most, however, date the modern militia movement to the rise in the 1970s and 1980s of Posse Comitatus, a violent, anti-Semitic, anti-tax, anti-government band of extremists prominent in several western states.

Militia membership increased dramatically in the mid-1990s, following upon a number of violent confrontations between elements of the radical right and the federal government, including at Ruby Ridge and Waco. Militia activity also flourished after the election of President Obama, seemingly in tandem with the rise of the Tea Party. Recently there has been yet another swell in militia activity. Militias have been involved in several high-profile standoffs with the federal government, including at the Bundy Ranch in 2014 and at the Occupation of the Malheur National Wildlife Refuge in 2016.[27]

Some of the more prominent groups in the Second Wave of militia activity, such as the Central Oregon Constitutional Guard (COCG) and the Oath Keepers, are not especially different than their predecessors. Certainly the rhetoric is familiar: B.J. Soper, one of the founders of the Central Oregon Constitutional Guard, cautions that "It doesn't say in our Constitution that you can't stand up and defend yourself. . . . We've let the government step over the line and rule us, and that was never the intent of this country."[28]

The COCG calls itself a self-defense organization. As a writer for the *Washington Post* notes, the enemy is clear: "Mainly, [Soper is] talking about the federal government, which he thinks is capable of unprovoked aggression against its own people. Soper started his group, which consists of about 30 men, women, and children from a handful of families, two years ago as a 'defensive unit' against 'all enemies foreign and domestic.'"[29] The COCG conducts paramilitary training sessions and "stockpiles supplies, practice survival skills and 'basic infantry' tactics, learn how to treat combat injuries . . . and train with their concealed handguns and combat-style rifles." The Constitution figures prominently in their worldview:

> Soper bristles when critics call him anti-government; he said he supports the government but just wants it to follow the Constitution. And he said calling his group 'armed' is as relevant as saying its members wear boots, because the Second Amendment gives every American the right to carry a gun. Soper, who carries a pocket Constitution with him everywhere, said he thinks the Constitution does not give the federal government the right to own land, and that the government's increasing emphasis on environmental regulations is putting ranchers, miners, loggers and others out of work and devastating local economies.[30]

Most militias insist they are peaceful and will resort to violence only if (most believe when) they are targeted by authorities. Nevertheless, the list of paramilitary groups and right-wing extremist organizations that have plotted or committed acts of terrorism and violence is long. Among them are the Order II, the Silent Brotherhood, the Arizona Patriots, the White Patriots Party, Posse Comitatus, and the KKK. Almost all of these groups were especially active in the 1980s, but there was right-wing terrorism in the 1990s as well, committed by such groups as Aryan Republican Army, the "Sons of Gestapo," and the Oklahoma Constitutional Militia.

Perhaps the best known example of a militia willing to use violence, however, was the Covenant, the Sword, and the Arm of the Lord (CSA). The CSA began as an evangelical, communal retreat in the early 1970s. Under the leadership of Minister James Ellison, the group became increasingly radical, helped along by Ellison's visions of a coming race war. Members attended gun shows and formed soft alliances with other right-wing groups, including Posse Comitatus, Aryan Nations, various chapters of the KKK, Elohim City, and others. They engaged in extensive paramilitary exercises at a mock-up village called Silhouette City, "complete with pop-up targets of blacks, Jews, and police officers wearing Star of David Badges."[31]

CSA was headquartered at a self-styled Aryan compound on the Arkansas-Missouri border, where it plotted and trained for assassinations of FBI agents and a United States District judge. CSA also concocted several plots to poison local water supplies and to bomb the Alfred P. Murrah Federal Building in Oklahoma City (well over 10 years before Timothy McVeigh and Terry Nichols did so). Most of the plans never came to fruition, but the CSA did commit several bombings and murders in the early to mid-1980s. In 1985, several members were arrested following a stand-off at their compound with federal agents that lasted several days.

The current crop of militias also includes organizations disposed to violence. One, the Crusaders, planned to attack a Somali mosque in Garden City, Kansas; three militia members were arrested before the attack could be carried out.[32] Militias have also made appearances at recent Alt-right demonstrations, including, notably, at rallies in Cal-Berkeley, the University of Florida, and the Unite the Right rally at the University of Virginia. Some of the militia groups involved in the riots at Charlottesville, such as the Pennsylvania Light Foot Militia and another group, the Three Percenters, justified their presence as both necessary to prevent disorder and as vital to protecting the First Amendment rights of the White Nationalists who organized the event. Some observers have begun to wonder if the militia movement has joined forces with the Alt-right: "Their presence as a private security force for an increasingly public coalition of white nationalist factions—Ku Klux Klan followers, neo-Nazis and 'alt-right' supporters—has transformed a movement that has already demonstrated a willingness to threaten violence."[33] Several militias involved themselves in the 2016 presidential election, including the Oath Keepers, who promised to monitor the polls, apparently fearing "expected attempts at voter fraud by leftists."[34]

WHAT IS A MILITIA? DEFINITIONS AND IDEOLOGIES

One way to understand the militia movement is to start with a definition. But we face a familiar problem: How do we distinguish (and should we distinguish?) between militias and a great variety of other groups and associations and clubs and hobbyists that do not call themselves militias, but do engage in some of the same activities and pursuits? Many but not all militias are conservative and Christian. Some militias cater to middle-aged white men playing weekend soldier, whereas others secret themselves and plan for armed insurrection by engaging in paramilitary tactics and training.

"The militia movement is comprised of a seemingly countless number of different groups and organizations that appear, disappear, and reassemble and reorganize with almost bewildering frequency."[35] Richard Abanes distinguishes between moderates, "conservative Christians dissatisfied by the current state of American politics," more radical participants, which "include both Christians and non-Christians who deny their US citizenship, drive without licenses, and refuse to pay income taxes," and "the most dangerous and unpredictable 'patriots'—Klansmen, neo-Nazis, and Christian Identity believers."[36] Abanes believes that "This loosely knit network of perhaps 5 to 12 million people may be one of the most diverse movements our nation has ever seen."[37] The militia movement's diversity, however, is fraternal rather than racial, ethnic, religious, or socioeconomic in nature. Of course there are exceptions, but most militia members are white, male, working class, Christian, and middle-aged. "This is not one unified movement," Berlet notes, "but a series of overlapping ones."[38]

A more useful, though no less messy, way to get a handle on the militia movement is to ask what militias believe. It is a messy task because there is no single, overarching principle to which every militia or every militia member will subscribe. One unifying element in the militia movement is fundamentalism, which may or may not have a religious cast to it, but almost always has a constitutional component. "Although *all* conservatism does *not* fit the mold" of religious fundamentalism,[39] militia members closely resemble religious fundamentalists (and in some cases they are religious fundamentalists) "in their zealotry for an ideological cause."[40]

CONSTITUTIONAL MILITIAS

Since the 1990s, some militias, like the Militia of Montana, the Michigan Militia, and the Ohio Unorganized Militia, have explicitly styled themselves as "Constitutional Militias." Unlike militia groups that are mostly concerned with resisting the New World Order, or ZOG, or inclined explicitly to Aryanism, constitutional militias consider themselves constitutional patriots,[41] as this CNN interview with a militia member reveals:

> Ling: Like in what way would you consider yourself an extremist?

> Silverback: The strict belief in the Constitution and the unwavering belief that the constitutional republic is what we should adhere to.

The constitutional militia movement is composed mostly of veterans, libertarians, and Second Amendment advocates who share a common belief in individual liberties and disdain for an abusive and tyrannical federal government that has no regard for constitutional limits.[42] Like their Founding heroes, who fought a like war against distant tyranny, constitutional militias campaign against federal oppression. This self-image helps militias to make the argument that far from posing a danger to the constitutional order, they are essential to preserving to it.

Constitutional militias hold fast to four fundamental truths. First, the people should be wary of the federal government, because all governments—and especially those that are at a remove from the people[43]—overreach and are vulnerable to corruption. Second, in light of this reasonable fear, the citizenry should be armed. Third, in order for the people to act on their fear, they must be organized (or organize themselves) into militias. Lastly, when governments seek to oppress the people, they begin by disarming them.[44]

Constitutional militias likewise hold that the original meaning of the Constitution has been lost to most citizens. This is why so much of the militia movement is directed to the project of constitutional literacy and to the study of the Founders and the Founding era, to getting the Constitution "right." In many militias, the Montana Militia is a good example, members are urged to purchase copies of the Constitution and to keep a copy on their person. Many militia members have memorized their favorite parts, along with collections of quotations from favored Founders, the Declaration of Independence, and other militia-sanctioned instructional materials.[45] W. Cleon Skousen's *Five Thousand Year Leap* is a favorite, as are the works of Justice Scalia (excepting his decision in *Heller*), David Barton, Kris Anne Hall, Mike Lee, Mark R. Levin, and a few others.

The foundational principles of militia constitutionalism, in addition to freedom of speech and originalism, are guns, property, and religion.

1. Guns

Like the right to own a firearm, the right to form a militia is an expression of the fundamental, God-given second amendment right of self–defense. For militias, there can be no compromise on such fundamental principles. Calls for firearm registration or waiting periods, like efforts to restrict the kinds of weapons civilians can own or to close gun show loopholes that allow purchasers to avoid federal law, are not a matter of how to balance Second Amendment rights with other imperatives, like protecting the peace, but instead a first step on the slippery slope to tyranny.

Militias see conspiracy behind every effort to regulate firearms, which they often stockpile in anticipation of forcible disarmament by the feds. It is not lost on militia men that both Ruby Ridge and Waco originated in federal weapons charges and then quickly escalated, in their telling, to murder. There is little doubt that federal authorities badly botched both incidents, but where some of us see gross incompetence with tragic consequences, many in the militia movement see a conspiracy to kill conservative religious Americans who wanted only to be let alone. Conspiracies of one sort or another are part of the life-blood of right-wing populism. As Chip Berlet notes, "The formation of movements such as the Tea Party and armed citizens' militias is facilitated in the US by the spadework done by previous right-wing movements that tell stories of elite conspiracies to subvert the nation. . . . The story embraced by the armed militias of the 1990s was that the government of the US was part of a secret plan to establish a one-world government as part of building a new world order."[46]

Conditioned by conspiracy thinking, militias see any and every call for gun control as just the first step, and not a very subtle one, toward the disarming and subjugation of Americans. The CNN interview again illustrates the point vividly:

> Ling: Why do you think there's been such an astronomical increase in the number of militias and patriot groups in this country over the last eight years?
>
> Silverback: I think a lot of it stems from an outgoing president that has been so outspoken against guns, an outgoing president that a lot of people feared was going to try to be a dictator and to stay in office—
>
> Ling: You're talking about President Obama?
>
> Silverback: Yes, yeah. Um, you know—
>
> Ling: That was a real fear?
>
> Silverback: I've heard it. . . . It may sound silly but every time a Democrat gets in office, people are afraid of their guns being taken away. They're afraid their rights are under attack.[47]

As David Neiwert has commented, "Taking away guns . . . was one of the militias' chief sources of paranoia in the 1990s,"[48] and it escalated during the Obama administration, accompanied by paranoid claims about secret FEMA concentration camps and other bizarre conspiracies involving the United Nations, the Federal Reserve, and other nefarious organizations.

2. Property

The specter of gun control looms large in militia thinking, and it overlaps with several other constitutional complaints. As evidenced by the Bundy and Malheur incidents, one of those complaints concerns federal ownership of land, especially in the west. (Racial fears play a role here as well. Some see federal ownership of rural lands as part of a plot to "drive white men off the land into the cities [and] to take away their guns and Second Amendment rights as well."[49]) As Thomas Halpern noted years before both of these incidents, "The militias reflect a general sense, present particularly in the western regions of the United States, that a man used to be able to stake out his piece of property, his homestead, to make a life for himself and his family, and do whatever he wanted to virtually be free of any kind of government oversight."[50] Like the First and Second amendments, the right to property is not a product of the social contract, not a right "given" to citizens in the Fifth Amendment. It is a divine or natural right, preconstitutional in the sense that it is independent of and superior to the Constitution. The Fifth Amendment does not *create* a right to property; it *recognizes* that we have a right to property.

Accordingly, the Alt-fifth amendment, like the alt-first and alt-second amendments, is absolute. A man's (I use the word consciously) property is his to do with as he pleases, subject only to whatever restrictions God envisioned. (I'm not sure what those are.) And like the Alt-first and the Alt-second amendments, the Alt-fifth amendment has a rich symbolic meaning for the radical right. The right to self-defense in the Alt-second amendment, for example, is tied to defending one's self, one's family and loved ones, and one's property. The conjunction of all three liberties is what gives incidents like Ruby Ridge and Waco such resonance on the right. The right to property means little without a right to protect it.[51]

Building on an anti-Federalist and Jeffersonian conception of property and liberty, militias believe property is essential to one's liberty and dignity as a free citizen. Property offers a man the possibility of independence, the chance to make his way in the world. Without the right to property he is no better than a subject, dependent upon others. The connection between property and citizenship is plainly evident in the related principle of freehold suffrage, common in the colonies, which provided that only property-holders could vote. The close connection between property and the right to vote highlights the relationship between property, citizenship, and full standing in the political community.

The right to property figures prominently in the militia movement because, in its view, impositions on property smack of tyranny. The armed militants who gathered at the Cliven Bundy ranch were there not only to support Bundy, who had claimed that the federal government had "stolen" his land, but to protest federal ownership of land in general. (The government had a court order directing Bundy to pay over $1 million in grazing fees for Bundy's use of federally owned land adjacent to Bundy's ranch in southeastern Nevada.) Bundy's argument was that the federal government has no constitutional authority to own vast tracts of lands in the western United States, and that the land he wanted to graze belongs to the "sovereign state of Nevada."

Similarly, the occupation that ended in violence (Patriots would say murder, referencing the shooting of LaVoy Finicum by Oregon State troopers) at the Malheur National Wildlife Refuge cannot be understood without appreciating the symbolic significance of property rights and constitutionalist rhetoric to the militia movement. These are hardened claims in the far right, especially in the west. The federal government's ownership of vast tracts of land in some western states is a physical sign, Bundy's compatriots argue, of the federal government's overreach. The land claim fits neatly into the thinking of the militia, Patriot, and Tenther movements.[52]

3. Religion

Another principal concern in the militia movement is freedom of religion. Some in the radical right see the events at the Branch Davidian compound in Waco as an attack on the religious beliefs of David Koresh and his followers. Koresh's religious beliefs (the Branch Davidians separated in 1955 from the Seventh-day Adventist Church), and his fear of federal authorities, led him to stockpile weapons in a secretive and closely guarded compound; he was eventually charged with federal weapons offenses. In militia ideology, the federal government's raid on the compound, in which 76 Branch Davidians died, including Koresh, was an unprovoked attack on citizens who desired nothing more than to be let alone to practice their faith. (Law enforcement authorities believed that in addition to federal weapons violations, Koresh practiced polygamy and had sexually abused several minors.)

Many on the far right likewise see religious persecution in the Ruby Ridge affair. Randy Weaver and his family had retreated to a twenty-acre isolated and heavily fortified compound near Naples, Idaho, to escape an evil world on the verge of the apocalypse. The Weavers were sought by agents from the Bureau of Alcohol, Tobacco, and Firearms for having sold an illegal sawed-off shotgun to an undercover ATF informant. Randy Weaver was arrested, charged, and released on his own recognizance; he then retreated to his compound on Ruby Ridge and refused to come out. A ten-day stand-off ensued, in which Weaver's son, Sammy, and wife, Vicki, were killed, as was a United States Marshall. The tragedy at Ruby Ridge was the perfect convergence of the several themes that animate the militia movement—religious faith, estrangement, firearms, private property—and paranoia.

The affinity between militias and religion goes well beyond Ruby Ridge or the Branch Davidians, however. One of the most significant features of the militia movement is its association with the Christian Identity movement. The convergence of Christian Identity and the contemporary militia movement dates from the 1970s and the 1980s. Not all militia members are part of the Christian Identity movement, and not all members of Christian Identity are militia members, but there is significant overlap, and many of the militia groups that sprouted in the 1980s and 1990s, including some members of Posse Comitatus, were connected in some way with Christian Identity, as were Randy and Vicki Wagner.

There is no litmus test one can use to distinguish adherents of Christian Identity from similar movements, such as the Christian Patriot Movement, Dominionists, Christian Reconstructionism, and dozens of other, sometimes fleeting groups and associations. There is no single text that sets out its central precepts; indeed, it is a mistake to think that Christian Identity has a comprehensive belief system beyond the overriding conviction that European whites are God's chosen, descended from Adam, and that other peoples are the descendants of Satan (African Americans) or of Cain (Jews).[53] Christian Identity is irredeemably anti-Semitic, believing that "Jews are not only wholly unconnected to the Israelites, but are the very children of the Devil, the literal biological offspring of a sexual dalliance between Satan and Eve in the Garden of Eden."[54]

Perhaps unsurprisingly, one of the organizing elements of Christian Identity ideology is the convergence between biblical law and the Founders' Constitution. Where they diverge, the Constitution is wrong and must give way to scripture. The divergence is more far-reaching than one might think. It includes claims that taxes are unbiblical, unjust, and unconstitutional, to take one example, to arguments about the sovereignty of the states, federalism, and that the Articles of Confederation supersede the Constitution of 1787.[55]

   Concern for traditional values helps to explain why the extremist right in general,[56] and Christian Identity especially, are attracted to the militia movement. It also helps to hide their racism from the squeamish and the mainstream liberal media. When members of the constitutional militias insist they are not racists, for instance, they mean they know better than to use the coarse language of racism. Instead they campaign for restoration of the "Constitution" in its original meaning, and for the world they imagine was intended by the Founders. Their constitution is not the Constitution of civil rights or of equality under the law for all Americans. It is instead a constitution of racial privilege. An example helps to make this point clear: Many in the militia movement dress their opposition to the civil rights movement and to programs like affirmative action in higher education or employment with appeals to a "color-blind" constitution instead of overt claims of racial privilege. Civil rights programs that make explicit use of race, they argue, betray the ideal of equal protection. (In more sophisticated treatments, they also condemn such programs as gross overreaches of federal power enabled by deliberate misinterpretations of the commerce power and disregard for the reserved Tenth Amendment powers of state and local government.)

   The original constitution, the Founders' constitution, the organic constitution, or whatever one wants to call it, was anything but color blind. It was (and is) built explicitly and purposefully on the worst forms of racial privilege. It institutionalized white superiority and in doing so brutalized African Americans and Native Americans. It denied them not only equality and liberty and the civil liberties so cherished by militia members—it denied their very humanity. I take up the point more fully later, but appeals to a color-blind constitution, or to traditional constitutional values are at best uninformed and more often disingenuous, a part of a racial project embraced by the far right that "ignores the social realities and implications of race, attempts to eliminate racial tension by disregarding race altogether, and thus permits ongoing racial discrimination in the private sphere."[57] Unlike the Alt-right, militias hide their racism behind coded appeals to the Constitution.

THE CONSTITUTIONALITY OF MILITIAS

The Constitution's provisions concerning militias stem from a complicated colonial history concerning the use of citizens' armies (think of the Minutemen of Massachusetts) and the rise of a standing Continental Army under the command of the Continental Congress and George Washington. Predictably, the concerns reflect many of the familiar tensions of federalism. Some anti-Federalists, for example, worried that a standing army would constitute a threat to the sovereignty and independence of the states. They argued that the Continental Army should be disbanded and replaced by state militias. Federalists, in contrast, thought that the experiences of funding the Revolutionary War and the necessity of a strong federal government counseled a strong and permanent federal army.

The Constitution reflects a compromise between these two positions. Read together, the relevant provisions call for the federal and state governments to share control of the militias. When the militias are called into federal service (a call they cannot lawfully resist under Article I), the Constitution provides that Congress has the authority to organize, arm, and discipline them. By virtue of Article II of the Constitution, the President is the commander in chief of the state militias when they are called into service; when not in federal service, state militias are under the command of state governors. The states retain the power to appoint officers and to oversee the training of the militias. It is important to emphasize that when Congress calls the state militias into service, it does so for the purpose of protecting the Union and suppressing insurrections. The supremacy clause of Article VI further underscores the point. This tells us that militias may not be formed to foment anti-government activity. (On the other hand, as we have seen, many of the members of private militias describe their efforts as pro-constitutional in purpose.)

The Constitution addresses militias in Article I; Section 8, clauses 15 and 16 granting Congress the power to "provide for organizing, arming, and disciplining the Militia," as well as, and in distinction to, the power to raise an army and a navy. Congress is granted the power to use the militia of the United States for three specific missions, as described in Article I, Section 8, clause 15: "to execute the laws of the Union, suppress insurrections, and repel invasions." Many of the constitutional issues surrounding militias, however, start with the Second Amendment, which begins with the phrase, "A well-regulated militia, being necessary to the security of a free State. . . . "

The sparse words of the Second Amendment raise a lot of questions. First among them is the matter of a "well-regulated Militia." What precisely is a militia? What does the qualifier "well-regulated" mean, and well-regulated by whom? Does the reference to the security of a free state mean that militias must be organized by the state? There is not much scholarly disagreement about what the word "militia" means, or at least about what it meant at the Founding. But the matter is more complicated once we leave academia. Anyone who looks into it is likely to run across several different meanings and uses of the word "militia," along with occasionally peculiar terminology, such as "state militia," "unorganized militia," "sedentary militia," "free militia," "irregular militia," and others.[58] This is another instance where the plain words of the constitutional text are far from plain. The text requires interpretation.

One interpretive question concerns the relationship between the opening words regarding militias and the subsequent language concerning the right of the people to keep and bear arms. As we saw, the relationship between the prefatory clause and the operative clause was a point of extended discussion in Justice Scalia's opinion for the Court in *Heller*. Scalia concluded that the prefatory clause (about the militia) is of little significance, or at least does not delimit the right alluded to in the operative clause (to own a firearm). Consequently, the right of the people to keep and bear arms is independent of their membership in a state militia. For most folks in the militia movement, however, the militia clause presumes that citizens have a pre-existing constitutional right to form militias, and that right in turn necessitates the operative clause. In other words, for the militias, the prefatory clause is both more and less important than one might think. It is more important because it recognizes a right to form and join a militia (also protected by the Alt-first amendment's right to association). It is less important, for some, because the right to own a firearm exists independent of one's membership in a militia.

Under federal law, the militia referenced in the Second Amendment and elsewhere in the Constitution takes the form of the National Guard in each of the states, as provided for in the Dick Act, passed in 1903.[59] The term "unorganized militia" also has a legal definition under the

Dick Act. It consists of able-bodied males between eighteen and forty-five years of age. Thus, under the Dick Act, every able-bodied male in the specified age range and who is not already in the armed forces or the National Guard is by definition part of the unorganized militia of the state in which he resides.

THE LEGALITY OF PRIVATE MILITIAS

The Constitution of 1787 makes no provision for private militias. As Robert J. Spitzer has noted, "From the colonial era on, Americans organized as militias did so—and sought to do so—under the recognition and control of the state or national governments. The Bill of Rights had just been ratified when Congress enacted the Uniform Militia Act of 1792, a law designed to bring greater uniformity and control to the nation's militias, which at the time were central to national defense."[60] In contemporary jurisprudence, it is equally clear that a lawful militia must be organized under the auspices of and subject to the control of the government. Any militia that purports to be private, or not under the authority of government, is not a militia in a strictly legal or constitutional sense. Congress almost certainly has the constitutional authority to make private militias illegal, albeit within the confines imposed by the First Amendment (more on the relationship between private militias and freedom of speech, below).

State governments can also make private militias illegal, and several have done so through statutes that criminalize private armies or paramilitary training by private organizations. In *Presser v. Illinois* (1886), the Supreme Court ruled that "Unless restrained by their own constitutions, state legislatures may enact statutes to control and regulate all organizations, drilling, and parading of military bodies and associations except those which are authorized by the militia laws of the United States."

In light of *Heller* and *McDonald*, some aspects of *Presser* are no longer good law. But its holding concerning state authority to prohibit private militias does not depend upon its now rejected interpretation of the Second Amendment. Two other cases help to make this clear, one from the 1940s, and one from the 1980s. The case from the 1980s, *Vietnamese Fishermen's Association v. Knights of the Ku Klux Klan*, was initiated by Morris Dees and the Southern Poverty Law Center and involved efforts by the KKK to terrorize Vietnamese fishermen in Galveston, Texas.[61] A federal district court in Texas issued an injunction against the KKK, barring it from organizing or maintaining a private army, in violation of Texas state law. The Court ruled that the Texas law did not violate either the First or the Second Amendment, and it specifically held that the "Second Amendment does not imply any general right for individuals to bear arms and form private armies."[62] The first part of that holding (about a general right of individuals to bear arms) may be incorrect in light of *Heller*, but the second claim (about private armies) does not depend upon the first. As the district court explained, quoting at length from a 1940s case from New York, *Application of Cassidy* (1947):

> There can be no justification for the organization of such an armed force. Its existence would be incompatible with the fundamental concept of our form of government. The inherent potential danger of any organized private militia, even if never used or even if ultimately placed at the disposal of the government, is obvious. Its existence would be sufficient, without more, to prevent a democratic form of government . . . from functioning freely, without coercion, and in accordance with the constitutional mandates.

Militias are not entirely beyond the safe haven of the First Amendment. Speech that simply criticizes government, no matter how sharply, or that talks openly of revolution or violent resistance to the state will be protected, provided it does not amount to incitement or intend to cause civil unrest or disorder. Hence, militia members that talk in the abstract about the possibility of armed resistance to state or federal authority—talk that simply advocates, to use the Supreme Court's terminology—are engaged in constitutionally protected speech.[63] Similarly, the right to associate with other citizens likely protects some of the associational activities of private militias, and this might even include some paramilitary training activities, so long as they are peaceable and do not violate other laws. Moreover, governmental authorities cannot make militias illegal or prohibit their activities simply because they disapprove of them or their message.[64] Insofar as militias are comprised simply of weekend soldiers dressed in camo and pretending to conduct pseudomilitary maneuvers, and not actively engaged in causing civic disorder or threatening others, their activity is protected by the First Amendment.

On the other hand, militia speech that incites others to illegal behavior, or that intentionally foments civil unrest and disorder, may be constitutionally proscribed.[65] Bona fide threats and criminal conspiracies are not protected by the First Amendment.[66] The logic is that speech that incites violence, whether against individuals or the state, not only does not advance any of the legitimate rationales for protecting speech, it undermines them. Consequently, narrowly drafted restrictions on militia speech, which target only what may be lawfully proscribed and which advance the state's undoubted interest in protecting individuals or the community, will not offend the First Amendment.

Approximately 40 states have laws that restrict some forms of paramilitary training or activity.[67] Punishments vary considerably. In Idaho, militias that train members to maim or kill with the intent to further "civil disorder" may be punished by up to 10 years in prison and/or up to a $50,000 fine. In Pennsylvania, training people to use guns or bombs with intent to further civil disorder is just a first-degree misdemeanor.

These statutes are often difficult to enforce, as they typically (and properly) require some evidence of intent and evidence of overt criminal activity.[68] There are several additional reasons why states don't always enforce these laws. Sometimes prosecutors have other, more significant charges they can bring against groups they think constitute a serious threat, including federal conspiracy charges and weapons charges, as well as extortion and obstruction of justice charges. The response of federal prosecutors to the militia members who gathered at Cliven Bundy's ranch is a good example of the resources available: "The federal government slapped the showdown's leaders, including Bundy, with a slew of federal charges, including conspiracy, extortion, obstruction of justice, and assault on a federal officer."[69]

The wisdom of neglect is open to dispute, but it is driven partly by a genuine concern not to infringe upon First Amendment rights. Some of it is also a calculation about whether enforcement is likely to drive more people into the movement, and some of it is simply about whether it is an efficient use of limited resources. If the militia movement becomes larger and/or more virulently anti-government, these considerations will have to be recalculated.

MILITIAS IN THE ALT-CONSTITUTION

The status of citizens' militias under the Alt-constitution hinges not only on specific interpretations of the Alt-second amendment, but also on somewhat larger, more inchoate understandings of federalism. The argument, in capsule form, is that most (well, all) efforts at gun control violate the second amendment right of individual self-defense and, importantly, its purpose to act as a bulwark against tyranny. Following this logic, private or citizens' or irregular or unorganized militias have an important role to play in protecting citizens from government gone badly. The National Rifle Association has been an especially vocal proponent of the anti-tyranny argument, on occasion calling government officials "jack-booted thugs" and warning of "a nefarious plot to disarm Americans."[70]

The argument for militias under the Alt-second amendment also claims that modern militias are the legitimate heirs to colonial militias and a logical extension of the right to bear arms. The Second Amendment, they argue, explicitly connects up the right to bear arms and the necessity of a well-regulated militia. Against the argument that "well-regulated" means under the auspices of government, Alt-second amendment theory holds that private militias *are* well-regulated, but self-regulated, and moreover that requiring state regulation would defeat one of the very reasons why citizens' militias exist. In short, the argument is that the Second Amendment affords constitutional protection for both the right to own a firearm and to join a private militia, and that the two reinforce each other. By extension, the Alt-second and the Alt-first amendments must also protect the various paramilitary training activities these groups engage in.

Insofar as militias stress the dangers of tyranny, the right of revolution, and the necessity of an armed citizenry, some of their "thinking mirrors the Framer's view of the [Second] Amendment."[71] But there are significant points of disagreement as well, especially regarding the Founders' fears of rebellion and civil war and their understanding of the "People."[72] More importantly, militias invoke the Constitution and other sacred texts, especially the Declaration of Independence, to clothe themselves with legitimacy and social status.

The same logic is behind the pronounced tendency amongst Gun Nuts to collect quotations from Founders both famous and obscure, often out of context, which purport to show the Founders intended us to take the words in the Second Amendment ("shall not be infringed") literally, or that the right to form a private citizens' militia is an inherent right, beyond the reach of any legitimate government.[73] One favorite is a Founder forgotten to many of us, but revered in certain circles, named Tench Coxe. Coxe was a delegate for Pennsylvania to the Continental Congress in 1788–1789 and often wrote under the pseudonym "A Pennsylvanian." Even a cursory look at pro-Second Amendment and pro-militia websites will find quotations from Coxe. Here is Coxe on the militias:

> Who are the militia? Are they not ourselves? Is it feared, then, that we shall turn our arms each man against his own bosom. Congress have no power to disarm the militia. Their swords, and every other terrible implement of the soldier, are the birthright of an American. . . . [T]he unlimited power of the sword is not in the hands of either the federal or state governments, but, where I trust in God it will ever remain, in the hands of the people.[74]

Coxe was also a great advocate of an individual right to own a firearm. Often unremarked, however, is that his views, although not unusual, were not universal either. Why is Coxe's theory of the Second Amendment to be preferred, say, to that of John Quincy Adams, who favored restricting the right to guns meant for hunting? Appeals to original meaning and Founders intent, as we have seen, are standard issue interpretive methodologies in the Alt-constitution. They rarely if ever yield a conclusive result, but much more is at stake than disputes about how to determine what the Constitution means.

In obvious contrast to their authority under the US Constitution, state and federal anti-militia states almost certainly offend the Alt-first amendment. Recall that the Alt-first amendment allows no restrictions on speech rights, including freedom of association. If the alt-first amendment is truly absolute, then even militia speech that counsels revolution should find protection under the Alt-first amendment, as would their training exercises and most other paramilitary activities. The more challenging question is whether the Alt-first amendment protects militia activities that incite others to rebellion, insurrection, and other criminal activities. The answer is yes and no. At the level of hypothetical abstraction, the Alt-first amendment can be absolutist and yet still offer no protection for illegal activity by holding to a distinction between "pure" speech (fully and absolutely protected, always) and symbolic speech and conduct, which may in limited circumstances be proscribed.[75] Both merit some degree of protection, but pure speech is more fully protected than symbolic speech. (Justice Black, a putative First Amendment absolutist, often took refuge in the distinction between speech and conduct.) And as we saw in Chapter 3, in free exercise cases courts often distinguish between religious beliefs, fully and always protected, and conduct, which may be regulated whenever the state has a rational basis for doing so.[76] Some of us (well, me) think the distinction between speech and conduct is simplistic, but judges have used it for a long time.

By adopting a similar rubric, the Alt-first amendment could hold fast to the claim that it is absolute. It might not protect militia violence, but it would protect the right of militia members to speak and to associate in the name of constitutional liberty and even to talk about revolution and resistance. The difference would be in where to draw the line between speech and conduct; under the Alt-first amendment the sphere of speech and association will expand, and the sphere of proscribable conduct will shrink. On the other hand, it is difficult to see what value anti-government speech has to militias if they have no corresponding constitutional right to act on it. Otherwise, it's *all* just talk. Or bluster.

Hence, in the Alt-constitution, the right to own a firearm and freedom of speech morph almost inevitably into a right to form armed militias. Even more broadly, militias preach the necessity of civic vigilance to protect liberty in general, and the specific liberties included in the Bill of Rights in particular, against governmental overreach and eventual tyranny. Any interpretation of the Alt-second amendment that frustrates that purpose or makes it more difficult for citizens to advance it must be wrong. So what we make of the constitutionality of militias under the Alt-constitution is not simply a question of determining what the Alt-first amendment requires, or even of what the Alt-second amendment demands. It requires that we read the Alt-first and the Alt-second amendments as a single piece. It is a way of interpreting the Alt-constitution that goes beyond self-contained inquiries into specific provisions and instead requires a comprehensive appeal to both the structure and the purpose of the Alt-constitution writ large, supplemented by an appeal to the Founders and a particular telling of history. The militias call upon a romantic (but imagined) vision of American history in which revolution and independence were won by men just like themselves, self-organized into small militias dedicated to the cause of liberty. On this telling, private militias are why we still have a Constitution, not a threat to it or incompatible with it.

A final qualification to the Alt-second amendment also requires us to consider it in light of the Alt-constitution writ large. As we shall see in Chapter 5, constitutional rights, including first and second amendment rights, belong only to full (or Sovereign) citizens. So of course the Alt-first and second amendments protect the speech and association rights of white males and their paramilitary play groups. They offer little or no protection at all, however, for the speech and associational rights of minorities and persons of color. White militias, no matter their ideology, rhetoric, or purpose, no matter how weaponized, are presumptively protected under the Alt-first amendment. Antifa, Black Lives Matter, BAMN, or other organizations and associations, on the other hand, are fair targets for regulation and proscription. The First Amendment prohibits these sorts of distinctions as viewpoint discrimination, and they raise questions under the equal protection clause of the Fourteenth Amendment too. We can explain a different result under the Alt-constitution only if we recognize that the Alt-first and second amendments cannot support a meaning that is at odds with the Alt-constitution in whole. In this instance, they must be read in light of what the Alt-constitution has to say about race, religion, and who qualifies for full citizenship in the American constitutional order.

CONCLUSION

Since the 1980s, arguably its heyday, the militia movement has waxed and waned in popularity, mostly in response to larger political events, such as the election of President Obama.[77] In short, the fears and anxieties that fueled the remarkable rise of the Tea Party movement (whose precepts have much in common with the beliefs of most militia members, though Tea Parties deny it vigorously) powered a resurgent militia movement, especially in the mid-west and the west.

Behind these anxieties is a narrative, however, that is larger than Barack Obama or the traitorous Left. The fear is of the federal government and its march to tyranny, which explains why at least some in the Tea Party could say their anger wasn't grounded in racism or antipathy toward a black president, but began earlier with a sense of betrayal by establishment conservatives and President Bush. I am among those who find these protests unconvincing: I don't recall hearing that anguished outrage before Obama was elected, and I don't recall anything like birtherism polluting the waters. But if fear of tyranny (and not of something or someone else) is what animates militias and Gun Nuts, it raises an interesting question: what will become of them now that Republicans control both the presidency and Congress?

Unless there is radical change in Washington or a full-scale retreat from the modern state, if not from modernity itself, there is little reason to think that the militia movement will subside soon. The enemy is a monstrously sized federal government that has no regard for liberty or for constitutional limits on its power and wants to take our guns.[78] The results of the 2016 presidential election may offer some immediate comfort to the alienated and fearful, but the long arc of militant extremism in the United States suggests that their fears run deep and will not be easily placated. Indeed, if President Trump disappoints them, we should expect entrenchment, if not additional violence. The Alt-second amendment, if not the Second Amendment we already have, almost guarantees it.

Chapter 5

COMMON LAW COURTS AND
SOVEREIGN CITIZENS

Bruce Doucette is a judge on one of America's most important courts, the "superior court of the continental United States of America." He and his court hear cases in such diverse jurisdictions as Alaska, Colorado, Florida, and presumably in several other (every other?) states and for nearly every kind of offense. In Costilla County, Colorado, for example, his court conducted a trial of several local officials for assorted crimes; the defendants were found guilty and ordered to resign their offices. (They didn't.)

If you have heard of Doucette, it is doubtless because of his much publicized association with the Bundy occupation in Oregon at the Malheur Wildlife Refuge in 2016. "Judge" Doucette promised to convene a citizen's grand jury to indict various federal officials and judges that he and members of the occupation accused of violating their oath to support the Constitution.[1] According to *The Oregonian*, "Doucette, a 54-year-old computer repairman, told the newspaper that 25 local residents 'would hear testimony and make decisions in private' before deciding whether to bring criminal charges. Those findings 'would be put in writing and made public.' . . . He didn't say what would come next."[2]

What came next were indictments, just as Doucette had intimated. Doucette and 7 other members of his 25-person Colorado People's Grand Jury were indicted by a Colorado grand jury (a real one).[3] According to the indictment, Doucette and others were engaged in a conspiracy in which one of them, having been convicted in a real court or having been treated unfavorably by a public official, would file a grievance against that official with the Colorado People's Grand Jury. Following a mock hearing or proceeding, the grand jury would then order the official to undertake some kind of corrective action or to resign. When, predictably, that did not occur, officers of the people's grand jury would file bogus liens or criminal complaints against the officials. "They would often serve the public servants at their homes, demanding they pay their 'debt' or be reported to a credit agency."[4]

Like the common law court on which Doucette sits, the "citizen's grand jury has roots in the Posse Comitatus movement, a sometimes violent, anti-Semitic, anti-tax, antigovernment brand of extremism."[5] Posse Comitatus dates from 1969 when Henry L. "Mike" Beach, a Portland business man, started the Citizen's Law Enforcement Research Committee. Beach also had ties with the Silver Shirts, an anti-Semitic white-supremacist organization modeled on Hitler's Brownshirts. According to the Oregon Historical Society, "Beach declared that a county's citizens, as defined by its laws, could deny state and federal authority to tax, regulate, and govern. . . . Followers, who sometimes formed their own government entities called 'townships,' appointed their owned public officials and believed only the county sheriff—not federal or state law enforcement—could enforce laws."[6] One Posse township, the "Constitutional Township of Tigerton Dells," sat on 570 acres on the Embarrass River in Northern Wisconsin. It had its own courts and appointed ambassadors to "other sovereign entities."[7] Outside Tigerton Dells hung signs that warned: "Federal Agents Keep Out; Survivors will be Prosecuted."[8] The "Blue Book," written by Beach, advised Posse members that governmental officials who enforced laws that Posse believed were unconstitutional or illegal should "be removed by the Posse to the most populated intersection of streets in the township and, at high noon, be hung by the neck, the body remaining until sundown as an example to those who would subvert the law."[9]

The Posse Comitatus movement was far from uniform and did not hold to a perfectly consistent philosophy.[10] But "At the heart of the Posse's political theory was the idea that citizens did not have to recognize any form of political authority higher than the county," a claim that "derives from English common law." Additionally, Posse members believed "that the only legitimate law was divinely given in the Bible and manifested in . . . the Articles of Confederation and Constitution, which restate that divine law."[11] The only legitimate power to interpret the law is "placed in common law associations and Christian grand juries, composed of only white, Christian males."[12] "Jews, minorities, and women have no legal standing in a Posse government."[13]

Doucette is not the only person on the far right who claims to have organized peoples' grand juries. John Darash (Vidurek), a retired carpenter from Poughkeepsie, New York, hopes to establish common-law grand juries in all 3,141 counties in the United States.[14] Darash is associated with a group called the National Liberty Alliance, which aims to "take back control of both our Judicial and Political Process"[15] with common law grand juries and common law courts, on which all adult Americans, when called for service by a jury administrator, must serve. According to the NLA, "It is the duty of ALL the People to respond to the Jury call. This is one of two ways where We the People self-govern by consenting or not to the government's request for an indictment, removal of an elected or appointed servant who breaches their oath, decides both facts and law in all trial cases and has the power of nullification." Common law grand juries and their companions, common law courts, are closely related to the Patriot and militia movements of the 1980s and 1990s.[16] Some observers, like the Southern Poverty Law Center, describe common law courts as "the most radical and active part of the antigovernment 'Patriot' movement,"[17] but some scholars think the connection between common law courts and the Patriot movement is less clear, if only because "the Patriot movement is too disorganized to have a clearly defined separation of powers or division of responsibilities."[18]

To my knowledge, no one in the Alt-right has invoked common law courts as part of its agenda, but the motivations that lay behind the common law courts movement is of a piece with much of Alt-right ideology, and especially of those strands that incline it to self-help (like the Alt-Knights and other paramilitary groups) and to white separatism. Like the Alt-right, the common law courts movement is white, often by design and always in fact.[19] Indeed, the single most important feature of the alt-common law is that it is organized around the idea of white supremacy. As noted by the Southern Poverty Law Center, "Behind the mountain of documents filed with county courts and computer-generated bank drafts lies an attempt to reverse a fundamental constitutional precept: all Americans are equal before the law."[20]

WHAT ARE COMMON LAW COURTS?

According to one definition, "Common law courts are courts organized at the local level outside the recognized judicial system that purportedly apply principles of common law to resolve disputes and adjudicate criminal matters."[21] Common law courts convene in bowling alleys, bingo halls, grange halls, taverns, and private homes. They purport to have all of the powers and trappings of authentic courts of law. Staffed by self-taught and self-appointed attorneys and volunteer judges, they mimic, often slavishly, the routines and procedures of real courts of law, issuing paper liens against defendants, drafting custody orders in divorce proceedings, imposing fines on litigants, resolving property disputes, and even issuing warrants for searches, seizures, and arrests. They claim the authority to punish those they convict and to hear and deny appeals. In some cases, they have gone so far as to declare local and federal officials who defy them as guilty of "capital" treason.[22]

In short, common law courts pretend to all of the powers and authorities of state-sanctioned courts, but common law courts are the courts of ochlocracy. Their authority is self-assumed and backed by threats of violence by the mobs who organize them. Threats of violence are integral to common law activism. Levin and Mitchell quote Leonard Ginter, one of 23 justices on a "national supreme court," as saying: "Go back to the time when somebody committed treason years ago, most of them were put on a scaffold to swing. That's what we need to do. If we do about 10 of them, the rest will straighten out."[23] Occasionally they seek to enforce their rulings through the apparatus of the county sheriff (the highest legal authority of the state they recognize as legitimate), but when that fails they appoint their own bailiffs and sheriffs and marshals. "As a last resort, some common-law courts call upon militia groups when the 'people have no place to go but to the constitutional militia.'"[24]

Just as importantly, these show courts are the visible manifestation of another common law principle: the persons involved in the common law court movement, advancing theories of the law and the Constitution that are not coherent enough to be called gibberish, claim immunity from the legal institutions and laws of the federal government. In its narrowest versions these surface as solemn proclamations by defendants in state and especially in federal courts that they do not recognize the jurisdiction of the court, typically followed by refusal to cooperate or to participate in the proceedings. (None of this has any bearing on whether the court in question will proceed anyway. It always does, sometimes with the defendant being tried in absentia, and sometimes with the defendant being held in contempt.) In its more ambitious versions it argues that a common law citizen is under no obligation to respect the authority of the state because he is not a member of that state—no need of a permit for a weapon, no need to register a car or license the driver, no need to pay social security or income or property taxes, no need to pursue a variance from a zoning board. Such a citizen must not accept the benefits of community or participate in it, not because it would be self-serving or hypocritical to do so, but because such participation creates a "contract of adhesion" by which one surrenders their status as a Sovereign Citizen for an inferior "federal" citizenship.

Common law courts sound ridiculous, but they are a very real threat to the many individuals who find themselves, usually unwittingly, caught up in them: "Thousands of people have been threatened, slapped with false liens against their property and 'convicted' of crimes such as 'treason' by these pseudo-legal, vigilante counterfeits of the real court system."[25] A typical example starts with a decision by a common law court to issue a lien against a person or his or her property, often without their knowledge. When that person attempts to sell the property the lien will show up and either prevent or delay the sale. Of course the lien is illegitimate and will not be enforced, but it will often take legal action, money, and time to clear it. It can cost thousands of dollars to "quiet title," or to remove the false property liens filed by common-law advocates.[26]

Often their targets are financial institutions, like banks, and their officers, who have earned enmity by virtue of foreclosure actions, or repossessions, or by calling or refusing to make loans. Admittedly, it can be difficult to work up much sympathy for the victims in such cases, but just as often the targets of this legal maneuvering—or caught in the crossfire—are county clerks and bailiffs and court recorders, who end up as targets of phony liens and enforcement actions themselves. In one case, a common law court in Montana filed a $500 million lien on the property of state Attorney General Joseph Mazurek.

One of the more novel uses of common courts is to file civil suits and liens to punish law officials for "nonperformance" of fictional duties imposed on them by common law "judicial" orders or bizarre readings of statutory or common law principles. In another case from Montana, a County Attorney, Nick Murnion, had a $500 million lien placed on his property based on his failure to prosecute the director of the Farmers Home Administration.[27] Murnion was also targeted by the Montana-based Freemen militia, who offered a $1 million bounty to anyone who would deliver him up to a common law court for trial.

I used the word "crossfire" above in both its figurative and its literal sense. Some public servants have been assaulted by individuals who claim to act under the authority of a common law court. Karen Mathews, a California county court recorder, was viciously attacked by an anti-government common law zealot: "Mathews . . . [had] been threatened, had bullets fired through her office windows, discovered a fake bomb planted under her car, and opened a package sent to her enclosing a single bullet and a chilling note: 'The next bullet will be directed to your head.'"[28]

The FBI calls the use of false liens and spurious lawsuits "paper terrorism."[29] Some estimates put the cost of coping with paper terrorism at many millions of dollars, which has led several states to enact legislation to cope with some of the problems.[30]

Some statutes make it easier for judges to dismiss frivolous lawsuits and to penalize those who file them. In one notorious case in Iowa, a judge fined 32 common law adherents $32,000 for filing a "just plain goofy" lawsuit.[31] Sometimes the legislation makes it easier for county clerks and court officials to refuse to file liens or complaints in the first place, or makes it easier to have them dismissed. In a highly publicized case in Missouri, more than a dozen people were jailed for filing a $10.8 million lien against a judge who refused to dismiss a speeding ticket.[32] Some laws criminalize participation in sham legal processes. The penalties attached to these statutes vary considerably and range from simple misdemeanors to felonies. In Montana, especially hard hit in the 1990s by the convergence of the militia and the common law court movements, politically motivated threats against public officials can be punished under the Anti-Intimidation Act of 1996 by fines of up to $50,000 and 10 years in prison.

COMMON LAW COURTS AND THE ALT-CONSTITUTION

The common law courts phenomenon draws upon almost every signifi-cant principle in the Alt-constitution, including freedom of expression; the second amendment; the right to property; qualifications for citizen-ship; and states' rights and federalism; as well as how to interpret the Constitution and who should interpret it. Behind the common law court movement, and the Sovereign Citizen Movement with which it is very closely associated, is a vision of an "idyllic American Republic com-posed of [f]reemen living virtuously with their families, free of taxes and regulation, subject only to 'godly' laws enforced by the county sheriff."[33] Making this vision a reality requires more than just talk. It requires the reinvention of the institutions (courts) and personnel (law enforcement and judicial officers) that comprise the modern state, remade in more acceptable form. As Susan Konick notes, "Out of a fiery gospel and a truncated version of the Constitution . . . a movement of people has created its own law. They call it 'common law' and their courts 'com-mon law courts' or 'our one Supreme Court.'"[34]

It also requires citizens to withdraw themselves from the jurisdiction of the modern administrative state. The Sovereign Citizen Movement (SCM) is famous for developing several elaborate and intricate theories of why and how a sovereign citizen can legally separate himself from the authority of the state. Some of these theories address the narrower but obviously related question of why Sovereign citizens are not subject to the jurisdiction of real courts. The arguments are painfully convoluted. One holds that federal and state courts, if they display a United States flag adorned with gold fringe, are *really* courts of admiralty whose prop-er jurisdiction extends only to maritime affairs. This may seem un-hinged, but for many in the common law movement it is rich with historical and symbolic significance. It draws directly upon the American colonists' hatred of the Stamp Act of 1765, which mandated the use of vice-admiralty courts to try violators of the law. Part of the colonists' opposition was addressed to the much despised writs of assis-tance, which authorized British custom officials, acting in concert with a local sheriff or justice of the peace, to conduct far-reaching searches for contraband and smuggled goods, based simply on an official's suspicion. One of the reasons colonial Americans objected to the Stamp Act was because cases in those courts were heard by royally appointed judges, not by local juries. Hence, when common law court advocates and Sovereign Citizens accuse our courts as acting as admiralty courts (as evidenced by the gold fringe on the flag), the objection to their jurisdiction is not just a (bizarre) narrow legal claim. It is an appeal to if not a reenactment of a glorious, patriotic history in which true Americans reject the legal institutions of an illegitimate, occupying government. (Flags in general are a matter of great affection in the radical right. The Gadsden flag, with a coiled snake and the words "Don't Tread on Me," is a staple at Tea Party, Patriot, and Militia events, and we all know about the Confederate flag.)

Other arguments challenge the legitimacy of standing courts by denying that they can hear cases that involve noncitizens (or Sovereign Citizens) who have withdrawn their consent from the social contract. Later in this chapter I'll review the various devices and strategies Sovereign Citizens use to effect their withdrawal; here I note simply that one of the consequences of withdrawing consent is said to be removing oneself from the jurisdiction of the courts of the state one has exited.

Some jurisdictional arguments appear to be more or less idiosyncratic to the defendant in question. The entertaining Texas case of *Greenstreet v. Heiskell* (1977) involved an effort by Greenstreet to remove a lien that had been placed on his crops.[35] Greenstreet made several claims disputing both the legality of the lien and the court's authority to adjudicate his case. In one document, Greenstreet argued that he had "by his own right and power [the right] to choose the applicable Law, within the proper territorial application [and] . . . he denies the above captioned court to assume jurisdiction, 'in Law' and in equity with the Supreme Courts [sic] Original jurisdiction." In another, even more elaborate and detailed filing, Greenstreet demanded that each and every officer of the court "reestablish his character by taking the Oath as presented by Edward Gale, Greenstreet, attached hereto, under penalty of perjury and treason, or in the alternative dismiss themselves as Foreign Alien Agents performing for a Foreign Principal," and stated that failure to comply would "constitute prima facia evidence and absolute facts that can not [sic] be disputed or denied that said Agents are Foreign Double Agents with full intent to overthrow our Constitutional Freely Associated Compact States of our Constitutional Republic and replace our De Jure 'Three Branch Government' with their One Branch Government of Executive Military Dictatorship of the communist Government of the District of Columbia and the United nations of foreign religion of Human sacrifice to the unnatural persons, 'corporate Government.'" (The judges did not take the oath Greenstreet demanded. I wonder what would have happened if they had?)

The *Greenstreet* case is representative of the sorts of fantastical propositions of law that characterize the common law court movement. How have courts presented with such claims responded? Pretty much as you would expect. In *Greenstreet*, the Texas court of appeals replied professionally to all of Greenstreet's claims and then dismissed his appeal. In a terse and admirably restrained footnote, the court noted that "We observe that the 'mythical judiciary' described as 'Our One Supreme Court for the Republic of Texas' does not exist. . . . Likewise . . .'The Common Law court for the Republic of Texas,' has been found to be nonexistent."

Greenstreet, it turns out, was well known to Texas judicial authorities, having been involved in other cases raising equally unique arguments of law. And he was persistent. Almost 20 years later, in *Greenstreet v. United States* (1996), he challenged the jurisdiction of the court with, in the court's words, "filings [that] have routinely been voluminous and difficult to comprehend," and even "reprehensible."

In another case, *Hilgeford v. Peoples Bank, Inc.* (1986), this one from Indiana, the defendant attempted to hold the federal judge hearing his case in contempt of his own common law court.[36] Judge William C. Lee described Hildgeford's claims as "self-serving, vexatious, bizarre, vexing, harassing, and frivolous." In *Vella v. McCammon* (1987) another federal case in which a district court judge considered the maritime/ gold fringed flag theory, the court dismissed the claims that it lacked "jurisdiction because the Court's flag has yellow fringes on it" as without merit [and] totally frivolous. Petitioner's claims have no arguable basis in law or fact and the appeal is not taken in good faith."[37]

Always these efforts to deny jurisdiction fail, but they are just one part of a larger scheme. The whole point of the common law movement is to separate one's self from the tyranny of the federal leviathan. This separation promises a very concrete and very attractive benefit: It frees one up from the obligations of "federal" (statutory, or inferior) citizenship, including the obligation to pay taxes. Freedom from taxation is an integral part of the common law movement, both at the level of jurisprudence (we shall see that the common law movement advances several pseudo-legal and constitutional arguments about why true citizens are under no obligation to pay taxes) and on a more entrepreneurial level. Many of the groups associated with common law courts peddle lectures and courses and books and tapes and forms dedicated to tax freedom. One favorite scam is essentially a fake church set up to evade taxes. Sovereign citizens obtain fake ecclesiastical credentials online or through mail-order catalogues.[38] This financial cheat is called the "Corporation Sole." (Sole/Soul. Clever, huh?) It begins with an application for incorporation as a minister or priest or religious leader of a pretextual religious organization. The next step is to apply for a tax exemption under federal tax law, USC 501(c)(3). If that sounds too complicated, for a mere $1,000 per person (think of how much money you'll save, though!), you can sign up for a seminar that will walk you through all of the steps necessary to file a phony Corporation Sole: "Participants are manipulated into believing that their counterfeit Corporation Sole provides a 'legal' way to avoid paying income taxes, child support, and other personal debts by hiding their assets in a tax exempt entity."[39]

Another favorite tool is called Redemption.[40] Redemption involves the use of bogus sight drafts (a real sight draft is a perfectly legitimate financial instrument) that draw upon secret bank accounts that citizens armed with the proper forms and words can "redeem" (redemption/ Redemption. Clever, huh?). The secret accounts are said to be worth approximately $630,000. "If only you know the right procedure—and the Redemptionists will gladly sell you the details—you will be able to withdraw funds from this account, which was supposedly created by the 1935 Social Security Act."[41] The legal arguments behind these claims aren't simply incoherent—they are preposterous.

Like the common law courts movement, the Sovereign Citizen movement is built on white racism. But not everyone in the common law movement is white or knowingly subscribes to its racist underpinnings. According to the American Bar Association and the Southern Poverty Law Center, some of the recent growth in the movement must be attributed to its adoption by militant movements organized by persons of color. A small but ambitious common law group in Louisiana, for example, laid claim to over 30 million acres in Louisiana (including a large tract of the Louisiana Purchase) and neighboring states. In May of 2000 federal agents from the FBI, the IRS, the US Customs Service, and the Louisiana state police, arrested Verdiacee 'Tiari' Washitaw-

Turner Goston El-Bey, leader (she calls herself the Empress) of a common law group called Washitaw de Dugdahmoundyah. She was charged with tax evasion and mail and wire fraud. As the SPLC notes, "Although her 'empire' is composed largely of black followers, much of its common-law ideology—including the notion that one can separate from the state and not pay taxes—comes directly from white supremacist groups."[42] The Redemption scam is especially popular in prisons and "Perhaps most surprisingly—given the white supremacist roots of the scam—redemption also has found favor among black nationalists, including those who call themselves Moorish Nationals and claim to be exempt from US laws."[43] Some scholars have argued that the driving force behind the common law court (and Sovereign Citizen) movement is as much economic hardship as anti-government paranoia or white nationalism.[44]

LEARNING THE ALT-COMMON LAW

Like the Alt-constitution, the Alt-common law is based on assumptions about what the law is (or rather, about which sources of law are legitimate), why is it authoritative, and about how (and when) to interpret it. Certain propositions of law are widely if not universally accepted in the Alt-common law movement, but like the (authentic) common law, people can and do argue about what the law requires and how it should be applied in specific cases.

The Alt-common law is a hash of famous, infamous (*Dred Scott* is much praised)[45] and obscure cases from England and United States (especially from the nineteenth century), quotations taken out of context from perfectly respectable academic and historical sources, including the Magna Carta and Blackstone, the *Federalist Papers*, federal commercial law (especially the Uniform Commercial Code), the Bible (especially the Book of Deuteronomy), Christian Identity theology, Dominionism, and Lockean social contract theory. Of these, the Bible is the final, authoritative word: "'The connection between the Bible and the Constitution is the common law,' one Freemen apologist wrote. 'The common law is Biblical law applied.'"[46]

To outsiders, however, the common law applied in common law courts by self-appointed common law judges is difficult to comprehend if not incomprehensible. Although I am trained in law (because I am trained in law?), was once licensed to practice law, and have taught constitutional law for more than three decades, I do not have a good grasp of the Alt-common law. I have read the cases and the commentaries, as well as the secondary scholarship, but I'm still confused about what it all means. Perhaps I am too impressed by my own erudition, but I think the reason I don't understand the Alt-common law is because it does not make sense. It is not supposed to make sense. Its purpose, rather, is simply to provide an impressive sounding veneer of legalism to self-serving arguments (the cynic in me wonders how that differs from any kind of legal argument). For its practitioners, the impenetrability of the Alt-common law has two distinct benefits. First, it makes such arguments impossible to engage on the merits, and an argument that cannot be engaged on the merits cannot be proven to be wrong. Second, it gives rise to a lucrative cottage industry of educational tapes and CDs and DVDs and podcasts that promise to explain the common law to novitiates.

A publication by John Darash (the retired carpenter we met earlier) and the National Liberty Alliance, a *Common Law Handbook for Sheriff's, Bailiff's, and Justice's* [sic] is a representative example. Although it does not say so explicitly (except on the back cover), the book is meant to help citizens form 25 person citizens' or common law grand juries in their county of residence and to "record" them with county clerks so they can go about the business of securing justice and administering the Alt-common law.

Immediately under the unwieldy title on the front cover of the *Handbook* is a quote from Psalms 89:14: "Justice and Judgment are the habitation of the throne mercy and truth shall go before thy face." Notably, the quote says nothing about what the common law requires, but it does do something more important: The explicit invocation of Bible verse tells us what the ultimate source of the common law is and what sort of authority it commands. Likewise, the very first entry on the very first page is a quote by William Penn that "Men must be governed by God or they will be ruled by tyrants."[47]

The rest of the *Handbook* follows no obvious organizational plan and there is no Introduction to explain it. I am tempted to say it asks a lot of its readers, to supply that framework and to discern why and what it all means, but that is probably wrong. A more probable explanation is that it assumes readers will intuit such things or that the meaning is (or should be) plain. The rest of the book is a long string of quotations from a variety of sources, including prominently scripture, the Constitution, cases decided by the Supreme Court, lower federal courts, state courts, the *Federalist Papers*, and occasionally academic treatises. With only a few exceptions, they are not annotated or explained. Section 1, for example, includes a collection of provisions from the United States Code, most of which concern deprivations of rights and various other statutory offenses, such as bribery and misprision of treason. The implicit message seems to be a warning to be on guard against governmental overreach and a catalogue of potential remedies in cases of governmental malfeasance.

Additional sections of the *Handbook* cover a miscellany of topics, including "The Real Law" (which is the common law), "Emergencies," (assertions that the United States is in a permanent state of emergency are a staple in the far right), "Courts of Record and Common law Courts," "Right to Practice Law" (open to any citizen and not subject to regulation by the state), and "History of the Sheriff" (as we have seen, the Sheriff is chief law enforcement officer). One of the most perplexing parts of the *Handbook* is Section 20, entitled "The Name Game— People or Citizen." The section begins with an unadorned quotation from the Fourteenth Amendment and then proceeds to offer quotations pertaining to several words highlighted in bold face—**Nation, Privilege, Persons, We the People, People, Ordain**, and **King**. I have no idea what point it wants to make, but it might have something to do with Sovereign citizenship versus federal citizenship. I think. . . . It is followed by a couple of pages that describe how the Constitution of the United States has been "usurped by the corporation: The CORPORATE UNITED STATES is not obligated nor accountable to the People except to make a profit for its stockholders as a corporation." The corporate, or "federal" United States dates from 1871 and replaced the "original united States." Note the capitalization—it is significant. "When the *federal United States* was formed in 1871 the adjective *"united"* was changed to the noun *"United"* because the *federal United States* is a corporation which word is not an adjective but a noun."[48] (Italics in the original.) Then there is something or other about the Federal Reserve and "international bankers" and how We the People are not citizens but "tenants and sharecroppers." It is difficult to follow the reasoning, but as with Section 20 on Citizens and Persons, it likely trades on widely shared conspiratorial tropes in the extreme right, among them fears of big government, international (read: Jewish) bankers, ZOG (Zionist Occupied Government), world government, and the New World Order. As we shall see, the corporate nature of the *federal United States* is important to explaining the differences between federal and sovereign citizenship. It also suggests a number of fixes one can use to remove one's self from the jurisdiction of the state/corporation and, just as importantly, to divest one's self of any financial obligations, such as taxes and fees for various licenses that one might otherwise accrue. To no one's surprise, these remedies are usually available at a modest cost and come with lots of promises but no guarantees, least of all a guarantee the IRS won't prosecute. In one tragic case, a farmer from Cairo, Nebraska, acting on advice from an organization called the National Agricultural Press Association, was shot and killed by a SWAT team after he threatened sheriff's deputies delivering a court order issued on behalf of a bank to which he owed money.[49]

One reason for the absence of any learned commentary or explanatory text in the *Handbook* and similar tracts reaches back to the interpretive principles of constitutional fundamentalism. If the words are plain in meaning, then they need no explanation by experts.[50] They say what they mean and they mean what they say, as the saying goes. This interpretive philosophy (appeal to the plain words first) recalls our discussion about *how* to interpret the Alt-constitution, and also of *who* has authority to interpret it. The various materials and sources collected in Sections 16 (Right to Practice Law) and 17 (Right to Assist) are premised on a truth that is unspoken because it is obvious to the common law courts movement: Because no expert knowledge or schooling is necessary to know the law, it is illegal (and unconstitutional) to restrict the practice of law to lawyers licensed by the state. The corollary is that the law is accessible to all citizens and, as the National Alliance *Handbook* claims, that any citizen can initiate, manage, and conclude his or her own legal affairs. The idea neatly mirrors one of the central interpretive premises of the Alt-constitution—that the meaning of the law/constitution can be known directly by any citizen who makes the effort. As we saw, this is a fundamentally Protestant if not Evangelical approach to constitutional interpretation. It is a methodology of interpretation perfectly suited to a movement suspicious of governments, judges, lawyers, and all manner of experts, most of whom are engaged in a conspiracy of one sort or another to deprive citizens of their constitutional and legal rights.

A related reason why the textbooks on the Alt-common law are typically just grab bags of quotes and cases is also grounded in interpretive methodology. What the law means is universal and objective. It does not depend on circumstance or situation or time, so there is no need to explain where a quotation, set in glorious isolation, comes from and no need to account for context, history, politics, economics, or culture. There is no need to consider how a provision or a phrase in the text interacts with others in the same text or decision, no need to consult the judgment of history or of later decisions that might call it into question or alter or elaborate upon its meaning. The Alt-common law, like the Alt-constitution, has little room for interpretive machinations like balancing or structuralism or appeals to aspirations—all tools of the disreputable "living" Constitution or the equally disreputable living law.

THE CONSTITUTIONALITY OF COMMON LAW COURTS

The supposed legality of common courts depends upon a peculiar interpretation of American legal history, a particular (and long rejected) theory regarding the nature and origins of the Constitution, and particular (and by now familiar) understandings about the meaning of a welter of individual constitutional provisions, including the First, Second, and Tenth Amendments. Of these, the First and the Tenth are the most significant.

COMMON LAW COURTS AND THE FIRST AMENDMENT

Proponents of common law courts often argue that these institutions are protected by the First Amendment freedoms of speech and association. This argument is not entirely facetious, but it does not go very far. Freedom of association almost certainly does protect the right of eight of my friends and myself to convene in my courtroom (complete with cushy sofas, a big flat screen, a tap . . . and nachos *Supreme*, because we are Supreme), just as it protects me when I preen about in a long black robe and a white wig and pretend to be the Chief Justice. And within certain narrowly prescribed limits, it will protect the nine of us even if we use these pseudo-judicial institutions to spout anti-government rhetoric or to dispute the legitimate authority of the Supreme Court that sits in the white marble temple at 1 First Street, NE, in Washington, DC. Most First Amendment scholars would categorize those statements as political speech and political association, which are, as we saw in Chapter 3, entitled to a very significant degree of protection under the First Amendment.

In similar fashion, if common law courts and the players in them are engaged in an act of symbolic protest through mimicry, then it is difficult to see why the First Amendment would not protect their protest. As Melle notes, "Arguably, such action is analogous to a theater production or reenactment of an historical event, where the message is inextricable from the conduct, and may therefore be proscribed only through content-neutral regulations. Furthermore, the public character of the subject matter—namely, political or government activity—suggests that the First Amendment protection is indeed robust."[51]

If the common law court movement is chiefly an ideology rather than a program of action or conduct, then it should be protected. But even as a call to action, it might still find refuge in the First Amendment. If the speech results in nonviolent political demonstrations, it should warrant some measure of protection.[52] Likewise, if the whole thing is just a financial scheme or a commercial venture, it may still qualify for limited protection under the First Amendment, provided it does not violate existing law (as in fraud, or tax evasion) or incite others to do so.

What the First Amendment will not protect is any effort to *exercise* the powers that belong to real courts, such as the powers to command parties and witnesses to appear, to compel testimony, to issue writs or orders of any kind with the intent of actually compelling people to comply, or to fine, punish, or incarcerate anyone. At any of those points, at the point where a common law court purports to exercise legitimate judicial powers, freedom of speech and association give way to the state's undoubted authority to exercise, as Max Weber wrote in *Politics as a Vocation*, a "monopoly of the legitimate use of physical force."[53] As we have seen, some common law courts have attempted to enforce their rulings, sometimes calling upon local citizens' militias to help.

Some have convicted public officials in absentia and sentenced them to death for "treason." Not only are such threats not protected by the First Amendment, they are almost always illegal.[54] Taking someone into custody by virtue of a common law court order, for example, would be false imprisonment, kidnapping, and would probably violate the criminal law in several other ways. Entering a home or a place of business under a warrant issued by a common law court would constitute trespass and possibly breaking and entering. Several states have criminalized the activities of common law courts, and the ADL has drafted model legislation that circumvents First Amendment concerns by requiring an element of "deliberate intention" or to act under "color of law" to "impersonate or falsely act as a public officer or tribunal . . . including . . . marshals, judges, prosecutors, sheriffs, deputies, court personnel or any law enforcement authority in connection with or relating to any legal process. . . ."[55]

COMMON LAW COURTS AND THE TENTH AMENDMENT: THE COMPACT THEORY OF THE UNION, REVISITED

Common law courts also trade heavily on the Tenth Amendment and a version of federalism in which state and local governments, and particularly county governments, are the penultimate legal authority (second only to the sovereignty of individual citizens). The highest legal official in the Alt-common law movement is the County Sheriff. The Sheriff has such an exalted authority because he (it is *he*, and he is white, as Attorney General Jeff Sessions intimated when, speaking before the National Sheriff's Association, spoke of the "Anglo-American heritage" of the role of the sheriff in American law enforcement)[56] is the chief law enforcement officer in the primary unit of government, the county. The logic traces to English common law and to popular mythology concerning the romantic role of the sheriff in English and early American constitutional history, but it is also grounded in the compact theory of the constitutional union. (See Chapter 2 for a full discussion of the compact theory.)

The compact theory of the Constitution is another of the "discarded shreds" of American constitutional history that help to make up the Alt-constitution.[57] It provides much of the edifice for the common law

courts movement by locating sovereign power in state and local governments, which are superior, both in constitutional authority and in constitutional time, to the federal government. It tells us why the common
law is a higher authority than constitutional law, why the sheriff is the
chief law enforcement officer, and why citizens' grand juries have the
power to indict not only other citizens but governmental officials.[58]

PERPETUAL EMERGENCY

A key component of the compact theory is its insistence, contra Lincoln, that the Union is *not* perpetual. Ironically, though, arguments
about perpetuity do form a significant part of common law constitutional theory. The claim is that by virtue of a series of presidential declarations, the United States has been in an official state of emergency since
1917. Why 1917? In 1917 Congress passed the Trading with the Enemy
Act, which authorized the President to regulate commercial transactions by United States citizens with nations declared by the President to
be enemies of the United States. President Roosevelt supposedly used
this authority to implement a number of emergency powers in 1933,
when he declared a bank holiday under the Emergency Bank Act. In so
doing, Roosevelt is said to have declared the American people themselves "enemies of the state" (referencing the 1917 legislation). "The
importance of the Emergency Banking Act to patriot history is difficult
to overstates," (note Levin and Mitchell), because it transformed the
United States into a "constitutional dictatorship. . . . The same theory
allows common-law court activists to contend that the United States has
been in a 'state of declared national emergency' since 1933."[59]

Under the state of emergency, common law theorists argue, the
United States moved off the gold standard to a system of Federal Reserve Notes, reducing the value of money and thereby depriving citizens of their property. The assault on private property also included the
de facto nationalization of property in the early 1930s because
"[v]irtually every industry or trade practice is now required to be licensed and controlled. . . ."[60]

The emergency powers claimed by President Roosevelt and his suc-
cessors figure prominently in the militant right's worldview because
they threaten, among others, the First, Second, Fifth, and Tenth

amendments. Moreover, emergency powers are said to have been (ab)used by federal authorities in their confrontations with various right-wing groups, including the Weavers at Ruby Ridge, the Branch Davidians at Waco, and the Bundy's and their fellow travelers at Malheur Wildlife Refuge.[61]

Under the compact theory, such abuses and assaults more than justify withdrawing from the constitutional compact. The Alt-common law then substitutes for the (illegitimate) constitutional amendments of the nineteenth century and the illegal administrative state of the twentieth century. Because the members of the common law court movement "believe that an illegitimate, usurper federal government has taken over," they believe they can repudiate the compact and "that they don't have to pay taxes, pull over their cars for police or obey any other law they don't like."[62]

What they don't like most of all is taxes.

Indeed, antipathy to taxes is an essential component of the common law courts movement. As I shall describe in more detail in Chapter 6, one expression of tax protest in the militant right takes the position that the Sixteenth Amendment and the federal income tax is unconstitutional. Interest in common law courts typically increase during times of economic hardship (and especially in 2008–2009, during the great recession). It should be no surprise, then, that much of the activity of common law courts involves Sovereign Citizens who have defaulted on tax obligations or debts they owe to private creditors. In sympathetic common law courts, Sovereign Citizens can quiet title on mortgaged properties, declare contracts null and void, and fight foreclosures and repossessions, often by issuing "judgments" against creditors.

The anti-tax component of the common law courts movement has fueled a "considerable library of 'books, literature, videotaped courses on 'common law,' and blank tax forms . . . that activists use to claim exemption from state and federal taxes."[63] Tax-relief and evasion courses are easily available online, and seminars are frequent in areas with large numbers of Patriots and militias, alienated audiences already inclined to doubt the legitimacy of the IRS and the federal government and often suffering from economic distress. One of the remarkable features of these courses (and of Alt-constitutionalism in general) is the trust and confidence the anti-taxers place in the magic of the law. For all of their paranoia and suspicion of judges, lawyers, and indeed of the law itself, Sovereign Citizens possess an almost preternatural faith in the transformative power of law and in magical, mystical incantations of legal language and legal sources to deliver them from their enemies. [64]

Much of the legal language in common law courts comes from the Uniform Commercial Code (UCC). Strictly speaking, the UCC is a model statute (which is to say, a recommendation) designed to standardize rules and regulations governing commercial transactions from state to state. It is not binding on any state except insofar as a state chooses to enact it, as the great majority of states have done. The UCC touches a wide variety of commercial transactions and relationships, such as the purchase and sale of property, contract law, and commercial law, including sales, leases, negotiable instruments, bank deposits and collections, funds transfers, letters of credit, bulk sales, documents of title, investment securities, and secured transactions. Appeals to obscure interpretations of the UCC abound because so much of the common law movement involves fraudulent checks, money orders, and wire transfers.

It is tempting to write off the anti-tax arguments of the common law movement to self-interest or greed, but the fact that the movement prospers most in times of economic hardship, if it does not rebuke that explanation, at least makes the movement more understandable. Most of the anti-tax crusade, though, is a scam run by grifters who dress their con up in appeals to the Constitution and the "American" tradition of resistance to unfair taxation which they foist upon their Sovereign Citizen marks.

I could point to dozens of examples. A site called "The Great IRS Hoax: Why We Don't Owe Income Tax" promotes both a free video and a book that "exposes the deception that misguided or malicious 'public servants' have foisted upon us all these years." [65] Like many other anti-tax resources, *The Great IRS Hoax* claims the tax codes are being "willfully misrepresented and illegally enforced by the IRS and state revenue agencies. . . . This willful misrepresentation and illegal enforcement is effected primarily through the abuse of words of art and presumption to deceive the hearer and violate due process of law. The deception is effected for financial reasons by those who benefit personally from the FRAUD." [66] (The site is unusual in that it offers its advice for free as a part of its "Christian Ministry.") Several YouTube videos offer testimony from "former IRS Officers" to explain why a federal income tax is "actually" illegal, and several other sites claim that the IRS and federal judges are engaged "in a monumental, criminal conspiracy to collect income taxes in violation of law."[67] Among those who called conspiracy was celebrated tax protester Irwin Schiff. Predictably, Schiff was convicted of tax evasion; he died in prison in 2015.

Another argument is that taxes are voluntary or are required only if one accepts some sort of benefit or enters into some kind of contractual relationship with the government. (Such arguments build on a radically individualistic understanding of consent and the social contract, a proposition that in structure is not very different from the arguments made in compact theory in favor of secession.) Sovereign Citizens often claim exemption from taxation by insisting that they accept nothing of value from the state and so owe nothing of value in return. Here the argument is that the federal income tax is contractual in nature, and that "the contract can be 'rescinded' by refusing to file returns."[68] One circuit court called this argument "imaginative, but totally without merit."[69]

Some anti-taxers hold that the filing requirements are a kind of self-incrimination prohibited by the Fifth Amendment, another inventive claim rejected by every (real) court that has heard it.[70]

Another argument holds that one's labor is property, "which, when exchanged for wages, produces no net gain subject to income as taxation."[71] This argument has been around a long time. It has also been dismissed for a long time. In the case of *Commissioner v. Glenshaw Glass Co.* (1955), the Supreme Court held that for purposes of determining gross income subject to taxation, there is no meaningful distinction between gain and capital.

My favorite anti-tax argument, however, is that the obligation to pay taxes violates the Thirteenth Amendment's prohibition of "involuntary servitude."[72] The argument starts with the "plain words" of the text. The Thirteenth Amendment provides that "Neither slavery nor involuntary servitude, except as a punishment for crime whereof the party shall have been duly convicted, shall exist within the United States, or any place subject to their jurisdiction." Apparently, what these words mean is that the state cannot obligate you to do anything unless it is in answer for a crime you committed.[73] In *Porth v. Brodrick*, the Tenth Circuit responded by noting that "If the requirements of the tax laws were to be classed as servitude, they would not be the kind of involuntary servitude referred to in the Thirteenth Amendment."[74]

Another version of the argument appeals to a *different*, forgotten Thirteenth Amendment. On May 10, 1810, Congress submitted to the states for ratification an amendment that prohibits titles of nobility (TONA). The necessity of such an amendment was a significant point of discussion when the "organic" constitution was sent to the states; Massachusetts, New Hampshire, New York, North Carolina, Rhode Island, and Virginia called for an amendment that would address the matter. Why was the issue so important? Titles of nobility were caught up with the intrigues of foreign affairs, concerns about patriotism and loyalty, and conceptions about aristocracy and equality.[75] The First Congress discussed the matter, but Congress took no action until 1813, when it sent an amendment to the states that would ban any American citizen from receiving any foreign title of nobility or receiving foreign favors, such as a pension, without congressional approval. The penalty was loss of citizenship.

By 1815, only 12 states had ratified TONA, an insufficient number. Nevertheless, some official publications prepared by the United States government in 1815 and for some years thereafter erroneously included TONA as the Thirteenth Amendment. TONA conspiracy theorists have long argued that TONA was in fact ratified, but that a complot devised by "lawyers, bankers, and foreign interests" have suppressed it to empower an "oligarchy" of lawyers that currently governs the United States.[76] For purposes of argument, let's assume that the Thirteenth Amendment (TONA) was in fact ratified (or may yet be. When Congress submitted TONA to the states, it did not include a time limit for ratification. Given the experience of the Twenty-seventh Amendment, which was proposed in 1789 but not ratified until 1992, one might argue that TONA is still on the table, awaiting ratification by the necessary additional 26 states), and that the real Thirteenth Amendment, regarding slavery and involuntary servitude, is not in truth a part of the Constitution, as some in the radical right argue. How does TONA establish that the income tax is unconstitutional? TONA prohibits "any title of nobility or honor." Invoking this language, tax protesters have argued variously that the title "taxpayer" is a title of nobility, and that that the term "person" as defined in the tax code is also a title of nobility. (Of what value is a title of nobility if everyone is a noble?) Both claims have been rejected by federal courts.[77]

SOVEREIGN CITIZENS

You may have heard of Jared Fogle. Jared was the Subway Sandwich guy. You probably remember the ad campaigns where Jared would dramatize his prodigious weight loss by holding up a pair of pants that was twice as large as he was. You probably also know that Fogle plead guilty in 2015 to traveling to engage in sexual conduct with a minor, and to distribution and receipt of child pornography. He was sentenced to 15 and a half years in a federal prison.

You may not know, however, that Fogle is a self-proclaimed "Sovereign Citizen" beyond the reach of state and federal law, and thus wrongfully imprisoned.[78] At least, that is what Fogle argued in a motion filed in 2017 in a federal court in Indiana. Judge Tanya Pratt dismissed the challenge, noting simply that "If Fogle is now claiming to be 'sovereign,' the Seventh Circuit has rejected theories of individual sovereignty, immunity from prosecution, and their ilk. . . . Regardless of his theory, Fogle's challenge of this court's jurisdiction is rejected."[79]

Sovereign Citizens claim they are not subject to laws they do not consent to, and so they are beyond the legal reach of all governmental authority. (Some will admit to the jurisdiction of a properly constituted citizens' grand jury, to a common law court, or a County Sheriff, as we saw above. The common law court movement goes hand in hand with the Sovereign Citizen movement.) Conveniently then, Sovereign Citizens need not pay taxes or fines. They do not need a drivers' license (this would violate a constitutional right to travel said to be in Article I, Section 9 of the Constitution), a license to marry, a license for their dogs, hunting or fishing permits, or a permit to carry a weapon. The property they own is not subject to zoning or land use regulations (much less to property taxes), and the contracts they enter into cannot be contested or enforced except in a common law court.

Sovereign Citizens in turn reject the benefits of citizenship, including Social Security and all other forms of social welfare, because accepting such benefits constitutes a "contact of adhesion" with the federal government and causes one to forfeit their Sovereign Citizenship for a lesser "federal" citizenship. Other contracts of adhesion result from voting, from using a zip code, from using credit cards, holding interest-bearing bank accounts, insurance policies, or purchasing securities and bonds. Some Sovereign Citizens refuse to work at wage-paying jobs because employers are required to withhold taxes and . . . therefore something, something contract of adhesion. Many Sovereigns invoke the UCC "to justify their bizarre claims; and some use weird forms of punctuation between their middle and last names in all kinds of documents."[80] Sovereign citizens cite the Bible, and especially the Old Testament, "which reference paying usury and taking money from the poor, such as Ezekiel 22:12–13, Proverbs 28:8, Deuteronomy 23:19, and Leviticus 25:36–37," to justify defaulting on credit card payments and bank loans. Some cite "Nehemiah 9:32–37 to bolster the belief that oppressive taxation results from sin. Also, 1 Kings 12:13–19 is used to justify rebellion against the government for oppressive taxation."[81]

This brief overview does not begin to fully describe the weird and fantastical universe of Sovereign Citizenship. Before I take up their constitutional arguments, however, we need to see why the Sovereign Citizen movement should be taken seriously. First, as the American Bar Association has warned, "These beliefs may sound silly, but sovereigns can be difficult to laugh off. For one thing, even though they don't believe they're subject to laws, they use laws as weapons . . . by filing false liens, false tax documents or spurious lawsuits. These can hurt the victim's credit, stymie attempts to sell or refinance property, and take years and thousands in legal fees to correct."[82] Consider a much publicized case in California involving a disputed foreclosure. In 2012, the Atta family locked up their Temecula, California, home and went on vacation. While they were away, the original owner of the house moved back in—uninvited. Victor Cheng had lost the house in foreclosure, but he filed a fraudulent deed with the county recorder's office, transferred the utilities into his name, and even tried to evict the Attas when they returned. During his prosecution for burglary, trespassing, and filing a false document, he insisted that he was not the person being prosecuted because the indictment spelled his name in all capital letters.[83] A quick Google search will turn up dozens of similar stories if not hundreds of articles about one or another of Sovereign Citizens who purport to be beyond the law in some matter.

More disturbing, some Sovereign Citizens defend their sovereignty with violence. Indeed, law enforcement authorities, including the FBI, consistently rank SCM as a significant domestic threat. The archives of the Southern Poverty Law Center include dozens of cases involving violent confrontations between Sovereign Citizens and law enforcement authorities.[84]

In one case from Alaska, two members of the Alaska Peacekeepers Militia, Lonnie and Karen Vernon, plotted to kill the United States District Court Judge Ralph Beistline, "who presided over a federal income tax case that ultimately cost the couple their home. The Vernons also admitted in their plea agreement to planning to kill an Internal Revenue Service official and Beistline's daughter and grandchildren."[85] In another case, from Florida, a Sovereign Citizen named John Ridge Emery III, acting at the behest of a friend who was also a Sovereign Citizen, gave a Charlotte County traffic judge an envelope he believed contained anthrax. Another much publicized case of Sovereign Citizen violence involved Jerry and Joseph Kane, a father and son active in the sovereign movement. Pulled over in Arkansas for a routine traffic stop, the Kanes murdered two West Memphis police officers. The elder Kane had previously been cited for driving without a license and for not wearing a seat belt. Kane was known to have complained of "Nazi checkpoints" and about being "enslaved" by judges who had convicted him. (It was reported that the younger Kane could recite the Bill of Rights from memory by age nine.)

Almost certainly the most famous case of violence, however, occurred on February 13, 1983, when Gordon Kahl, a self-described Christian Patriot, was involved in a shootout with United States marshals on the outskirts of Medina, North Dakota. Kahl was leaving a Posse Comitatus meeting when marshals tried to serve him an arrest warrant for failing to appear. One marshal died at the scene and a second died later. Several other persons were wounded, including Kahl's son. Kahl killed another police officer in a subsequent confrontation, and was himself shot and killed by law enforcement officers in June 1983. In a manifesto much cited in the extreme right, Kahl advanced a number of themes that are prominent in a wide variety of militant organizations, among them that taxes are "a tithe to the synagogue of Satan" and the necessity of restoring the common law, which was lost when "statutory law," at the hands of "Jewish Communists," was substituted for the Constitution. "Today, Gordon Kahl is looked upon as a modern-day patriot martyr by many sovereign citizens, militia extremists and other radicals on the alt-right."[86]

As with the Tea Party, Christian Patriots, Constitutionalists, and the militia movement, the SCM is composed of persons who subscribe to a few central, shared precepts but who also disagree amongst themselves about many of the finer points of the sovereign creed. I use the word creed deliberately, because for many in SCM, there is a distinct religious component to the movement. "Sovereign citizens believe that God created man to be sovereign—'free' of man-made laws and government regulation. They believe their doctrine is inspired, sanctioned and sustained by God. It consists of universal divine truths concealed to humanity by the world's most powerful leaders and business elites."[87] In addition, many Sovereign Citizens are anti-Semitic and/or white nationalists, and almost all are religious and constitutional fundamentalists.

In "God's Law: Universal Truth According to Religious Sovereign Citizens" (2015), Spencer Dew and Jamie Wight identify several characteristics of the SCM, all of which incorporate an element of religiosity and constitutional fundamentalism, including the conviction that beliefs about the law are also religious beliefs. "Religious discourse and legal discourse are understood as one and the same. . . . Rather than 'every man a priest,' for religious sovereigns 'every individual a lawyer.' Indeed, the sovereign citizen movement could perhaps best be described as populist folk magic: everyone can become expert in the law, and use that expertise to change their lives."[88]

Sovereign Citizens speak a private language with a distinctive vocabulary. Among its many stock phrases and terms of art are "14th Amendment Citizen" (an inferior form of citizenship); "Accepted for Value" (if written on a bill or an invoice it means the bill will be paid out of a secret Treasury Direct Account, set up by the government for every citizen when one is born. Go ahead—try it); "Bill of Exchange" (see Accepted for Value); "Common law Court"; "yellow flag fringe" (indicating an admiralty court); "Name in all capital letters" (one's name in all caps signifies the corporate shell of a person, as opposed to the flesh-and-blood person—similar to "Name Punctuation," in which the addition of punctuation indicates a flesh and blood person, and its absence means a corporate shell); "Negative Averment" (a device Sovereigns use to shift the burden of proof by reframing statements as questions);

"Redemption" (a process sovereigns use to separate a person's flesh-and-blood body from their corporate shell. Since only the corporate shell is subject to taxes, traffic laws, and license requirements, the ability to separate the two is the key to liberating people from such requirements); and "Truth language."

They also adopt a weird set of linguistic rules designed to mimic the secret language of the law. One such rule is that all sentences must start with the preposition "for," have a minimum of 13 words, and use more nouns than verbs. Many of these stock phrases and terms do in fact parrot the language of law, another example of the naïve magical legalism that characterizes the common law courts movement. As the SPLC notes, Sovereigns "believe that if they can find just the right combination of words, punctuation, paper, ink color and timing, they can have anything they want—freedom from taxes, unlimited wealth, and life without licenses, fees or laws, are all just a few strangely worded documents away. It's the modern-day equivalent of 'abracadabra.'"[89]

THESE SOVEREIGN UNITED STATES

Most of the substantive propositions Sovereigns hold are similar to those that comprise the belief system of the common law courts movement, and indeed the two movements are close relatives. Both are grounded in the fundamentalist conception of the Constitution we discussed in earlier chapters—one that stresses the literality of the text and which requires a "holy crusade to become informed."[90] They both invoke an alternative constitutional history of the United States, a story that involves a glorious beginning, a fall from grace induced by Satan and his progeny (in this account, international bankers and Jews), sin, and especially greed, but one that holds the promise and possibility of redemption. There is some disagreement within the SCM about when all of this happened. Passage of the Trading with the Enemy Act of 1917 or of the Emergency Banking Act in 1933 and the roughly contemporaneous abandonment of the gold standard, are both popular launching points. But some other SCMs, citing the work of Gertrude Coogan, author of a favored tract called *Money Creators* (1935), think it all started with the Civil War, which wasn't about slavery, or states' rights, but rather was part of "a conspiracy by 'certain bankers' and 'internationalists' to weaken America for future economic exploitation."[91]

Whenever it happened, what matters in this story is that the constitution and the common law were stolen or subverted by a conspiracy of international bankers, lawyers, and liberal politicians and replaced by a new system governed by admiralty law and the Uniform Commercial Code. In this new (world) order, most citizens are not really citizens at all. They are "federal" (or Fourteenth Amendment) citizens entitled to none of the liberties guaranteed in the Bill of Rights, more akin to employees or slaves.

At its core, SCM ideology is not simply a deeply religious worldview. Nor is it simply racist.[92] It is also a profoundly legalistic worldview in which Sovereign Citizens have no attachments except those they choose to assume. Implicit in their legalism is an almost Lockean conception of constitutional contract theory. Whereas in traditional contract theory the legitimacy of the social contract is secured by an act of collective consent at a distinct and identifiable moment in the past, and ratified on an ongoing basis through various mechanisms of tacit consent, the SCM movement holds to a radically individualistic account of Lockean social contract theory, in which an individual's consent to the social contract must be explicit, contemporaneous, and continuous.

HOW TO ASSERT ONE'S "SOVEREIGNTY"

Because all of a Sovereign Citizen's attachments and legal obligations must be consensual, they can all be renounced . . . if one knows how. SCMs attend classes and conferences where they teach each other the convoluted mechanics of Redemption and the common law. They peddle books and CDs and DVDs, IM, "like" each other on Facebook and subscribe to YouTube channels, listen to dedicated radio programs and Podcasts, and share links to sympathetic websites.[93]

In theory, reclaiming one's status as a Sovereign Citizen ought not to be too difficult. Since a Sovereign claims to be bound only by his consent, the obvious solution is to not give it, or to withdraw it if given. In practice, the process is incredibly convoluted. First, Sovereigns hold that most individuals have unknowingly consented to being downgraded to the inferior form of federal citizenship in all sorts of nonobvious if not nefarious ways. Again using the language of law, SCMs argue that "contracts of adhesion" amount to giving one's consent. In traditional contract theory, a contract of adhesion is one in which one party offers something on a take-it or leave-it basis, or where there is no room for negotiation. SCMs think that Sovereigns forfeit their sovereign citizenship in exchange for the inferior form of citizenship when they enter into contracts of adhesion with the state. Moreover, they think that pretty much every form issued by the government, and certainly any form you *sign*, is such a contract. Birth certificates, drivers' licenses (licenses of *every* kind), tax forms, paychecks that withhold state and federal taxes, Social Security cards, credit cards, and even voter registration forms are all said to be contracts of adhesion. In some accounts, "any individual using a Social Security number or zip code has unknowingly consented to be governed as resident of the District of Columbia," in other words, to being a US citizen rather than a state citizen or a sovereign citizen, "and abdicated his or her rights as a citizen of a republic . . . with the accompanying loss of constitutional rights."[94]

How does one extract one's self from this vast web of adhesion? Through an elaborate process called Redemption (fittingly, a term rich with both religious and legal meaning) in which a Sovereign thoroughly extricates himself from every contract and renounces any tangible governmental benefit. (We saw earlier that another redemption scam is popular in the common law courts movement.) As one might expect, the process is another example of the power of magical legalism, full of forms and solemn declarations. It begins by filing a formal "notice of intent" to reclaim one's sovereignty, followed by a formal declaration of sovereignty, then an oath, and then another notice (this one of protest when one uses a Federal Reserve note), and by revoking pretty much every other form or license, including, obviously, one's driver's license, birth certificate, Social Security and other all forms of social welfare, closing credit cards and bank accounts, removing one's children from public schools, refusing to post or to accept mail that has a zip code, and no doubt an unholy host of other forms and contracts and licenses. Some Sovereigns even make their own license plates: "a sovereign citizen group in Oregon actually sold 'Kingdom of Heaven' license plates, passports, and driver's licenses to fellow sovereign citizens entitling them to be members of God's Kingdom."[95] Another organization, called "The Embassy of Heaven: Under the Jurisdiction of the Kingdom of

Heaven," sells license plates and vehicle registrations for a one-time fee of $40. The Embassy advises drivers pulled over by police officers to:

> State that you are a citizen of Heaven traveling upon the highways in the Kingdom of Heaven, for the purpose of evangelizing, in obedience to our Lord and Savior Jesus Christ. If they try to claim you are on the highways in the State, remind them that the highways are multi-jurisdictional. If you were using the highways in the State, you would need their permission in the form of a State license. But, since you are using the highways in the Kingdom of Heaven, you cannot be trespassing upon the State. They normally will try to have you acknowledge that you are in their State. Remember, there is no communion between light and darkness. Stay in the Kingdom of Heaven, regardless of their pressure.[96]

The Embassy acknowledges that these arguments may not satisfy the officer. For that reason, "We suggest purchasing an inexpensive, older, reliable car for evangelizing. If you drive a $500 sedan and the police confiscate it, your losses will be minimal."[97] ($500 is not a typo.)

Redemption also requires Sovereigns to create fictitious persons that are distinct from their "flesh and blood" sovereign persons. In SCM legal theory, every person has two identities—one is a real person and one is a strawman or corporate fiction. The distinction is a consequence of the federal government's decision to abandon the gold standard in 1933. No longer backed by gold, the new monetary system secures its debt with collateral, which is its citizens, or rather, their future earnings. It does so by creating secret accounts and identities for every citizen at birth. Hence, birth certificates are a registration system, as evidenced by the fact that most certificates spell out the child's name in capital letters. "Since most certificates use all capital letters to spell out a baby's name, JOHN DOE, for example, is actually the name of the corporate shell identity, or 'straw man,' while John Doe is the baby's 'real' flesh-and-blood name. As the child grows older, most of his legal documents will utilize capital letters, which means that his state-issued driver's license, his marriage license, his car registration, his criminal court records, his cable TV bill and correspondence from the IRS all will pertain to his corporate shell, not his real, sovereign identity."[98] The government uses the birth certificate to create a secret Treasury account for that person, "which it funds with an amount ranging from

$600,000 to $20 million, depending on the particular variant of the sovereign belief system. By setting up this account, every newborn's rights are cleverly split between those held by the flesh-and-blood baby and the ones assigned to his or her corporate shell account."[99]

A key claim in this byzantine theory is that the government's jurisdiction extends only to the fictitious strawman. By filing the correct forms in the correct sequence, a Sovereign Citizen can redeem their citizenship, a process that usually includes a demand for compensation, typically in the millions of dollars, for the government's continued use of the strawman. Moreover, through Redemption, Sovereign Citizens can draw on the strawman account by writing checks and sight drafts. In all subsequent transactions, by using deliberate misspellings of their name, or all capital letters, or peculiar forms of punctuation, Sovereigns distinguish the fictitious corporate shell of a person from the flesh-and-blood person. Since only the corporate shell is subject to taxes, traffic laws and license requirements, the ability to separate the two is the key to renouncing the obligations unwittingly assumed. Once you reject your strawman identity, your physical person is no longer liable for the strawman's debts.

CONCLUSION

Like common law courts, the Sovereign Citizen movement is constitutional nonsense on stilts,[100] composed of arguments that are bizarre and trivial. Predictably, the IRS and federal courts treat such nonsense as nonsense. Several prominent proponents of Redemption, including Roger Elvick, one of its founders, have been convicted of various conspiracy and tax evasion charges and have served lengthy prison sentences. Sadly, though, the Redemption scam causes legal problems for the gullible as well as the duplicitous. The IRS encounters it often enough to include it on its list of frivolous positions that may result in the imposition of a $5,000 penalty when used as the basis for an inaccurate tax return.[101]

For believers, it makes no sense to ask if Redemption works or to demand evidence that it might, if only. Fundamentalism, religious, constitutional, or some intoxicating mix of both, has no need of evidence.

Chapter 6

INAUTHENTIC AND ILLEGITIMATE

Contesting the Reconstruction Amendments and Beyond

Like our Constitution, the Alt-constitution extends well beyond words on paper. Both include a number of other texts, assumptions, philosophies, and historical understandings. The Alt-constitution "plus" includes, for almost everyone in the radical right, parts of the Bible and the Declaration of Independence. For many, it includes the Articles of Confederation and, for some, it reaches to the Mayflower Compact, restores the "lost" Thirteenth Amendment, and incorporates a veritable host of favorite quotes from favorite Founders, both prominent and obscure.

Most scholars and judges are comfortable with the idea that the Constitution includes things that aren't actually in the document, like certain customs and conventions, as well as certain historical understandings, and perhaps even certain philosophical presuppositions. Most scholars and judges are equally comfortable with the idea that parts of the constitutional document are irrelevant, archaic, or just a bad idea. Favorite examples include the Preamble, the Ninth Amendment, and the privileges and immunities clause of the Fourteenth Amendment, all of which are often said to have little or no legal significance. We might refer to this constitution as the "Constitution-minus" (the disfavored or illegitimate parts).

Adjudging what the Constitution includes and excludes forces us to ask about the meaning and relevance of history to how we read the Constitution. Asking what the Constitution includes and what it excludes requires us to think about the relevance of what its authors intended it to mean and about the relevance of what *we* think it means. These sorts of questions are hardly unique to the Constitution. They should seem familiar to any student of the Bible, Torah, the Quran, or any other sacred text. Should the canonical Gospels include the gnostic gospels or the Books of Earnest or The Shepherd of Hermas? Does the Torah include the rabbinical commentaries?

In approaching these questions, constitutional fundamentalists often distinguish between the organic constitution and the rest of the constitutional document. The organic constitution, sometimes called the original constitution, the Founders' constitution, or the authentic constitution,[1] includes only certain, selected parts of what we ordinarily think of as the constitutional document. The other (inauthentic and illegitimate) provisions are "in" the text, in the sense that anyone can pick up the document and see that they are there, but they don't count. What makes some parts of the Constitution authentic and legitimate and others not? And why does it matter? The first question is the easiest to answer. The organic constitution includes what the Founders produced at the Convention (the Miracle at Philadelphia) and the first ten amendments, minus the unloved parts that come later in constitutional time.

Why does the organic or authentic constitution include some provisions and not others? The answer to that question is more complicated. It starts with the conviction that what happened at Philadelphia wasn't *metaphorically* a miracle, but *truly* a miracle. For constitutional fundamentalists, the Miracle at Philadelphia, like Genesis, is not simply an allegorical creation story. It ascribes a higher law background and authority to the Constitution and makes obedience to it as compelling as religious obedience. It ascribes a higher if not saintly status not only to the *work* of the Founders, but to the Founders themselves, and in so doing it sanctifies a particular way of reading and interpreting their work. By implication, those parts of the Constitution that come later and bear no evidence of divine touch are of a different character. They are the work of man alone, and as such, susceptible of error. Indeed, because the disfavored parts are (only) the work of sinful or imperfect

humans, they may actually contravene or subvert the Founders' constitution, in which case the false should be exposed and condemned by the
faithful.

There is surprisingly little disagreement in Alt-constitutional thought
about what parts of the Constitution don't count. The Alt-constitution
does not include the Thirteenth (or, one version of it, anyway), Fourteenth, Fifteenth, Sixteenth, and Seventeenth Amendments. Some of
the more idiosyncratic elements of the far right would also strike the
Nineteenth Amendment.

THE THIRTEENTH, FOURTEENTH, AND FIFTEENTH AMENDMENTS

The most important thing any constitution does is to delineate the qualifications, benefits, and burdens of citizenship.[2] Indeed, questions
about citizenship, about who qualifies for inclusion in the exalted status
of We the People, have driven most episodes of constitutional conflict
in the United States. Sometimes the conflicts and the questions that
drive it are explicit and transparent, as in the Civil War and Reconstruction; or in the Japanese-American Internments of World Wars I and II;
or in disputes about immigration; school desegregation; and affirmative
action. Sometimes they percolate just beneath the surface, as in disputes about gun control, law and order, voter fraud, and hate speech, to
name just a few. It should be no surprise, therefore, that questions
surrounding citizenship mark the clearest point of divide between the
Constitution of the United States and the Alt-constitution.

The Founders' Constitution indicates that only natural citizens can
hold the office of president, and in a few other places it references
some of the incidents and duties of citizenship, including jury service,
voting, and taxation. The organic Constitution is more notable for what
it does not say about citizenship. Its silence on the matter partly reflects
widely held assumptions at the Founding about who was fit to be a
citizen and why, but it also reflects a calculated decision not to talk too
loudly about the one thing that could bring the whole project down. It is
remarkable that the Constitution of 1787 has so much to say about
slavery without actually using the word. On the other hand, no one
needed to *say* that African Americans were not citizens.

We cannot fully understand the Alt-constitution, however, without locating its origins in the Civil War and Reconstruction, when several of the key elements of radical right ideology, including its understandings of federalism, race, citizenship, and the Fourteenth Amendment, began to crystalize. The Reconstruction era ushered in a profound change in the American constitutional order, especially regarding the relationship between the states and the federal government. Before the Civil War, for example, the Bill of Rights did not apply to state governments. Moreover, as the Supreme Court had (disastrously) ruled in *Dred Scott v. Sandford* (1857), African Americans were not citizens, and thus not eligible for whatever few protections the federal Constitution offered citizens against hostile state governments. As a consequence, African Americans had no constitutional rights they could enforce against slave states and, as the Court wrote, "no rights which the white man was bound to respect." *Dred Scott* did not make African Americans second class citizens; it ruled that they were not citizens at all. The Reconstruction Amendments meant to correct *Dred Scott* and to make the Bill of Rights applicable to state and local governments.

Occasioned by the rise of the Radical Republicans in Congress after the Civil War (so-called because congressional Republicans, unlike Presidents Lincoln and Johnson, were disinclined to make nice with the rebellious states), the Reconstruction amendments were not simply about reconstructing the Southern states. The Thirteenth, Fourteenth, and Fifteenth Amendments amounted to a fundamental reconstruction of the American constitutional order, if not to a third constitutional revolution. They revolutionized several key principles of the American constitutional order, including our notions about who qualifies for citizenship, about the reach of the Bill of Rights, and concerning the relationship between the states and the federal government. (The Alt-constitution, we shall see, has no use for the Fourteenth Amendment.)

Southern opposition to Reconstruction was organized around a series of claims provoked by each of those transformations, including (1) states' rights and the doctrine of nullification; (2) the necessity of gun ownership and private militias to protect Southern whites; (3) white supremacy, white nationalism, or white separatism (on the right, there are subtle but significant differences between these); and (4) exclusive racial definitions of citizenship. These claims continue to resonate with a significant part of the extreme right.

In Alt-constitutional terms, then, the commitment to white superiority takes a number of different forms. Some in the Alt-right and the radical right embrace doctrines of nullification. Others embrace quixotic theories of political and cultural secession[3] (and of freedom of association) that would allow whites to form race-restrictive enclaves and compounds. Perhaps the most unsettling arguments, however, attack the Fourteenth Amendment directly. One organization, the neo-Confederate League of the South, has described the Fourteenth Amendment as the most "nefarious consequence of the Reconstruction."[4]

Before we take up the radical right's specific objections to the Fourteenth and the other two Reconstruction amendments, however, there is a point of terminology. In Chapter 5, we addressed a favorite argument of anti-tax protesters that there is a lost, or forgotten, or suppressed Thirteenth Amendment (TONA), outlawing all titles of nobility. *That* version of the Thirteenth Amendment counts as part of the Alt-constitution, not only because it provides a useful resource for anti-tax arguments, but also because it was first proposed during the ratification debates, sent to the states in 1810, and supposedly ratified in 1815. The "lost" Thirteenth Amendment, unlike the Reconstruction Thirteenth, can plausibly be attributed to the sainted Founders.

Interestingly, there is yet a third Thirteenth Amendment, and it is the version most consistent with the overall tenor of the Alt-constitution. The so-called "Corwin" amendment was named for Representative Thomas Corwin of Ohio, its sponsor in the House. The proposed amendment was submitted to the states for ratification in March 1861. It provided that "No amendment shall be made to the Constitution which will authorize or give to Congress the power to abolish or interfere, within any State, with the domestic institutions thereof, including that of persons held to labor or service by the laws of said State." The language may seem oblique, but the point was obvious enough: If ratified, *this* Thirteenth Amendment would have protected slavery from being abolished by constitutional amendment, or from abolition, or interference by Congress. (Most historians see the Corwin Amendment as a last gasp effort to forestall secession, and as especially designed to persuade the border states.) Its subsequent history is a complicated matter. Depending upon how, what, and who counts the votes, the Corwin Amendment may have been ratified by five states (Kentucky, Ohio, Rhode Island, Maryland, and Illinois) and one proto-state, the

Restored Government of Virginia (which would become West Virginia), some of which later tried to rescind their votes. The ratification process was short-circuited, of course, by the Civil War. I don't know of anyone who takes seriously the idea that the Corwin Thirteenth Amendment was duly ratified, but its move through Congress and signature by President Buchanan (Buchanan's signature was purely symbolic; the Constitution does not require the President to sign off on amendments) are evidence of the importance of states' rights and slavery to a proper understanding of the constitutional order. (Like the Constitution itself, the Corwin Amendment avoids the word slavery.) Even more telling, some argue, is President Lincoln's reference to the Corwin Amendment in his First Inaugural Address:

> I understand a proposed amendment to the Constitution—which amendment, however, I have not seen—has passed Congress, to the effect that the Federal Government shall never interfere with the domestic institutions of the States, including that of persons held to service . . . holding such a provision to now be implied constitutional law, I have no objection to its being made express and irrevocable.

Lincoln's reference to "express and irrevocable" illuminates two extraordinary features of the Corwin Amendment. First, the Amendment was only a modest change insofar as it purported to make express what its proponents thought was already implicit in the Constitution. In Alt-constitutional theory, the Corwin/Thirteenth sheds light on what the Constitution, properly interpreted, *really* means, which is why President Buchanan described it as "explanatory."[5] Second, the Corwin amendment, if modest in that sense, was extraordinary in its ambition to make what it protected (slavery), an unamendable, "irrevocable," and perpetual part of the Constitution. If ratified, the Corwin amendment would be one of only two parts of the Constitution that cannot be changed by constitutional amendment. The other provision, you will remember, is Article V's guarantee to the states of equal representation in the Senate, not unrelated to the question of slavery. The Corwin amendment may not be a part of the true Constitution, but for the far right, it does tell us what the Constitution means (or meant)—that it was expressly and irrevocably committed to protecting the institution of slavery and white supremacy.

Under the Alt-constitution, the Thirteenth Amendment that *was* (supposedly) ratified as one of the Reconstruction Amendments, which outlaws slavery and involuntary servitude, is not part of the "authentic" constitution. There are two arguments why the Reconstruction amendments are illegitimate. The first is a deeply legalistic and technical tale of procedural mistakes and constitutional improprieties, salted with allegations of deception and fraud. For obvious reasons, this is precisely the kind of argument that appeals to so many in the extreme right. The second argument is of an altogether different character. It appeals to the subtleties of constitutional theory.

I. THE ARGUMENT FROM PROCEDURAL IRREGULARITIES

The argument from procedural impropriety is a dark fairy tale about arm-twisting, bullying, and inventive math. The Thirteenth Amendment was ratified by 27 states of the then 36 states of the Union, including, importantly, Virginia, Louisiana, Arkansas, South Carolina, Alabama, North Carolina, and Georgia. Without the votes of these seven Southern states the Thirteenth Amendment would have failed. But those seven positive votes, the argument runs, were coerced by threats from Congress that the Southern states would remain under military law and would not be readmitted to the Union unless they agreed to ratify the Amendment. Coerced consent is no consent at all, and so the Thirteenth Amendment must be illegitimate.[6]

The argument that the Fourteenth Amendment is unconstitutional starts with the observation that the Congress that proposed it had no Southern representatives (I'll let you guess why) and so was an illegitimate body with no power to submit the Amendment to the states for ratification. Moreover, opponents point to vote-counting shenanigans in both the Senate and the House to meet the constitutional requirement that two-thirds of both Houses approve of the amendment before transmitting it to the states.

At the time, ratification required affirmative votes in 28 of the 37 states that made up the Union. Those who say that the Fourteenth Amendment was not properly ratified point to several problems in the ratification process. By March 17, 1867, the argument goes, the Amendment had been officially rejected and Secretary of State William

Seward had reported that fact to Congress. Congress, however, rejected Seward's report and passed the Military Reconstruction Acts, which put 10 of the 11 southern states into five military occupation zones. (Tennessee was spared because alone among the Southern states, it had voted to ratify the Fourteenth Amendment.) In addition, the Reconstruction Acts further disfranchised most white voters in occupied states, declared that their Senators and Representatives could not be seated in Congress, and provided that they must ratify the Fourteenth Amendment as a condition for rejoining the Union. Unsurprisingly, and unwillingly, 7 of the 10 affected states "ratified" the Amendment.

But by then the landscape had changed dramatically. Two more States had rejected the proposed Amendment and New Jersey and Ohio had rescinded their positive votes. There were two votes in Oregon as well—the first was favorable but improper; on a revote, Oregon voted in the negative. On July 20, 1868, Secretary of State Seward again declared that the proposed Fourteenth Amendment had been defeated. Congress disagreed, choosing to count all positive notes, no matter when they occurred, and notwithstanding declared rescissions. On July 28, 1868, Secretary of State Seward certified that the Amendment "has become valid to all intents and purposes as a part of the Constitution of the United States."

2. THE ARGUMENT FROM CONSTITUTIONAL THEORY

The argument from constitutional theory takes us back to the Corwin version of the Thirteenth Amendment. Assume for a moment that the Fourteenth Amendment was ratified by the states without a hint of procedural impropriety. Is there some way in which a constitutional amendment, passed in complete compliance with every constitutional rule we can imagine, could still be "unconstitutional"? Can a constitutional amendment be unconstitutional?

Imagine a Twenty-eighth Amendment that provides "The thirteenth article of amendment to the Constitution of the United States is hereby repealed." If the language sounds familiar it is because I have lifted it from the Twenty-first Amendment, which repealed the Eighteenth Amendment and ended prohibition. My imaginary Twenty-eighth Amendment repeals the constitutional prohibition of slavery and involuntary servitude. Imagine too that the proposed Amendment is properly ratified by three-fourths of the states, as Article V requires. There are no questions about procedure, no funny or disputed votes, no approvals followed by rescissions—everything is in order. Is the Twenty-eighth Amendment part of the Constitution? What would we say about an amendment that purported to repeal the First Amendment? Or the Second Amendment? (see chapter 4).

Before you dismiss my questions as the sort only a professor with too much time on his hands might ask, you might think back to Chief Justice Roy Moore's senatorial campaign in Alabama in 2017. It was somewhat overshadowed by other matters (I'm sure you know what those were), but Moore also made news for stating that "getting rid of constitutional amendments after the Tenth Amendment would 'eliminate many problems' in the way the US government is structured."[7] Moore's comments were first directed to the Seventeenth Amendment, which we will take up later in this chapter, but he also spoke critically of the Fourteenth. In response to a comment by a radio host that "the Fourteenth Amendment was only approved at the point of the gun," Moore replied, "Yeah, it had very serious problems with its approval by the states. . . . The danger in the Fourteenth Amendment, which was to restrict, it has been a restriction on the states using the first Ten Amendments by and through the Fourteenth Amendment."[8]

If there is an argument that my hypothetical repealing amendment is unconstitutional, it will likely look like this: Some principles in the Constitution are so important, so fundamental, so essential to the very idea of what the Constitution is and what it means, that repealing them would be tantamount to dismantling the Constitution itself—akin to a constitutional revolution, not an amendment. Implicit in the guarantee of equal representation in the Senate, and plainly in the Corwin Amendment, is precisely the idea that some principles in the Constitution are unamenable, perpetual, beyond the reach of We the People except through revolution.

The claim that a constitutional amendment, especially one that undoubtedly complies with all of the relevant "rules" concerning how the process works, could still be unconstitutional, is not entirely novel. As we saw in Chapter 2, in *Leser v. Garnett* (1922), the Supreme Court was asked to declare the Nineteenth Amendment (extending the vote to women) unconstitutional.

For those who dispute the constitutionality of the Fourteenth Amendment, it is no accident that the one principle identified as beyond amendment in the Constitution (equal state suffrage in the Senate) concerns federalism (and by implication slavery). If the Fourteenth Amendment is unconstitutional, then, it would be because it upsets the relationship between the states and the federal government that the Founders so carefully set in place in the organic, original constitution. The Fourteenth purports to authorize the federal government to do precisely what the Corwin Amendment claimed no amendment could ever do: "the power to abolish or interfere, within any State . . . the domestic institutions" of any State. (By "domestic institutions," it meant chiefly slavery.)

The Supreme Court recognized the revolutionary reach of the Reconstruction Amendments (and especially of the Fourteenth), but tried to muffle it in the *Slaughterhouse Cases* in 1873. Justice Miller concluded that one possible interpretation of the privileges and immunities clause—that it made the Bill of Rights applicable to the states—could not possibly be correct, precisely because it would work a fundamental transformation in the federal character of the constitutional order. (This was Roy Moore's point.) Faced with a reading of the Fourteenth that would make the Bill of Rights applicable to the states, a majority of the Court in *Slaughterhouse* shrank. The Court ruled instead that the Fourteenth Amendment had only the very limited purpose of guaranteeing newly freed African Americans the constitutional rights that attach to "citizenship of the United States." What were those rights? Notably, they did not include many of the rights listed in the Bill of Rights, but happily, they did include protection on the "high seas" and from foreign governments.

In his dissent, Justice Swayne described the true purpose of the Reconstruction Amendments in grandiloquent terms:

> Fairly construed, these amendments may be said to rise to the dignity of a new Magna Carta. The thirteenth blotted out slavery and forbade forever its restoration. It struck the fetters from four millions of human beings, and raised them at once to the sphere of freemen. . . . Before the war, it could have been done only by the States where the institution existed, acting severally and separately from each other. The power then rested wholly with them.

Justices Miller and Swayne were both correct. The Reconstruction Amendments *were* a constitutional revolution. Swayne embraced it; Miller tried to subvert it.

In the Alt-constitution narrative, the Reconstruction Amendments are unconstitutional because they are fundamentally at odds with the vision of constitutional life set out at the Founding. There is some truth in this claim: The Fourteenth Amendment cannot be reconciled with the Founders' Constitution. The Founders' Constitution was built on the erroneous belief that states, because close to their citizens, were less of a threat to liberty than the new national government. The Fourteenth Amendment meant, in part, to correct that mistake.

But the Founders' Constitution was more than simply mistaken about from where threats to liberty would originate. It was flawed in the most significant way we can imagine. The Founders' constitution did not simply tolerate slavery. It entrenched it in the very fabric of the new constitutional order. It made slavery an immutable part of the Constitution (and the Corwin Amendment simply made the point clear). It may be shocking to hear, but Chief Justice Taney's decision in *Dred Scott*, although not the only possible reading, was a defensible reading of that Constitution, a Constitution that Senator Stephen Douglas, debating Lincoln, described as, "[M]ade on the white basis. It was made by white men for the benefit white men and their posterity forever."[9] (Note Senator Douglas's allusion to the Preamble—it is a Preamble by and for whites.) What ought to offend us almost as much as the terrible rhetoric and appalling result in *Dred Scott* is the distinct possibility that the Court reached the "right" decision—not a morally correct decision, but "right" in the sense that it correctly divined what the Founders' constitution, seen through the lenses of intent and originalism, thought about the status of African Americans in the original constitutional order.[10]

One final word on the Corwin Amendment. When Congress submitted it to the states it did not include an expiration date for ratification. A Republican representative in the Texas statehouse introduced a joint resolution to ratify it in 1963.

THE FOURTEENTH AMENDMENT: THE CITIZENSHIP CLAUSE. TWO KINDS OF CITIZENSHIP, SOVEREIGN AND FEDERAL

Distaste for the Fourteenth Amendment is the single most important and unifying thread of constitutional thought across the many and diverse elements of the extremist right. This is because the Fourteenth's offense to constitutional government runs deeper than just insults to proper procedure and indignities to the sovereignties of state government. The Fourteenth is part and parcel of a grand conspiracy to rescind the liberties of American citizens by diminishing what it means to be a citizen. The Fourteenth Amendment changed what citizenship *is* and who can qualify for it.

The Fourteenth effected this momentous change in the meaning of citizenship by repudiating the decision in *Dred Scott*. Section 1 of the Fourteenth Amendment corrects *Dred Scott* by providing that "All persons born or naturalized in the United States, and subject to the jurisdiction thereof, are citizens of the United States and of the State wherein they reside." The meaning of the citizenship clause should be clear: *Any* person born or naturalized in the United States is a citizen. The Fourteenth thus establishes the principle of birthright citizenship, or what lawyers sometimes call *jus soli*, in contradistinction to *jus sanguinis*, in which citizenship is determined by parentage.

This significance of this change cannot be overstated. As Eric Foner has observed, "[B]irthright citizenship . . . make[s] the United States (along with Canada) unique in the developed world [. . . . Birthright citizenship is one expression of the commitment to equality and the expansion of national consciousness that marked Reconstruction. . . . Birthright citizenship is one legacy of the titanic struggle of the Reconstruction era to create a genuine democracy grounded in the principle of equality."[11] The Fourteenth Amendment's embrace of the constitutional ideal of equality therefore runs deeper than just its explicit guarantee that all persons shall be guaranteed the equal protection of the law. It embeds equality in the most fundamental decision every community has to make about itself—about who to include and who to exclude.

Another way to understand the significance of the Fourteenth Amendment is to ask: What part of the organic or original or Founders'

Constitution did the Fourteenth Amendment amend? The best answer is this: The citizenship clause of the Fourteenth amends the Preamble. It clarifies who We the People are. This is the point so thoroughly missed by the Alt-right and its sympathizers. Writing in *Taki's Mag* (a self-described Libertarian "fanzine" that often features essays sympathetic to the Alt-right; Richard Spencer was once an editor), Pat Buchanan says:

> The Constitution, agreed upon by the Founding Fathers in Philadelphia in 1789, begins, 'We the people. . . .' And who were these 'people'? In *Federalist* No. 2, John Jay writes of them as 'one united people . . . descended from the same ancestors, speaking the same language, professing the same religion, attached to the same principles of government, very similar in their manners and customs. . . .' If such are the elements of nationhood and peoplehood, can we still speak of Americans as one nation and one people? We no longer have the same ancestors. They are of every color and from every country. We do not speak one language, but rather English, Spanish and a host of others. We long ago ceased to profess the same religion. We are Evangelical Christians, mainstream Protestants, Catholics, Jews, Mormons, Muslims, Hindus and Buddhists, agnostics and atheists. *Federalist* No. 2 celebrated our unity. Today's elites proclaim that our diversity is our strength. But is this true or a tenet of trendy ideology?[12]

The ideology Buchanan disparages isn't "trendy." It dates at least to the Fourteenth Amendment (if not to the Declaration of Independence), in which we emphatically rejected Buchanan's definition of the preambular people.

Jason Sims likewise argues that for the Founders, We the People were and should be white. In *American Renaissance*, a white superiority/white culture website, Sims argues that:

> The framers of the Constitution agreed that homogeneity of race, mores, language, and religion were the foundation of harmony and a viable republic. They understood that excessive diversity means that politics become a zero-sum game among competing and antagonistic groups. . . . A sound understanding of race has always been part of our nation, and America cannot endure without a return to such an understanding.[13]

Sims' invocation of the Founders ends the discussion. They cannot have been wrong, but the Fourteenth Amendment, the work of mere men, can be, and is.

For others in the radical right, the argument is not simply that We the People means white people. Some attack one of the self-evident truths set out by the Declaration of Independence—that all men are created equal. Sam Francis (formerly a columnist and editor at the *Washington Times*; now deceased) argued, for example, that "the most casual acquaintance with the realities of American history shows that the idea that America is or has been a universal nation, that it defines itself through the proposition that 'all men are created equal,' is a myth. . . . Indeed, it is something less than a myth, it is a mere propaganda line invoked to justify . . . the total reconstruction and re-definition of the United States as a multiracial, multicultural, and transnational swamp."[14]

Likewise, an e-book entitled *Cuckservative: How "Conservatives" Betrayed America* (2015), authored by two prominent Alt-right personalities, Vox Day and John Red Eagle, argues that the People referenced in the Preamble secured the Blessings of Liberty for the Founding generation and their posterity: "The blessings of liberty are not to be secured to all the nations of the world, to the tired and huddled masses, or to the wretched refuse of the teeming shores of other lands. They are to be secured to our children, and their children, and their children's children. To sacrifice their interests to the interests of children in other lands is to betray both past and future America."[15] Necessarily implicit is a rejection of a vision of equality that encompasses any of us who would not and could not have qualified as We the People who wrote the Declaration.[16] A YouTube video by Jared Taylor of *American Renaissance* similarly notes that all elements of the Alt-right "all agree [on] one thing: equality is a dangerous myth. Races are different. . . . Most people prefer the culture created by their own race and prefer to be around people like themselves."[17]

There is an important and sad sense in which these sorts of claims cannot be easily dismissed. When the Alt-right and others in the extreme right rail about immigration, they call upon a long history of anti-immigrationism. That history includes the Alien and Sedition Acts of 1798 (in addition to its freedom of speech implications, the Act explicitly linked citizenship to white immigration),[18] the Page Act of 1875, the

Chinese Exclusion Act of 1882, the Immigration Act of 1924, the American eugenics movement (Supreme Court Justice Oliver Wendell Holmes Jr. was a voice in this movement), President Eisenhower's Operation Wetback (yes, that is really what it was called), the REAL ID Act of 2005, and many anti-immigration policies enacted at the state level.

Slaughterhouse did not challenge the concept of birthright citizenship directly; it simply made it less meaningful. Many voices in the radical right, and some in the conservative movement more broadly, *do* want to abolish birthright citizenship. One of them is President Trump, as he indicated in his proposals for immigration reform when he was candidate Trump. And according to the *Huffington Post*, at least five of the other Republican candidates for the presidency agreed that birthright citizenship should be abolished.

There are several reasons why the extreme right wants to get rid of birthright citizenship. Birthright citizenship is an immigration problem, the argument goes, because it entices immigrants to enter the country illegally to have children (thus the slur "anchor babies") who will be United States citizens by birth. The Trump campaign claimed that there are about 400,000 children born to undocumented immigrants every year. Most estimates put the number at about 300,000, but it is certainly a mistake (and offensive) to think that all of these children were born in the United States simply to gain citizenship in the United States.[19]

For the Alt-right, the case for repealing birthright citizenship hinges on white purity and protecting the "integrity" of white culture. Some in the Alt-right, such as Richard Spencer, openly defend white supremacy and white nationalism. Others in the Alt-right (and in the Alt-Lite and Alt-White fraternities) prefer to talk about preserving Western culture or European heritage, but the object is the same. "Alt-right supporters point out that America was 80 percent white in 1980, but is barely 60 percent white today. They denounce rising rates of interracial marriage, liberal immigration policies, the Black Lives Matter movement, and the targeting of 'white privilege' by academics and the media."[20]

Sometimes the arguments are about demographic change and the prospect that whites will soon no longer constitute a majority of the population. (A popular version of this is a projection by the US Census Bureau that whites will be a minority by 2044.[21]) Sometimes the arguments are cast in terms of population overgrowth, or economic harm to working-class Americans, or skyrocketing social welfare costs, or crime rates.[22] And for some, birthright citizenship heralds a demographic change that means electoral trouble for Republicans.[23] For many conservatives the birthright citizenship problem is about winning and losing elections, chiefly because the assumption is that these children will not be white and consequently will not vote for conservatives. No matter the reason for anxiety, be it border security, overpopulation, identity, culture, or elections, the obvious solution is to get rid of birthright citizenship.[24] How best to do that is a matter of some disagreement. President Trump and some others think the fix is fairly straightforward because they argue that the Fourteenth Amendment, interpreted correctly, does not protect birthright citizenship. Speaking on the campaign trail, Trump said that his plan to roll back birthright citizenship for children of illegal immigrants would be constitutional because "many of the great scholars say that anchor babies are not covered" by the Fourteenth Amendment.[25] So those who think the Fourteenth Amendment is a victim of willful misinterpretation, like President Trump, can hope at some point to persuade the Supreme Court to correct the error.

There *are* a few well-known constitutional law scholars who take this position. They typically argue that the Founders of the Fourteenth Amendment did not intend it to establish birthright citizenship, or that this conclusion was not the original understanding.[26] (As it turns out, originalism is not much of a help on the question, but it rarely is. In the view of most scholars,[27] the best originalist readings of the citizenship clause actually support birthright citizenship.) But there is little doubt that this is the minority view. Most scholars think that repealing birthright citizenship requires a constitutional amendment.[28]

So those who think the Fourteenth itself is the problem must pursue the course of constitutional amendment. In the late 1980s, a Los Angeles attorney, William Daniel Johnson, created a group called "the League of Pace Amendment Advocates" to make the case for repeal. Johnson achieved brief notoriety in 2016, when Trump's campaign named him one of its delegates to the 2016 Republican National Convention. Campaign officials blamed Johnson's inclusion on a "database error."

The Pace Amendment was Johnson's idea, writing under the pseudonym of James O. Pace. The Pace Amendment would repeal the Fourteenth and Fifteenth amendments and deport almost all non-whites from the United States. (Indigenous Americans and Hawaiians would be maintained in tribal reservations instead of being deported.)

The Pace Amendment provides that:

> No person shall be a citizen of the United States unless he is a non-Hispanic white of the European race, in whom there is no ascertainable trace of Negro blood, nor more than one-eighth Mongolian, Asian, Asia Minor, Middle Eastern, Semitic, Near Eastern, American Indian, Malay or other non-European or non-white blood, provided that Hispanic whites, defined as anyone with an Hispanic ancestor, may be citizens if, in addition to meeting the aforesaid ascertainable trace and percentage tests, they are in appearance indistinguishable from Americans whose ancestral home is in the British Isles or Northwestern Europe. . . .

(I can't help but wonder how many of us cannot satisfy the definition, but I suspect it's a lot. I propose we start by inquiring into the racial lineage of William Daniel Johnson and then systematically work our way through everyone who claims to be a member of the militant right.)

Another advocate of repealing the Fourteenth, Robert Wangrud, is a longtime proponent of "white law" and of the "common law." (See Chapter 5.) Wangrud claims that:

> At the time of the adoption of the Preamble, the phrase 'We The People' was known and understood to mean the people of the white race and none other. The Preamble emanated from and for the people so designated by the words 'to ourselves and our posterity' (Dred Scott v. Sandford, 19 How. [60 US] 393, 406–07, 410–11), and it is known that the men that framed the Preamble and the Constitution were all of the white race and the Christian faith. The people fully understood that those words secured the intent of all that followed for that one people (the white race), and them alone.[29]

Note the approving citation to *Dred Scott*.

Parenthetically, in the Alt-right immigration is also a First Amendment issue. Some in the Alt-right have taken facetiously to talking about a "Zeroth" Amendment that, unless repealed, forecloses all efforts at immigration reform. According to Steve Sailer, writing in *Taki's Magazine,* the Zeroth Amendment provides "that American citizens should get no say in who gets to move to America because huddled masses of non-Americans possess civil rights to immigrate, no questions asked. And this Zeroth Amendment overrides the obsolete First Amendment, so you aren't allowed to question it."[30]

TWO KINDS OF CITIZENSHIP, SOVEREIGN AND FEDERAL

Some objections to the Fourteenth Amendment go well beyond birthright citizenship, demography, or threats to white culture. The Fourteenth Amendment is also at the heart of a vast conspiracy to divest (true) Americans of their constitutional liberties and of their very citizenship. Sovereign Citizens argue that the citizenship clause created two classes of citizenship—citizens of a state and citizens of the United States. The latter category, they argue, was designed to make citizens into mere subjects (or, in some accounts, employees). The argument recalls the distinction in the Sovereign Citizen Movement between Sovereign Citizens and federal citizens, or between "de jure" and "de facto" citizens, or between Preambular Citizens and Fourteenth Amendment citizens.

Federal citizenship is plainly inferior to Sovereign Citizenship. Unlike Fourteenth Amendment citizens, Sovereign Citizens have inalienable natural rights "that are recognized, secured, and protected by [the] state Constitution against State actions and against federal intrusion."[31] Among these are speech; property; the right to own a weapon (to defend one's self and one's property); the right to travel; and the right to fully participate in civic life, including the right to be governed only by the authority of the common law and a properly appointed county sheriff.

Why would anyone agree to exchange their full citizenship for an inferior form? The answer, we saw in Chapter 5, hides in the chicanery of contracts of adhesion implicit in Social Security, drivers' licenses, zip codes, and so on.

If the Fourteenth Amendment and all manner of contracts and forms are part of an Orwellian conspiracy, how can a diligent Sovereign Citizen protect himself from inadvertently entering into or from being tricked into signing an unrevealed contract? As we saw in Chapter 5, the answer lies in the talismanic power of legal magicalism.[32] All potential obligations can be averted by writing "U.C.C. 1–207" on the document in question, including driver's licenses, social security cards, and banknotes.[33] I have said repeatedly that the Alt-constitution is white. Nowhere is the point more obvious than here. Sovereign Citizens typically hold that the miserly citizenship created by the Fourteenth Amendment is the only sort of citizenship available to African Americans and to other minorities. As Leonard Zeskind has written, "A racial theory is deeply embedded in this concept of citizenship, which postulates rights and responsibilities for sovereign white Christians different from that of Fourteenth Amendment citizens—that is, everyone else."[34]

Some Sovereigns argue that nothing about the distinction between Sovereign and federal citizenship is racist or even racial. Evidence for this, they say, is the fact that membership in the diminutive class of federal citizenship includes many (duped) whites. One of the great appeals of the SCM is its promise to free white citizens who have unwittingly become mere federal citizens from the heavy handed, all-inclusive jurisdiction of the federal government. What this overlooks, though, is that most Sovereigns also believe that the freedom of this elevated citizenship extends only to people who would have qualified for full citizenship when the Constitution was written and ratified. (Think *Dred Scott*.)

Preambular citizenship, in other words, includes only those persons who would have qualified for full citizenship when the Constitution was ratified—which is to say, white males. The Preamble's invocation of "We" must be understood as it was "originally" understood, as including only some Americans. Only whites can be Sovereign Citizens, but not all whites are Sovereign.

THE SIXTEENTH, SEVENTEENTH, AND NINETEENTH AMENDMENTS

The Alt-constitution has no use for the Sixteenth, Seventeenth, and perhaps the Nineteenth amendments. The Eighteenth, which prohibited the production, transport, and sale of alcohol, raises no complaint because it was repealed by the Twenty-first Amendment, although one can find in some fundamentalist circles a call for the repeal of the repeal. (As I write this I am living in one of the "dry" townships in the otherwise perfect state of Maine.)

THE SIXTEENTH AMENDMENT

Many of the specific objections to the Sixteenth Amendment originated in the tax protest movement of the 1950s. One of the leaders of the movement was Arthur Porth. Porth sued the IRS to recover $135 that he had paid in federal income taxes in 1951, claiming that the Sixteenth Amendment was "illegal and unconstitutional." The interesting part is *why* he thought so. Porth argued that the tax had put him in a state of "involuntary servitude" (and hence violates the Thirteenth Amendment) and that the "Federal tax legislation enacted after the ratification of the Sixteenth Amendment has given rise to such a mass of ambiguous, contradictory, inequitable and unjust rules, regulations and methods of procedure, that the taxpayer's rights as a citizen of the United States have been placed in jeopardy because the present and existing tax laws, rules, regulations and methods of procedure have compelled him to assume unreasonable duties, obligations and burdens." In *Porth v. Broderick* (1954), a federal court of appeals noted that "Apparently the taxpayer, while recognizing the taxing power of the United States, attacks both the legality of the Sixteenth Amendment and the constitutionality of the Federal tax laws, rules and regulations enacted pursuant thereto. . . . The claim is clearly unsubstantial and without merit." In a later tax year Porth submitted a blank tax return, arguing that the required disclosures on the form violated his Fifth Amendment right against self-incrimination. (Nope.)[35]

Sovereign Citizens often claim that they are common law citizens or "natural freemen" beyond the jurisdiction of the IRS because they are "free born, white, preamble, sovereign, natural, individual common-law 'de jure citizens' [who] are alien to the federal government.'"[36] Some tax protesters invoke the free exercise clause of the First Amendment. In one case, a protester claimed that his religious scruples prevented him from "entering into contracts with the inhabitants of the land," a reference to Old Testament prohibitions of dealing with the Canaanites.

In *The Law That Never Was: The Fraud of the 16th Amendment and Personal Income Tax* (1985), William J. Benson and Martin J. "Red" Beckman argue that the Sixteenth Amendment is unconstitutional because it was not properly ratified. *The Law That Never Was* is a sacred text in the tax protest movement, even though its central claims have been repeatedly rejected by scholars and judges. The gist of the book's argument is that the Sixteenth Amendment was not properly ratified because there were variations in wording, punctuation, capitalization, and pluralization in the language of the Amendment said to be ratified. Benson also claimed to have found documents suggesting that some states that had been certified as having ratified the Amendment never voted to ratify it, or even voted against ratification.

Benson was tried and convicted in federal court for tax evasion and willful failure to file tax returns. The court that upheld his conviction gave no weight to Benson's argument that the Sixteenth Amendment is unconstitutional.[37] In another notable federal court case, an appeals court dismissed most of Benson and Beckman's arguments. In *Miller v. United States* (1989), a clearly exasperated circuit court wrote that:

> The movement's manifesto, Benson and Beckman's *The Law That Never Was*, is a collection of documents relating to the ratification of the sixteenth amendment, and is intended to be both a call to arms for the movement and 'exhibit A' in the trials of tax protesters who argue that the sixteenth amendment was illegally ratified. ('The tax protestor will be the great American hero of 1985 just as in 1776. It was tax protestors, not any political party, or judge or prosecutor who gave us our great Constitutional Republican form of government. The tax protest is more American than baseball, hot dogs, apple pie or Chevrolet!!'). In the eyes of the authors, the most damning evidence of the illegality of sixteenth amendment is a 1913 memorandum from the Solicitor of the Department of State to then Secretary of State Knox outlining the minor grammatical discrepancies in the instruments ratified in many of the states. . . . [The defendant] insists that because the states did not approve exactly the same text, the amendment did not go into effect.

The court concluded that these arguments had no merit.

The extreme right's objection to the Sixteenth Amendment is not limited to alleged improprieties in the ratification process. Nor is it just about liberty or property or taxation without representation. There is an equally fundamental objection in principle to the enormity of the modern administrative state. Tax laws are "the most obvious sign of the active modern state."[38] The Sixteenth is also objectionable, therefore, precisely because the growth of the federal leviathan was made possible through the instrumentality of taxation.

If the Sixteenth Amendment feeds the beast, then the solution is plain: Starve the beast. (I use the word "beast" because it captures the language and imagery that is so popular in the tax-protest movement. It also alludes to the conspiratorial strain characteristic of Alt-constitutional theory.) There is, predictably, some disagreement about how to starve the beast. For many years the primary tool has been to challenge the Sixteenth Amendment directly with the IRS and in federal courts. Indeed, an entire industry has grown up around this strategy: "Tax protesters have built a considerable library of 'books, literature, [and] videotaped courses. . . . Numerous Internet-based groups [sell] their own documentation which claims to give a sovereign a program for taxes with 'no tax liability."[39]

Somewhat surprisingly, such claims continue to crowd the dockets of federal courts, even though they have no track record of success. The *Miller* court addressed this question as well, saying:

> We find it hard to understand why the long and unbroken line of cases upholding the constitutionality of the sixteenth amendment generally, and those specifically rejecting the argument advanced in *The Law That Never Was*, have not persuaded Miller and his compatriots to seek a more effective forum for airing their attack on the federal income tax structure. . . . Miller and his fellow protesters would be well advised to take their objections to the federal income tax structure to a more appropriate forum.

Why would anyone expect courts to look favorably upon such challenges? The answer lies once more in the naïve, almost childlike faith that Sovereign Citizens, Patriots, Constitutionalists, and militias have in magical legalism and the redemptive power of the "law" properly understood.

The other fix is to pass a constitutional amendment to repeal the Sixteenth Amendment. In some quarters, repealing the Sixteenth is near a holy crusade.[40] At the 2012 Republican National Convention, for example, the party platform said that "In any restructuring of federal taxation, to guard against hypertaxation of the American people, any value added tax or national sales tax must be tied to the simultaneous repeal of the Sixteenth Amendment, which established the federal income tax."[41] The 2016 platform made the same claim.[42] Calls for repeal are a staple in the Tea Party,[43] among conservative politicians (like Rick Perry),[44] and on conservative editorial pages.[45]

One reason why the repeal movement has not had more traction is a suspicion that it would not change much and might make things worse. Thus:

> Eliminating Congress' power to tax income, as many supporters of a national sales tax propose, would require more than merely repealing the 16th Amendment. We would have to ratify an amendment prohibiting Congress from imposing any income tax as well as estate, gift, and gross receipts taxes. Otherwise, Congress could rely on the earlier Supreme Court decisions to continue collecting these and other related taxes. And as the residents of Canada and Western Europe could tell us, we'd probably end up with the worst of both tax worlds: paying both a national sales tax and an income tax.[46]

Such arguments are irrelevant in the Alt-constitution, which likely provides that sales taxes also violate the Fifth Amendment right to property, and maybe even the Thirteenth.

THE SEVENTEENTH AMENDMENT

In the spring of 2018, the Arizona state legislature took up a proposal that would authorize the state legislature to decide which candidates for the United States Senate can appear on state ballots. Republican legislators would nominate two Republicans and Democrats would nominate two Democrats, and those would be the only choices. The bill includes no method for independents or third-party candidates to be nominated.

The Arizona legislation is an attack on another part of the Constitution that many conservatives, and not only extremists, think should be repealed—the Seventeenth Amendment. The Seventeenth Amendment provides that the Senate of the United States shall be composed of two Senators from each state, elected by the people thereof, for six years. Prior to its adoption, Senators were chosen directly by state legislatures.

The Seventeenth Amendment might not seem like an obvious candidate for repeal by constitutional fundamentalists, but in fact it is a favorite target. In the past few years, political commentator Mark Levin; Justice Antonin Scalia; Governors Rick Perry (who described the Seventeenth as enacted in "a fit of populist rage")[47] and Mike Huckabee; and Senators Ted Cruz, Mike Lee, and Jeff Flake have all pressed for its repeal. It is largely true, if somewhat simplistic to argue, as do proponents of repeal, that "The Progressives that pushed for the Seventeenth Amendment in the belief that the cure for democracy's shortcomings is more democracy, did not address the fundamental purpose for the Senate: to protect the sovereignty of the states against the encroachment of national government into the states' meaningful interest in addressing their people's needs."[48] As Roy Moore observed of the Seventeenth Amendment, "[S]ome of these amendments have completely tried to wreck the form of government that our forefathers intended."[49]

For many in the radical right, the Seventeenth Amendment ushered in a fundamental transformation of the constitutional order from a constitutional *republic*, to a constitutional *democracy*, and not for the better. In a republic, the argument runs, the people govern through the sage mediation of representatives chosen for their wisdom and public mindedness. In a democracy, the people govern directly. Skousen puts the matter concisely: the problem with the Seventeenth Amendment is that it makes Senators vulnerable to "popular pressure."[50]

Before the Seventeenth Amendment was passed, the argument holds, states had considerable influence in Washington by virtue of their voice in the Senate. Because they owed their office to state legislatures, individual Senators were attentive to the concerns and interests of their states. Set loose of that direct accountability, Senators are increasingly "national" political actors; many aspire to a national (presidential or vice presidential or cabinet) office. The rise of a national media and a twenty-four hour news cycle only exacerbates the attenuation between state and Senator.

Scrapping the Seventeenth Amendment appeals to constitutional fundamentalists because it simultaneously explains and offers a potential cure for the malady of big government. State control over the selection of Senators was meant to be one of the brakes on the growth of federal power at state expense. "Once that power was removed by the 17th Amendment," the argument goes, "state governments lost their pull in Washington, leading to a bigger, greedier, and more powerful federal government at the expense of states' rights and interests."[51] Hence, "it is no coincidence that the national government began its exponential growth following the passage of the 17th Amendment, just as soon as there was no longer a competing interest that could stop it."[52]

There is some merit in these arguments. The Founders did indeed envision a Senate reflective of and attentive to the states. Indeed, they promulgated a constitutional rule that guarantees every state two seats in the Senate—a requirement that, whatever its merits, is deeply antidemocratic in purpose and in effect. It is worth asking why the Founders embraced such a rule. What was so important and why? (The answer has as much to do with slavery as with principled defenses of federalism.)

It is far from clear, though, that the Seventeenth Amendment is the reason why the Senate no longer serves the cause of federalism as forcefully as some would like.[53] The reasons for the Senate's transformation into an arena for senatorial ambition in national politics have more to do with the transformation of American politics in general. In addition, some scholars question the practical wisdom of repealing the Seventeenth Amendment. Some of us think a return to the old system would do more to diminish the states, even if it would appear to give them a louder voice in the Senate. One reason for thinking so is what political scientists call the problem of "second-order" elections, a phenomenon in which voters cast their vote in one election based upon their preferences in another one. So instead of strengthening states and cultivating strong democracy, direct selection of senators may lead voters to vote for *state* officers based upon their calculation of *national* interests: "[N]ational issues, including things state legislatures have no control over, from the Iraq war to monetary policy, now play a huge role in state elections, meaning that state officials are less accountable on state issues than they should be."⁵⁴ If this is so, then repealing the Seventeenth Amendment might actually diminish the dignity and autonomy of the states, while also ensuring that the voice that is heard in the Senate is not the state's.

So it is not at all clear that enhancing federalism provides a good reason for repealing the Seventeenth Amendment, but admittedly it's not beyond thinking. The real reasons why the far right dislikes the Seventeenth Amendment, however, are grounded, predictably if quietly, in racism. Like several of the other constitutional amendments ratified after the Civil War, notably the Fifteenth and the Nineteenth, but also the Twenty-fourth and the Twenty-sixth, the Seventeenth Amendment is part of the great democratization of the American electoral system that occurred in the nineteenth and twentieth centuries. All of these amendments extended the vote to groups that had previously been disfranchised. In comparison to the Fourteenth Amendment, these extensions provoked only minor constitutional anxieties. Even in the most extreme fringes of the Alt-right one is hard pressed to find an explicit argument against the Fifteenth Amendment as such. Objections are usually cast against the Reconstruction Amendments as a package, which has the effect of taking some of the sting out of direct and blatant opposition to extending the vote to African Americans, but achieves the same purpose.

In contrast, the Seventeenth Amendment does not expand the electorate, but it does do something comparable and just as important: It expands the power and responsibilities of the electorate by extending its jurisdiction to encompass powerful institutions that were previously immunized from We the People. That expansion of authority, indeed, the very process of democratization, cannot be applauded if you think We the People includes some people who should not be counted as full citizens. In other words, what's wrong with the Seventeenth Amendment (and the Fifteenth, certainly, and the Nineteenth possibly) is the Fourteenth Amendment and birthright citizenship. We have seen already that the Alt-constitution has no use for the Fourteenth Amendment. If the Fourteenth cannot be undone, then repealing the Seventeenth would help at least a little by limiting its reach and effect. And unlike a direct assault on the Fourteenth, which necessarily smacks of racism, an attack on the Seventeenth Amendment can proceed on grounds of federalism and good government. In short, restricting the franchise to original or Sovereign or preambular citizens is the preferred course, but limiting what can be voted on or who can be voted for (as repealing the Seventeenth would do) is a passable second choice and can be defended as a choice the Founders themselves made.

THE NINETEENTH AMENDMENT

In contrast to the other disputed amendments, the Nineteenth Amendment is not a prominent talking point in Alt-constitutional jurisprudence. This might seem odd. The radical right has always been overwhelming male in membership and ideology (a demographic no less true of the Alt-right than of the militia movement and its other predecessors). Many of the "soldiers in the alt-right's fractious army regularly insult women on digital platforms such as Twitter, 4chan, and Reddit."[55] Richard Spencer famously opined that women shouldn't make foreign policy because their "vindictiveness knows no bounds."[56]

Nevertheless, any student of the militant right knows that "Women have always been part of white extremist groups" and many have held positions of prominence.[57] Additionally, the Alt-right's continued vitality as a political movement means that it would be impolitic and unwise to engage in a campaign to deny women the right to vote. Welcoming women is not a principled position borne of some fundamental commitment to gender or human equality; it's a calculated decision. As Lana Lokteff, a prominent female voice in the Alt-right, has observed, "The question of why they've embarked on this crusade has a practical answer: No movement can survive on men alone."[58]

In some circles, though, and especially among some Christian conservatives, the Nineteenth Amendment cannot be part of the Alt-constitution because it violates God's law. Adhering to the literal word of the Bible (citing Isaiah 3:12) and certain of the writings of Apostles Paul and Timothy, some Christian Fundamentalists believe women should be excluded from pastoring, ordination, and even teaching men. The husband is considered the head of the household, as indicated in 1 Corinthians 14:34 and 1 Timothy 2:12. Women care for children and maintain the house; men run the family, businesses, and churches. Only men are called to do the work of governing.

In a course on American government available for purchase on Amazon, called "Law and Government: An Introductory Study Course," former Alabama Chief Justice and Republican candidate for Senate Roy Moore tells students that women should not be permitted to run for elected office. "If women do run for office, the course argues, people have a moral obligation not to vote for them. The course is also critical of the women's suffrage movement"[59] and of the Nineteenth Amendment.

There is, of course, no serious movement to repeal the Nineteenth Amendment, although a brief Twitterstorm in October 2016 seemed to suggest such a movement was afoot. The hashtag #Repealthe19th appeared shortly after a report in the *Washington Post* indicated Trump would win the election handily if only men could vote. "But despite numerous media outlets reporting #Repealthe19th as a genuine call to strike the amendment, there didn't appear to be anyone seriously suggesting women's right to vote be rescinded in order to facilitate a Trump win."[60] The Alt-constitution includes the Nineteenth Amendment because, at least for now, it has to.

CONCLUSION

The Fourteenth Amendment, like the other contested amendments in the Constitution, enhances the project of democratic self-governance by expanding the electorate and by redefining who qualifies for citizenship. It is true, then, as its critics so often complain, that the Fourteenth Amendment amounted to a constitutional revolution. It amended the definition of We the People in the Preamble and advanced our understanding of human equality. It is as much a part of the Constitution as the Preamble itself, but better.

It is not the Founders' Constitution but the Reconstruction constitution that best captures the ringing ideals of the Declaration of Independence. In extending the work of the Founders by making good on the ideals they espoused, we do not dishonor them. We embrace their work and make their Constitution our own.

CONCLUSION

Why It Matters

It has been six years or more since the talk I heard at a small library in a small town in Maine. Now on Thursday mornings, at another small library in another small town (this one in Connecticut), I meet with a study group of concerned citizens to talk about the Constitution and other things. I hope to listen more than talk, no small ambition for a newly retired professor, but I try to remember that I have a responsibility not to let some falsehoods and fictions pass without polite challenge.

Why should we care about the Alt-constitution? What does it matter if the radical right misappropriates the Constitution and invokes fairy tales about the Founding to give their political platform a veneer of constitutional rectitude? The answer is clear: Just as some elements in the radical right's politics have begun to enter mainstream political thought, there is reason to worry that constitutional extremism may begin to influence how the rest of us think about the Constitution. The only firewall between the Alt-constitution and the veridical Constitution is for those who know better to speak out.

At the heart of the Alt-constitution is a preoccupation with the most important of political questions: Who are we? If there is a common thread to the many varied and disparate elements of conservative political thought in the United States, it is that single question of identity, of who belongs and who does not belong.[1] This anxiety explains why so much of the ideology of the radical right is caught up with the Constitution. Every dispute about what the Constitution means and how it should be interpreted and by whom is caught up with the question of who makes up We the People and, no less significantly, what we believe. "We" are always a matter of conversation and contest, and because we are, so is the Constitution. The Constitution, like who we are, is a question.

Nowhere is this clearer than in how we read the Preamble.[2] The radical right insists that "We the People" includes only those of us with a certain racial and religious and cultural heritage, and they invoke the Constitution in whole and in several of its parts to give dignity to their argument. The Alt-preamble is grounded in suspicion and fear. As David H. Bennett argues, "If there has been political extremism of the Right in American history, it is found in large measure in . . . efforts to combat peoples and ideas that were seen as alien threats to a cherished but embattled American 'way of life.'"[3] Fear of the other—of other races, peoples, religions, and cultures—is a challenge to the nation's democratic traditions[4] and to the noble ambitions of the Preamble.

Constitutional fundamentalists are right to see the Preamble as the key to the Constitution, but they do not understand what it means. Too many of us think the Constitution is a conservative project—conservative not like Republicans, or Libertarians, or Birchers, or Constitutionalists, or the Tea Party, or the Alt-right, but conservative in the sense that the reason for writing anything down is to preserve it. But as Michael Walzer and other scholars have observed, the Constitution is also a radical project, "opening the way for, if not actually stimulating social change."[5] The progressive character of the Constitution begins with the Preamble. Read in the generous spirit the Founders intended but did not achieve, the Preamble is inclusive, welcoming, and hopeful. The Preamble tells us the Constitution is *our* work. It tells us not even the Constitution is set in stone, that it is not a religious artifact but a call to action, an injunction to make it, and us, better.

Constitutional fundamentalists see the Constitution as an immutable object of faith and veneration. They are precisely the people Thomas Jefferson alluded to when he observed that "Some men look at constitutions with sanctimonious reverence, and deem them like the ark of the covenant, too sacred to be touched. They ascribe to the men of the preceding age a wisdom more than human, and suppose what they did to be beyond amendment."[6] Like James Madison, John Adams, Noah Webster, Alexander Hamilton, and George Washington, Jefferson saw the Constitution not in sacred terms but in instrumental terms, as a "means to achieve the public good. This includes, as the Preamble announces, preserving justice, our liberties, and the general welfare."[7]

Constitutional fundamentalism discourages us from thinking critically about the Constitution and about how it might be obsolete, flawed, or even objectionable. Constitution worship renders us incapable of doing precisely what the Preamble instructs citizens to do: To ask whether we are making reasonable progress toward securing the Blessings of Liberty for our children and ourselves.[8]

HOW TO BE A CONSTITUTIONAL PATRIOT

The radical right uses constitutional history as a weapon in its ongoing struggle to define America.[9] Getting the Constitution 'right' necessitates a concerted effort to teach citizens that the Constitution, rightly understood, instantiates and sanctifies a particular conservative worldview. It is no wonder that civic education and constitutional literacy programs are a booming business in the far right. Hardly a meeting of the Tea Party,[10] or the Oath Keepers, or the Constitutional Sheriffs, or a militia can be found that does not peddle a variety of pamphlets, books, CDs, audio books, and tapes about the Constitution and the Founders. There are constitution camps[11] and constitution coloring books for kids[12] and centers for the study of the Constitution and even, a little ominously, a program in "Constitution Combat Training (CCT),"[13] all meant to preach constitutional truth and to win converts to the cult of the Constitution that once was. One camp, cleverly called ConstitutionBootCamp.com, proclaims loudly that "The Constitution is in Crisis"[14] (for which I should get royalties, but don't).[15] Another site, Save It! Read It! ~ Powered by the Moms at AsAMom.org, features lectures by Kris Anne Hall and includes sections dedicated to youth education and homeschoolers. (The Constitution for kids is almost a cottage industry, featuring books like *Founders' Fables: Ten Tales for Future Patriots*[16] and *Ethan and Emily, the Tuttle Twins*.)[17] There are even rock bands that exalt the Founders and the Constitution, like "Madison Rising," which describes itself as "America's Most Patriotic rock band" and likes to incorporate conservative political themes into its songs. (A writer for the *New York Post* described the band as the "Monkees of conservatism.")[18] Those who feel the need to cite obscure legal cases and want the veneer of academic legitimacy can consult "The DixieLand Law Journal," which includes "briefs and other legal materials . . . which cover subjects . . . of interest to the concerned American."[19] It is a civic education that inculcates reverence and devotion instead of critical thinking and engagement. Education isn't the point so much as engaging in patriotic rituals.

The speaker I heard all those years ago in a small library called herself a "Constitutional Patriot." Constitutional patriotism *is* a vital civic virtue. But what does it mean to be a constitutional patriot? No one should doubt that constitutional fundamentalists are constitutional patriots, but their patriotism "is more of a holy crusade than a conscientious effort to become informed."[20] We need a conception of constitutional patriotism grounded in critical thinking, not cheerleading.

* * *

Constitutional patriotism properly understood has nothing to do with Founder worship or with insisting that the meaning of the Constitution was settled long ago by (Christian white) men more saintly than us. What constitutional patriotism demands is a citizenry educated in the "meaning and value of the ideals that characterize a constitutional way of life."[21] True constitutional patriotism therefore rejects the constitutional idolatry of the Alt-constitution, but neither is it dispassionate or noncommittal about the virtues of our constitutional order.[22]

How do we achieve this kind of constitutional literacy? It cannot be done in constitution camps or by memorizing the Constitution like verse or by teaching school children about the miracle at Philadelphia. It cannot be done by forcing schoolkids (or football players) to salute the flag or say the pledge of allegiance. Instead, it requires us to rethink what citizens need to know about the Constitution. It requires a civic education that equips citizens with the capacity to reason and with the skills necessary to make wise choices. It must include instruction in the meaning of "equality, liberty, government under law, tolerance, and other such constitutional values."[23]

The place to begin is with the Constitution itself. Citizens must be taught to read the Constitution instead of memorizing it. Citizens must be taught also *how* to read the Constitution. As Garret Epps has argued,

"At its most basic level, reading the Constitution requires the tools that Vladimir Nabokov urged readers to bring to any text: imagination, memory, a dictionary and a willingness to use all three when the going gets tough."[24] Reading the Constitution means thinking about it, what it says, and what it does not say, and why. It requires a working knowledge of American history, the Founding, and the Founders. It requires some knowledge and understanding of the choices the Founders made, and the ones they *might* have made, concerning how to allocate power between the states and the federal government, regarding the separation of powers, and about civil liberties. It also requires us to confront the reality of slavery and how it was built into the very fabric of the constitutional order. Studies show that students lack a basic knowledge of the critical role slavery played in shaping our constitutional history and the impact it continues to have on race relations in America.[25]

More than answers to multiple choice questions, constitutional patriotism requires instruction in the constitutional virtues. The constitutional virtues are the traits, dispositions, and habits that sustain a constitutional way of life.[26] Constitutional virtues include civic habits and practices[27] like civility, tending, friendship,[28] future-mindedness, honesty, humility, empathy, and love. They make self-government in a community of strangers possible.[29]

Of the constitutional virtues, civility and empathy are the most important.[30] Civility (not to be confused with politeness or decorum)[31] because it makes possible discussion and dialogue with those who are different from us; empathy because it enables us to imagine ourselves as others who are different. David Neiwert has also emphasized the need of empathy in civic life—respect, civility, and empathy for others "simply means being a part of a democracy, which is enriched by its diversity."[32] For Neiwert, empathy is a civic virtue that progressives and liberals must cultivate to converse with "those from rural areas," in the flyover, red states.[33] I am not as sure that liberal disdain for rural America is a significant problem, but I do think, as does Danielle Allen, that "When citizenly relations are shot through with distrust, efforts to solve collective problems inevitably founder."[34] Democracy "depends on trustful talk among strangers."[35]

Where do citizens learn empathy, civility, and the other constitutional virtues? Civic virtues flourish in the third spaces of American life, or in what I have called civic spaces, like bowling alleys,[36] coffee shops,[37] barber shops, PTAs, Little League, and . . . in discussion groups in libraries. In civic spaces, citizens learn how to engage and interact with one another by engaging and interacting with one another. It is an education deeply, inescapably Tocquevillian in character. It is a vision of civic education that is both formal and informal—precisely the sort of education one gets by learning how to live with other citizens, not all of whom look like you, or think like you, or believe what you believe. Civility and empathy, as John Dewey might have written, are best learned in the life of the community, not in a classroom.[38]

To ask Americans to take up the real Constitution, and not simply to revere it from afar, is a heavy burden to put on citizens who are busy with the all-encompassing demands of family, work, and leisure. We cannot ask citizens to become constitutional scholars, expert on the fine and subtle nuances of case law, well-versed in the strengths and weaknesses of various methods of constitutional interpretation. Indeed, it might be hazardous to the Constitution. Madison warned in *Federalist* #49 of "The danger of disturbing the public tranquility by interesting too strongly the public passions."[39] Madison's warning seems especially prescient when one digs deep into the thinking of constitutional fundamentalists.

Robert Brent Toplin has observed that, "True believers . . . are reluctant to question the basic assumptions of their ideology. . . . The radicals' faith promotes the politics of obeisance, not questioning."[40] But questioning the Constitution is precisely what we need to do to keep it from becoming a stale religious artifact. A community built on Constitution worship and genuflection, and on fear of our fellows cannot be what the Founders intended for us. Tragically, it is precisely when we are most fearful that we turn to Constitution worship. Max Lerner made just this point in another fearful time in American history. Writing in 1937, Lerner observed that citizens "live in a jungle of fear, filled with phantoms of what they have heard and imagined and been told." In this world, the Founders become "giants against the sky," and the "Constitution and Supreme Court are symbols of an ancient sureness and a comforting stability."[41]

❊ ❊ ❊

No matter what it pretends to, the Alt-constitution does not honor the Founders. The Alt-constitution is a dangerous distortion of their work and of the true Constitution. Its claims of fealty and patriotism notwithstanding, it actually subverts the very project it claims to honor by undermining the civic virtues necessary to sustain a healthy constitutional order. Paradoxically, constitutional fundamentalism threatens the very thing it celebrates.

There *is* a role for admiration, and perhaps even veneration, in how we think about and teach the Constitution. One of my teachers liked to distinguish between venerating the Constitution and venerating the Founding. The latter we should indeed venerate, but "for the virtues it represents, not for the constitution it produced."[42] If we should venerate the Founders, we should esteem them not for what they gave us (the Constitution of 1787) but rather for what they imagined themselves to be demonstrating for all of us: "namely, humanity's capacity for 'establishing good government from reflection and choice.'"[43] In venerating what the Founders *did*, instead of what they *wrote*, we can imagine ourselves as engaged in the same constitutional project, a living project that asks us to make important choices about what the Constitution means and what it asks of us.

To do less is to live in fear and not in the spirit of "mature deliberation."[44] To do less is to be a subject, not a citizen, of the Constitution.

SELECTED BIBLIOGRAPHY

BOOKS

Abanes, Richard. *American Militias: Rebellion, Racism and Religion*. Downers Grove, IL: InterVarsity Press, 1996.

Allen, Danielle S. *Talking with Strangers: Anxieties of Citizenship since Brown v. Board of Education*. Chicago: University of Chicago Press, 2004.

Barber, Sotirios A. *Constitutional Failure*. Lawrenceville: University Press of Kansas, 2014.

Barkun, Michael. *Religion and the Racist Right: The Origins of the Christian Identity Movement*, rev. ed. Chapel Hill: University of North Carolina Press, 1997.

Batchis, Wayne. *The Right's First Amendment: The Politics of Free Speech and the Return of Conservative Libertarianism*. Stanford: Stanford University Press, 2016.

Bennett, David H. *The Party of Fear: The American Far Right from Nativism to the Militia Movement*. New York: Vintage Press, 1995.

Berger, J.M. *Without Prejudice: What Sovereign Citizens Believe*. Washington, DC: George Washington University, 2016.

Bowen, Catherine Drinker. *Miracle at Philadelphia*. Boston: Back Bay Books, 1986.

Corcoran, James. *Bitter Harvest: Gordon Kahl and the Posse Comitatus: Murder in the Heartland*. New York: Viking Press, 1990.

Dees, Morris. *Gathering Storm: America's Militia Threat*. New York: Harper, 1997.

Dew, Spencer and Jamie Wight. "God's Law: Universal Truth According to Religious Sovereign Citizens." (Oct. 15, 2015): https://divinity.uchicago.edu/sightings/gods-law-universal-truth-according-religious-sovereign-citizens

Dionne, E.J., Jr. *Why the Right Went Wrong: Conservatism—From Goldwater to Trump and Beyond*. New York: Simon and Schuster, 2016.

Finn, John E. *Peopling the Constitution*. Lawrenceville: University Press of Kansas, 2014.

Fletcher, Jeannine Hill. *The Sin of White Supremacy: Christianity, Racism, & Religious Diversity in America*. Ossining, NY: Orbis Books, 2017.

Fukuyama, Francis. *Trust: The Social Virtues and the Creation of Prosperity*. New York: The Free Press, 1995.

Graber, Mark A. *Dred Scott and the Problem of Constitutional Evil*. Cambridge: Cambridge University Press, 2008.

Green, Stephen K. *Inventing a Christian America: The Myth of the Religious Founding*. New York: Oxford University Press, 2015.

Halpern, Thomas, and Brian Levin. *The Limits of Dissent: The Constitutional Status of Armed Civilian Militias*. Amherst, MA: Aletheia Press, 1996.

Hawley, George. *Making Sense of the Alt-Right*. New York: Columbia University Press, 2017.

Karl, Jonathan. *The Right to Bear Arms: The Rise of America's New Militias*. New York: Harper, 1995.

Lepore, Jill. *The Whites of Their Eyes: The Tea Party's Revolution and the Battle over American History*. Princeton: Princeton University Press, 2011.

Levitas, Daniel. *The Terrorist Next Door: The Militia Movement and the Radical Right*. New York: St. Martin's Griffin, 2004.

Levinson, Sanford, ed. *Nullification and Secession in Modern Constitutional Thought*. Lawrenceville: University Press of Kansas, 2016.

Lichtman, Allan J. *White Protestant Nation: the Rise of the American Conservative Movement*. New York: Atlantic Monthly Press, 2008.

Matsuda, Mari J. "Public Response to Racist Speech" in *Words That Wound*. Edited by Mari J. Matsuda, Charles R. Lawrence III, Richard Delgado, and Kimberle Williams Crenshaw. Boulder, CO: Westview Press; 1993.

McIlwain, Charles. *Constitutionalism: Ancient and Modern*. Ithaca: Cornell University Press, 1947.

Mering, Sabine von, and Timothy Wyman McCarty, eds. *Right-Wing Radicalism Today: Perspectives from Europe and the US*. London: Routledge, 2013.

Mulloy, D.J. *American Extremism: History, Politics, and the Militia Movement*. New York: Routledge, 2004.

Murphy, Paul V. *The Rebuke of History: The Southern Agrarians and American Conservative Thought*. Chapel Hill: University of North Carolina Press, 2001.

Nash, George, H. *The Conservative Intellectual Movement in America Since 1945*. Wilmington, DE: Intercollegiate Studies Institute, 2006.

Neiwert, David. *Alt-America: The Rise of the Radical Right in the Age of Trump*. New York: Verso, 2017.

Neiwert, David. *In God's Country: The Patriot Movement and the Pacific Northwest*. Pullman: Washington State University Press, 1999.

Simi, Pete, and Robert Futrell. *American Swastika: Inside the White Power Movement's Hidden Spaces of Hate*. 2nd ed. New York: Rowman & Littlefield, 2015.

Skocpol, Theda, and Vanessa Williams, *The Tea Party and the Remaking of Republican Conservatism*. New York: Oxford University Press, 2016.

Skousen, W. Cleon. *The Making of America: The Substance and the Meaning of the Constitution*. Washington, DC: National Center for Constitutional Studies, 1986.

Stock, Catherine McNicol. *Rural Radicals: Righteous Rage in the American Grain*. Ithaca: Cornell University Press, 2017.

Taylors, M. *What is the Alt-Right?* Scotts Valley, CA: CreateSpace Independent Publishing Platform, 2016.

Thomas, George. *The Founders and the Idea of a National University*. New York: Cambridge University Press, 2014.

Throckmorton, Warren, and Michael Coulter. *Getting Jefferson Right: Fact Checking Claims about Our Third President*. Grove City, PA: Salem Grove Press, 2012.

Toplin, Robert Brent. *Radical Conservatism: The Right's Political Religion*. Lawrenceville: University Press of Kansas, 2006.

Whittington, Keith E. *Speak Freely: Why Universities Must Defend Free Speech*. Princeton: Princeton University Press, 2018.

Winant, Howard. "Behind Blue Eyes: Whiteness and Contemporary U.S. Racial Politics," in *Off White: Readings on Power, Privilege, and Resistance*. 2nd ed. Edited by Michelle Fine, Lois Weis, Linda C. Powell, and L. Mun Wong. New York: Routledge, 2004.

Zernicke, Kate. *Boiling Mad: Inside Tea Party America*. New York: Times Books, 2010.

Zeskind, Leonard. *Blood and Politics: The History of the White Nationalist Movement from the Margins to the Mainstream*. New York: Farrar, Straus & Giroux, 2009.

ARTICLES

Bailey, Jeremy D. "Should We Venerate That Which We Cannot Love? James Madison on Constitutional Imperfection," *Political Research Quarterly* 65, no. 732 (2012).

Chaloupka, William. "The County Supremacy and Militia Movements: Federalism as an Issue on the Radical Right," *Publius* 26, no. 161 (1995).

Bryant, Douglas H. "Unorthodox and Paradox: Revisiting the Ratification of the Fourteenth Amendment," *University of Alabama Law Review* 53, no. 555 (2002).

Corwin, Edward S. "The 'Higher Law' Background of American Constitutional Law," *Harvard Law Review* 42, no. 365 (1929).

Huhn, Wilson. "Political Alienation in America and the Legal Premises of the Patriot Movement," *Gonzaga Law Review* 34, no. 417 (1999).

Jackson, Christopher S. "The Inane Gospel of Tax Protest: Resist Rendering Unto Caesar - Whatever His Demands," *Gonzaga Law Review* 32, no. 291 (1996–97).

Levin, Daniel Lessard, and Malcom W. Mitchell. "A Law Unto Themselves: The Ideology of the Common Law Court Movement," *South Dakota Law Review* 44, no. 9 (1999).

Melle, Julia. "Illogical Extremes: The Sovereign Citizens Movement and the First Amendment," *Temple Political and Civil Rights Law Review* 22, no. 554 (2013).

Neiwert, David. "Ash on the Sills: The Significance of the Patriot Movement in America," *Montana Law Review* 58, no. 1 (1997).

Schmidt, Christopher W. "The Tea Party and the Constitution," *Hastings Constitutional Law Quarterly* 39, no. 193 (2011).

Schmidt, Christopher W. "Popular Constitutionalism on the Right: Lessons from the Tea Party," *Denver University Law Review* 88, no. 523 (2011).

Silversmith, Jol A. "The Missing Thirteenth Amendment: Constitutional Nonsense and Titles of Nobility," *Southern California Interdisciplinary Law Review* 8, no. 577 (1999).

Smith, Thompson P. "The Patriot Movement," *Valparaiso University Law Review* 32, no. 269 (1997).

Sullivan, Francis X. "The Usurping Octopus of Jurisdictional Authority: The Legal Theories of the Sovereign Citizen Movement," *Wisconsin Law Review* no. 1 (1999).

Theret, Michelle. "Sovereign Citizens: A Homegrown Terrorist Threat and its Negative Impact on South Carolina," *South Carolina Law Review* 63, no. 853 (2012).

Vache, James M., and Mark Edward DeForrest. "Truth or Consequences: The Jurisprudential Errors of the Militant Far Far-Right," *Gonzaga Law Review* 32, no. 593 (1997–1997).

NOTES

INTRODUCTION

1. George Hawley has a nice discussion of Clinton's much publicized speech on the Alt-right. George Hawley, *Making Sense of the Alt-right* (New York: Columbia University Press, 2017), 121–128.

2. For example, see Anthony Smith, "Donald Trump's Star of David Hillary Clinton Meme was created by White Supremacists," July 3, 2016, https://mic.com/articles/147711/donald-trump-s- star-of-david-hillary-clinton-meme-was-created-by-white-supremacists#.ACdgKUf0C T.

3. In the spring of 2017, several news reports detailed the rise of paramilitary organizations like the Proud Boys; the Fraternal Order of the Alt-Knights; the Oath Keepers; and others, who purport to "police" right-wing demonstrations against leftists (sometimes called Antifa) counter protesters. See Alan Feuer and Jeremy W. Peters, "Fringe Groups Revel as Protests Turn Violent," *The New York Times*, June 2, 2017, https://www.nytimes.com/2017/06/02/us/politics/white-nationalists-alt-knights-protests-colleges.html. The Southern Poverty Law Center estimates that over 100 people have been killed or injured by "alleged perpetrators influenced by the so-called 'Alt-right.'" Keegan Hankes and Alex Amend, "The Alt-right is Killing People," February 5, 2018, https://www.splcenter.org/20180205/Alt-right-killing-people.

4. Oliver Willis, "What is the 'Alt-right?' A Guide To The White Nationalist Movement Now Leading Conservative Media," August 25, 2016, https://www.mediamatters.org/blog/2016/08/25/what-Alt-right-guide-white-nationalist-movement-now-leading-conservative-media/212643.

5. See David Neiwert, *Alt-America: The Rise of the Radical Right in the Age of Trump* (New York: Verso Books, 2017), 292. "Right-wing extremism has

always been woven into the American political and social landscape: the nativists, the paranoid conspiracists, the racists, the white supremacists, white nationalists, xenophobes, and misogynists."

6. "It is clear that the Alt-right is much younger, on average, than previous iterations of the racial right in America." Hawley, *Making Sense of the Alt-right*, 77.

7. David Neiwert, "'Ash on the Sills,' The Patriot Movement," *Montana Law Review* 58, no. 1, (1997): 23. Neiwert's description is of the Patriot Movement, but it works just as well for the Alt-right.

8. Southern Poverty Law Center, "Alt-right," https://www.splcenter.org/fighting-hate/extremist-files/ideology/alternative-right.

9. George Hawley, *Making Sense of the Alt-right*, 3.

10. Hawley, *Making Sense of the Alt-right*, 91; see also 18; 60.

11. See Jeffrey C. Isaac, "Charlottesville and Trump: David Duke Explains Neo-Nazi Violence to You," *Public Seminar*, August 12, 2017, http://www.publicseminar.org/2017/08/charlottesville-and-trump/#.WY90NOmQxPZ.

12. Neiwert, *Alt-America*, 216.

13. Neiwert, *Alt-America*, 33.

14. See Julia Melle, "Illogical Extremes: The Sovereign Citizens Movement and the First Amendment," *Temple Political and Civil Rights Law Review* 22, no. 2 (2013): 566.

15. Hawley, *Making Sense of the Alt-right*.

16. Susan P. Koniak, "The Chosen People in Our Wilderness," *Michigan Law Review* 95, no. 6 (1997): 1761, 1764.

17. See Carl Schmitt, *The Concept of the Political*. Translated and with an Introduction by George Schwab; with a Foreword by Tracy B. Strong; and Notes by Leo Strauss (Chicago: University of Chicago Press, 2007). It is worth recalling that Schmitt, the Crown Jurist of the Third Reich, was a scholar of jurisprudence.

18. This was the title of the rally (also known as the Charlottesville rally) in Charlottesville, Virginia, from August 11–12, 2017.

19. Susan P. Koniak, Review of "Rural Radicals" and "Gathering Storm," *Michigan Law Review* 95, no. 6 (1997): 1761.

20. Darren J. Mulloy, *American Extremism: History, Politics, and the Militia Movement* (New York: Routledge, 2004), 78.

21. In addition to Lepore, *Whites of Their Eyes*, 16; see Barkun, *Religion and the Racist Right*; and Mulloy, *American Extremism*, 78; see Angela P. Harris, "Vultures in Eagles Clothing," *Michigan Journal of Law and Race* 10, no. 2 (2005): 269. See also Garry Wills, *Inventing America: Jefferson's Declaration of Independence* (New York: Doubleday, 1978).

22. See generally Hawley, *Making Sense of the Alt-right*; and Neiwert, *Alt-America*.

23. Luke O'Brien, "My Journey to the Center of the Alt-right," *Huffington Post,* November 3, 2016, http://highline.huffingtonpost.com/articles/en/Alt-right/.

24. Howard Winant, "Behind Blue Eyes: Whiteness and Contemporary US Racial Politics," in Michelle Fine, et al., *Off White: Readings on Power, Privilege, and Resistance* 2d ed. (New York: Routledge, 2004), 5–16.

25. Winant "Behind Blue Eyes," 5–16.

26. Audrea Lim, "The Alt-right's Asian Fetish," *New York Times*, January 6, 2018, https://www.nytimes.com/2018/01/06/opinion/sunday/Alt-right-asian-fetish.html.

27. Lim, "The Alt-right's Asian Fetish," 6–7.

28. George Michael, "The Seeds of the Alt-right, America's Emergent Right-wing Populist Movement," *The Conversation*, August 14, 2017, https://theconversation.com/the-seeds-of-the-Alt-right-americas-emergent-right-wing-populist-movement-69036?sg=998c49eb-6937-4773-8331-e12cb52584ac&sp=1&sr=1.

29. Michael, "The Seeds of the Alt-right."

30. O'Brien, "My Journey to the Center of the Alt-right."

31. The phrasing is from Michael Barkun, *Religion and the Racist Right: The Origins of the Christian Identity Movement,* rev. ed. (Chapel Hill: University of North Carolina Press, 1997).

32. Hawley, *Making Sense of the Alt-right*, 101.

33. Jill Lepore, *The Whites of Their Eyes: The Tea Party's Revolution and the Battle over American History* (Princeton: Princeton University Press, 2010), 16.

34. Barkun, *Religion and the Racist Right*, 284.

35. Robert Brent Toplin, *Radical Conservatism: The Right's Political Religion* (Lawrenceville: University Press of Kansas, 2006), 35.

36. Catherine Drinker Bowen, *Miracle at Philadelphia* (Boston: Back Bay Books, 1986). See also Chapter 2.

37. Christopher W. Schmidt, "The Tea Party and the Constitution," *Hastings Constitutional Law Quarterly* 39, no. 1 (2011): 193.

38. I take this up more fully in Chapter 2. See generally Mulloy, *American Extremism*, 42–44.

39. I discuss this more fully in Chapters 2 and 6. See also David Neiwert, *In God's Country: The Patriot Movement and the Pacific Northwest* (Pullman: Washington State University Press, 1999), 11; 35.

40. Vox Day, "Who Killed Conservatism," June 9, 2016, https://vox-day.blogspot.com/2016/06/who-killed-conservatism.html.

41. Richard Spencer, "What It Means to Be Alt-right: A Meta-political Manifesto for the Alt-right Movement," August 11, 2017, https://altright.com/2017/08/11/what-it-means-to-be-Alt-right/.

42. Hawley, *Making Sense of the Alt-right*, 11–50; Neiwert, *Alt-America*.

43. Hawley, *Making Sense of the Alt-right*, 91.

44. Greg Johnson, "George Hawley's Making Sense of the Alt-right," September, 2017, https://www.counter-currents.com/2017/09/george-hawleys-making-sense-of-the-Alt-right/.

45. Umberto Eco, *The Prague Cemetery* (New York: Houghton Mifflin Harcourt, 2011), 342: "Someone said that patriotism is the last refuge of cowards; those without moral principles usually wrap a flag around themselves, and those bastards always talk about the purity of race."

CHAPTER 1. MAPPING THE ALT-RIGHT AND THE LIKE

1. Carl Schmitt, *The Concept of the Political* translated and with an Introduction by George Schwab (Chicago: University of Chicago Press, 2007).

2. See Julie Zauzmer, "You have to be Christian to Truly be American? Many People in the US say so," *Washington Post*, February 1, 2017, https://www.washingtonpost.com/news/acts-of-faith/wp/2017/02/01/you-have-to-be-christian-to-truly-be-american-people-in-the-us-are-far-more-likely-to-say-so/?ICID=ref_fark&tid=sm_fb&utm_content=link&utm_medium =website&utm_source=fark&utm_term=.54b0925e4a4e.

3. "Alt Right: A Primer about the New White Supremacy," https://www.adl.org/education/resources/backgrounders/Alt-right-a-primer-about-the-new-white-supremacy?referrer=https%3A //www.google.com/#.WC0zSforLIU.

4. Alan Rappeport, "From the Right, a New Slur for G.O.P. Candidates," *New York Times*, August 13, 2015, https://www.nytimes.com/2015/08/13/us/from-the-right-a-new-slur-for-gop-candidates.html?_r=0.

5. Olivia Nuzzi, "Five Myths About the Alt-right," November 28, 2016, http://www.chicagotribune.com/news/opinion/commentary/ct-Alt-right-white-supremacy-neo-nazis-20161128-story.html.

6. Alfred W. Clark, "What is a #Cuckservative?" *Occam's Razor,* July 15, 2015, https://occamsrazormag.wordpress.com/2015/07/15/what-is-a-cuckserva-tive-nrx/

7. Oliver Willis, "What is The 'Alt-right'"? A Guide to the White Nationalist Movement Now Leading Conservative Media," August 25, 2016, http://mediamatters.org/blog/2016/08/25/what-Alt-right-guide-white-nationalist-movement-now-leading-conservative-media/212643.

8. Alan Rappeport, "From the Right, a New Slur for G.O.P. Candidates." *New York Times*, August 13, 2015.

9. https://angrywhitemen.org/cucktionary/, March, 2014.

10. https://angrywhitemen.org/cucktionary/, March, 2014.

11. https://www.adl.org/education/resources/backgrounders/Alt-right-a-primer-about-the-new-white-supremacy. The 14 words refer to the expression, "We must secure the existence of our people and a future for white children."

12. http://www.adl.org/combating-hate/domestic-extremism-terrorism/c/Alt-right-a-primer-about-the.html

13. See Dani Di Placido, "'How 'Pepe The Frog' Became A Symbol Of Hatred," *Forbes Magazine,* May 9, 2017, https://www.forbes.com/sites/danidiplacido/2017/05/09/how-pepe-the-frog-became-a-symbol-of-hatred/#1e546e41426b.

14. Pepe first appeared on MySpace, with no racial or anti-Semitic connotations. "Q & A with Matt Furie," Know Your Meme, January 25, 2011, http://knowyourmeme.com/blog/interviews/qa-with-matt-furie.

15. "Hate on Display" Hate Symbols Database," https://www.adl.org/education/references/hate-symbols.

16. "Pepe the Frog Meme Branded a 'Hate Symbol,'" *BBC News,* September 28, 2016, accessed November 16, 2016.

17. Cooper Fleishman and Anthony Smith, "(((Echoes))), Exposed: The Secret Symbol Neo-Nazis Use to Target Jews Online," June 1, 2016, https://mic.com/articles/144228/echoes-exposed-the-secret-symbol-neo-nazis-use-to-target-jews-online#.Z7PywD1GM.

18. "ADL to Add (((Echo))) Symbol, Used by Anti-Semites on Twitter, to Online Hate Symbols Database," June 6, 2016, https://www.adl.org/news/press-releases/adl-to-add-echo-symbol-used-by-anti-semites-on-twitter-to-online-hate-symbols.

19. Mitchell Sunderland, "Can't Shake It Off: How Taylor Swift Became a Nazi Idol: Nazis and members of the 'alt-right' consider Taylor Swift an Aryan pop queen who is "red pilling" America into a race war through her pop hits," May 23, 2016, https://broadly.vice.com/en_us/article/ae5x8a/cant-shake-it-off-how-taylor-swift-became-a-nazi-idol.

20. https://dstormer6em3i4km.onion.link/papa-johns-pizzas-disgusted-with-anti-white-nfl-pulls-ads/.

21. NPR Staff, "What You Need To Know About The Alt-right Movement," August 26, 2016, http://www.npr.org/2016/08/26/491452721/the-history-of-the-Alt-right.

22. George Hawley, *Making Sense of the Alt-right* (New York: Columbia University Press, 2017), 17.

23. Hawley, *Making Sense of the Alt-right,* 17–18.

24.   Kevin Sullivan, "Primed to Fight the Government," *The Washington Post*, May 21, 2016, http://www.washingtonpost.com/sf/national/2016/05/21/armed-with-guns-and-constitutions-the-patriot-movement-sees-america-under-threat/.

25.   "SPLC report: Bundy ranch standoff was highly coordinated, reflecting threat of larger far-right militia movement," July 9, 2014, https://www.splcenter.org/news/2014/07/10/splc-report-bundy-ranch-standoff-was-highly-coordinated-reflecting-threat-larger-far-right. See also George Zornick, "The 12 Scariest Findings in the New Report on the Bundy Ranch Standoff," *The Nation,* July 2014, https://www.thenation.com/article/12-scariest-parts-new-report-bundy-ranch-standoff/.

26.   "SPLC report."

27.   "SPLC report."

28.   Mike Levine, "Feds File Charges against More Alleged Militants Tied to 'Bundy Ranch' Standoff," *ABC News*, March 3, 2016, http://abcnews.go.com/US/feds-file-charges-alleged-militants-tied-bundy-ranch/story?id=37374437.

29.   http://sipseystreetirregulars.blogspot.com/.

30.   Sullivan, "Primed to Fight the Government."

31.   Sullivan, "Primed to Fight the Government."

32.   Sullivan, "Primed to Fight the Government."

33.   Sullivan, "Primed to Fight the Government."

34.   Sullivan, "Primed to Fight the Government."

35.   "About Oath Keepers," https://www.oathkeepers.org/about/.

36.   "About Oath Keepers," https://www.oathkeepers.org/about/.

37.   Elias Alias, "Ten Orders We Will Not Obey," January 25, 2015, https://www.oathkeepers.org/10-orders-we-will-not-obey/.

38.   Quoted in David Neiwert, *Alt-America: The Rise of the Radical Right in the Age of Trump* (New York: Verso Books, 2017), 151.

39.   Neiwert, *Alt-America,* 151. See also Justine Sharrock, "Oath Keepers and the Age of Treason," *Mother Jones*, March, 2010, http://www.motherjones.com/politics/2010/02/oath-keepers/.

40.   "What is the ideology of the Alt Right?," http://www.adl.org/combating-hate/domestic-extremism-terrorism/c/Alt-right-a-primer-about-the.html.

41.   Richard Spencer, "What it Means to be Alt-right," AltRight.com, August 11, 2017, https://altright.com/2017/08/11/what-it-means-to-be-Alt-right/.

42.   https://www.adl.org/education/resources/backgrounders/traditionalist-youth-network#.VrpKqOZkZME.

43.   http://www.adl.org/combating-hate/domestic-extremism-terrorism/c/Alt-right-a-primer-about-the.html.

44. Shane Burley, "Disunite the Right: The Growing Divides in the Pepe Coalition," 2017.

45. For one detailed account of conflict between the Alt-right and the Alt-Lite regarding a free speech rally in Washington, DC, in June, 2017, see Burley, "Disunite the Right: The Growing Divides in the Pepe Coalition," 2017.

46. Luke O'Brien, "My Journey to the Center of the Alt-right," *Huffington Post,* November 3, 2016, http://highline.huffingtonpost.com/articles/en/Alt-right/.

47. Hawley, *Making Sense of the Alt-right*, 144.

48. David Gilmour, "From 'Alt-right' to white supremacy: A guide to far-right terminology," *The Daily Dot,* November 28, 2017, https://www.dailydot.com/layer8/white-supremacy-Alt-right/.

49. Shane Burley, "Disunite the Right: The Growing Divides in the Pepe Coalition," September 19, 2017.

50. Hawley, *Making Sense of the Alt-right*, 148.

51. https://altright.com/author/radix/.

52. https://nationalpolicy.institute/donate-9-15/.

53. Neiwert, *Alt-America*, 244.

54. Chuck Todd, Mark Murray, and Carrie Dann, "The Alt-right is Coming to the White House," November 14, 2016, http://www.nbcnews.com/politics/first-read/Alt-right-coming-white-house-n683456.

55. Stephen Piggot, "Is Breitbart.com Becoming the Media Arm of the 'Alt-right'?" April 28, 2016, https://www.splcenter.org/hatewatch/2016/04/28/breitbartcom-becoming-media-arm-Alt-right (Southern Poverty Law Center).

56. William Hicks, "Meet Hatreon, the New Favorite Website of the Alt-right," *Newsweek,* August 4, 2017, http://www.newsweek.com/hatreon-Alt-right-richard-spencer-andrew-anglin-white-nationalism-white-644546.

57. In keeping with the victimization theme, Alt-righters are remarkably quick to complain when they themselves are doxxed. For several examples, see M. Taylors, *What is the Alt-right?* (Self-published e-book, 2016), 24–26.

58. Tom Porter, "The Alt-right is Using Leaked NATO Psychological Warfare Tactics to Spread White Supremacism Globally," *Newsweek,* October 24, 2017, http://www.newsweek.com/Alt-right-using-leaked-nato-psychological-wafare-tactics-subvert-democracy-and-691457?amp=1&utm_source=fark&utm_medium=website&utm_content=link&ICID=ref_fark.

59. Larry Kohler-Esses, "Group Tied To Accused Charlottesville Killer Purged From Internet," August 14, 2017, http://forward.com/news/breaking-news/379977/the-far-right-group-that-accused-killer-james-fields-rallied-with-has-been/.

60. Andrew Wyrich, "Neo-Nazi site Daily Stormer is back on the web as Punished Stormer," *The Daily Dot,* August 24, 2017, https://www.dailydot.com/layer8/daily-stormer-punished-stormer/.

61. For an overview, see Martin Bouchard, ed., *Social Networks, Terrorism and Counter-terrorism: Radical and Connected* (London: Routledge Press, 2015).

62. See Richard Spencer, "The Conservative Write," *Takimag,* August 6, 2008, http://takimag.com/article/the_conservativewrite#axzz4RUGQpBOE. Spencer acknowledges, though, that the idea was inspired by Paul Gottfried, who himself denies being a member of the Alt-right. See Paul Gottfried, "The Decline and Rise of the Alternative Right," *American Renaissance,* August, 2018, http://www.amren.com/news/2016/08/the-decline-and-rise-of-the-alternative-right.

63. "Whose Alt Right Is It Anyway?" *Southern Poverty Law Center,* August 2018, https://www.splcenter.org/hatewatch/2016/08/25/whose-Alt-right-it-anyway.

64. "Home," The National Policy Institute, http://www.npiamerica.org/.

65. "Richard Bertrand Spencer," *Southern Poverty Law Center,* https://www.splcenter.org/fighting-hate/extremist-files/individual/richard-bertrand-spencer-0.

66. Josh Harikson, "Meet the Dapper White Nationalist Who Wins Even if Trump Loses," *Mother Jones,* October 2016, http://www.motherjones.com/politics/2016/10/richard-spencer-trump-Alt-right-white-nationalist.

67. "Richard Bertrand Spencer," *Southern Poverty Law Center.*

68. Hawley, *Making Sense of the Alt-right,* 59.

69. https://altright.com/.

70. "Richard Bertrand Spencer," *Southern Poverty Law Center* https://www.splcenter.org/fighting-hate/extremist-files/individual/richard-bertrand-spencer-0.

71. Richard B. Spencer, "Exiled," *Radix Journal* http://www.radixjournal.com/journal/2016/7/14/exiled.

72. Hawley, *Making Sense of the Alt-right,* 60-61.

73. David Ng, "Gamergate advocate Milo Yiannopoulos blames feminists for SXSW debacle," *Los Angeles Times,* October 29, 2015, http://www.latimes.com/entertainment/la-et-milo-yiannopoulos-gamergate-feminists-20151028-story.html.

74. Mike Isaac, "Twitter Bars Milo Yiannopoulos in Wake of Leslie Jones's Reports of Abuse," *The New York Times,* July 20, 2016, http://www.nytimes.com/2016/07/20/technology/twitter-bars-milo-yiannopoulos-in-crackdown-on-abusive-comments.html.

75. Elle Hunt, "Milo Yiannopoulos, rightwing writer, permanently banned from Twitter," *The Guardian,* July 20, 2016, https://www.theguardian.com/technology/2016/jul/20/milo-yiannopoulos-nero-permanently-banned-twitter.

76. David Ng, "Gamergate advocate Milo Yiannopoulos blames feminists for SXSW debacle," *Los Angeles Times,* October 29, 2015, http://www.latimes.com/entertainment/la-et-milo-yiannopoulos-gamergate-feminists-20151028-story.html.

77. Hunt, "Milo Yiannopoulos, rightwing writer, permanently banned from Twitter."

78. Elle Hunt, "Milo Yiannopoulos." Nafeez Ahmed, "Milo Yiannopoulos and his far-right support base want the 'freedom' to harass women they disagree with," *Medium,* January 14, 2014, https://medium.com/insurge-intelligence/online-harassment-epidemic-against-women-reveals-a-crisis-of-masculinity-84d979b1ea7b#.d6gp55508.

79. Hunt, "Milo Yiannopoulos."

80. Hawley has a good discussion of the Alt-lite and its differences with the Alt-right, Hawley, *Making Sense of the Alt-right,* 140–148.

81. http://www.wallbuilders.com/ABTOverview.asp.

82. "Influential Evangelicals—David Barton," *Time Magazine,* February 7, 2005, http://content.time.com/time/specials/packages/article/0,28804,1993235_1993243_1993261,00.html.

83. "David Barton: Propaganda Masquerading as History," September, 2006, http://www.rightwingwatch.org/report/david-barton-propaganda-masquerading-as-history/.

84. Bob Smietana, "Thomas Nelson drops 'Jefferson Lies' book over historical errors," *The Tennessean*, August 10, 2012, http://mytnnews.com/blog/2012/08/10/thomas-nelson-drops-jefferson-lies-book-over-historical-errors/.

85. "David Barton: Propaganda Masquerading as History."

86. "David Barton: Propaganda Masquerading as History."

87. Paul Harris, "The Born-Again Birther Debate," *The Guardian,* April 21, 2011, https://www.theguardian.com/commentisfree/cifamerica/2011/apr/21/barack-obama-us-elections-2012.

88. Sullivan, "Founding Fervor," *The Washington Post,* November 6, 2016, http://www.washingtonpost.com/sf/national/2016/11/06/meet-the-woman-who-spends-260-days-a-year-preaching-the-constitution/.

89. Sullivan, "Founding Fervor."

90. Sullivan, "Founding Fervor."

91. Kris Anne Hall, "How Supreme is the Supreme Court?" *Liberty First,* February 11, 2015, http://krisannehall.com/supreme-supreme-court/.

92.   Kevin Sullivan, "Founding Fervor," *The Washington Post,* November 6, 2016, http://www.washingtonpost.com/sf/national/2016/11/06/meet-the-woman-who-spends-260-days-a-year-preaching-the-constitution/.

93.   Kris Anne Hall, "The Origin of American Religious Liberty," *Kris Anne Hall Television Show,* May 4, 2016, http://krisannehall.com/origin-american-religious-liberty/.

94.   Sullivan, "Founding Fervor."

95.   Kris Anne Hall, "Cartoons and Reasonable Speech," *Liberty First,* May 5, 2015, http://krisannehall.com/cartoons-and-reasonable-speech/.

96.   "About Us," *Constitutional Sheriffs and Peace Officers Association,* https://cspoa.org/about/.

97.   Sheriff Richard Mack, *The County Sheriff: America's Last Hope* (self-published, 2009).

98.   "Resolution Drafted by the 2014 Resolution–Constitutional Sheriffs and Peace Officers Association," *Constitutional Sheriffs and Peace Officers Association,* http://cspoa.org/2014-resolution/.

99.   "Resolution Drafted by the 2014 Resolution–Constitutional Sheriffs."

100. Hawley, *Making Sense of the Alt-right,* 159-175.

101. Greg Johnson, "George Hawley's Making Sense of the Alt-right," *Counter-Currents,* September, 2017, https://www.counter-currents.com/2017/09/george-hawleys-making-sense-of-the-Alt-right/.

102. Hawley writes, "People bearing the Alt-Lite label are a frequent target of criticism from both the left and the far right. To the Alt-right, the Alt-Lite is problematic because it threatens to weaken the movement's core message." Hawley, *Making Sense of the Alt-right,* 147.

103. "League of the South," https://en.wikipedia.org/wiki/League_of_the_South.

CHAPTER 2. UNDERSTANDING THE ALT-CONSTITUTION

1.   Gary J. Jacobsohn, *Constitutional Identity* (Cambridge: Harvard University Press, 2010).

2.   See, for example, D.J. Mulloy, *American Extremism: History, Politics, and the Militia Movement* (New York: Routledge, 2004).

3.   Letter from George Washington to Lafayette, (7 February 1788), National Archives Online. https://founders.archives.gov/documents/Washington/04-06-02-0079.

4. Letter from James Madison to Thomas Jefferson (24 October 1787), Papers 10:207–15 http://press-pubs.uchicago.edu/founders/documents/v1ch17s22.html.

5. Warren E. Burger, "Foreword," in Catherine Drinker Bowen, *Miracle At Philadelphia: The Story of the Constitutional Convention May–September 1787* (Boston: Little, Brown, 1986).

6. Jill Lepore, *The Whites of Their Eyes: The Tea Party's Revolution and the Battle over American History* (Princeton: Princeton University Press, 2010), 14–16.

7. For a discussion, see Lawrence Rosenthal and Christine Trost, *Steep: The Precipitous Rise of the Tea Party* (Berkeley: University of California Press, 2012), 259–260.

8. "David Barton—The 25 Most Influential Evangelicals in America," TIME.com, February 7, 2005, http://content.time.com/time/specials/packages/article/0,28804,1993235_1993243_1993261,00.html.

9. Skipp Porteous of the Massachusetts-based Institute for First Amendment Studies reported that Barton was listed as a speaker at a 1991 summer retreat in Colorado sponsored by Scriptures for America, a far-right Christian Identity ministry headed by Pastor Pete Peters, which has been linked to neo-Nazi groups. See Bill Luckett (1997-06-20), "Speaker Accused of Racist Ties: Christian Coalition denies Barton's links to white supremacists," June 20, 1997, (PDF). *Casper Star-Tribune,* archived from the original (PDF) July 18, 2013.

10. https://wallbuilders.com/about-us/.

11. https://wallbuilders.com/constitution-alive/.

12. Ronald Mann, "Introduction," to *The Five Thousand Year Leap: Twenty-Eight Great Ideas That Are Changing the World,* 10th ed., W. Cleon Skousen (Washington, DC: National Center for Constitutional Studies, 1981).

13. Chris Rodda, "No, Mr. Beck, Our Constitution Is Not Based on the Book of Deuteronomy," July 9, 2010, https://www.alternet.org/story/147497/hey_glenn_beck,_our_constitution_is_not_based_on_the_bible.

14. For a more detailed criticism of Barton's work, see also Chris Rodda, "Hey Glenn Beck."

15. For a detailed account, and an important overview of the extreme right's long-standing preoccupation with the Constitution, see Garret Epps, "Stealing the Constitution: Inside the right's campaign to hijack our country's founding text—and how to fight back," *The Nation,* January 20, 2011, https://www.thenation.com/article/stealing-constitution/.

16. See Alexander Zaitchik, "Fringe Mormon Group Makes Myths with Glenn Beck's Help," February 23, 2011, https://www.splcenter.org/fighting-hate/intelligence-report/2011/fringe-mormon-group-makes-myths-glenn-beck%E2%80%99s-help. See also Jeffey Rosen, "Radical Constitutionalism,"

New York Times Magazine, November 26, 2010, http://www.nytimes.com/
2010/11/28/magazine/28FOB-idealab-t.html.

17. https://www.splcenter.org/fighting-hate/intelligence-report/2011/fringe-
mormon-group-makes-myths-glenn-beck%E2%80%99s-help.

18. https://www.splcenter.org/fighting-hate/intelligence-report/2011/fringe-
mormon-group-makes-myths-glenn-beck%E2%80%99s-help.

19. *The Five Thousand Year Leap: Twenty-Eight Great Ideas That Are
Changing the World,* 10th ed. (Washington, DC: National Center for Constitutional Studies, 1981).

20. Sean Wilentz, "ConFounding Fathers: The Tea Party's Cold War
Roots," *The New Yorker,* October 18, 2010, https://www.newyorker.com/maga-
zine/2010/10/18/confounding-fathers.

21. Richard Hofstadter, "The Paranoid Style in American Politics," *Harpers'
Magazine,* November, 1964, https://harpers.org/archive/1964/11/the-paranoid-
style-in-american-politics/.

22. Charles Howard McIlwain, *Constitutionalism: Ancient and Modern,* re-
vised edition (Carmel, IN: Liberty Fund Inc., 2010).

23. McIlwain, *Constitutionalism.*

24. Edward S. Corwin, "The 'Higher Law' Background of American Constitutional Law," *Harvard Law Review* 42, no. 3 (1929): 365.

25. McIlwain, *Constitutionalism.*

26. Corwin, "The 'Higher Law'."

27. Susan P. Koniak, "The Chosen People in our Wilderness," *Michigan
Law Review* 95, no. 6 (1997): 1761, 1777.

28. Letter from Thomas Jefferson to Alexander Donald, 1788, ME 6:425.
National Archive Online, https://founders.archives.gov/documents/Jefferson/
01-12-02-0602.

29. Awr Hawkins, "What Thomas Jefferson Meant by 'Unalienable Rights'"
(September 23, 2013), http://www.breitbart.com/big-government/2013/09/23/
what-did-thomas-jefferson-mean-by-unalienable-rights/.

30. For a nice overview, see Kate Zernike, *Boiling Mad: Behind the Lines in
Tea Party America* (New York: St. Martin's Griffin, 2010), Chapter 4. For a
more extended study, see Christopher W. Schmidt's incisive study of Tea Party
constitutionalism in "The Tea Party and the Constitution," *Hastings Constitutional Law Quarterly* 39, no. 101 (2011): 193.

31. Sotirios A. Barber and James E. Fleming, *Constitutional Interpretation:
The Basic Questions* (New York: Oxford University Press, 2007).

32. The academic literature on originalism is quite good. Leading treat-
ments include Ilan Wurman, *A Debt Against the Living: An Introduction to
Originalism* (New York: Cambridge University Press, 2017); and Jack Balkin,
Living Originalism (Cambridge: Harvard University Press, 2011). See also my

discussion in *Peopling the Constitution* (Lawrence: University Press of Kansas, 2014), 140ff. For an extensive critique, see Terence Ball and JGA Pocock, eds., *Conceptual Change and the Constitution* (Lawrence: University Press of Kansas, 1988).

33. Debra Cassens Weiss, "Justice Thomas fans create website dedicated to his originalist jurisprudence," *American Bar Association Journal,* October 21, 2016, http://www.abajournal.com/news/article/justice_thomas_fans_create_website_dedicated_to_his_originalist_jurisprudence.

34. Robert Brent Toplin, *Radical Conservatism: The Right's Political Religion* (Lawrence: University Press of Kansas, 2006), 20.

35. Cass Sunstein, *Radicals in Robes: Why Right-Wing Courts are Bad for America* (New York: Perseus, 2005), xiv.

36. Walter F. Murphy, "Who Shall Interpret? The Quest for the Ultimate Constitutional Interpreter," *Review of Politics* 43, no. 3 (1986): 401.

37. Theda Skocpol and Vanessa Williams, *The Tea Party and the Remaking of Republican Conservatism* (New York: Oxford University Press, 2016), 50-51. Comparisons between vaguely "Protestant" and "Catholic" approaches to constitutional interpretation are fairly common in academic literature. The seminal piece is by Sandy Levinson, "On Interpretation: The Adultery Clause of the Ten Commandments," *Southern California Law Review* 58, no. 2 (1985): 719; see also Levinson, *Constitutional Faith* (Princeton: Princeton University Press, 2008). See also the nice discussion of this point by Christopher W. Schmidt, "The Tea Party and the Constitution," *Hastings Constitutional Law Quarterly* 39, no. 101 (2011): 193.

38. See note 37. See also D.J. Mulloy, *American Extremism: History, Politics, and the Militia Movement* (New York: Routledge, 2004), 42.

39. http://campconstitution.net/camp-constitution-speakers-bureau/.

40. Interestingly, Barton's work has been roundly criticized by scholars of faith as well, to little effect. For representative treatments, see Greg Forster, "David Barton's Errors," *First Things*, August 8, 2012, https://www.firstthings.com/blogs/firstthoughts/2012/08/david-bartons-errors/; and Warren Throckmorton and Michael Coulter, *Getting Jefferson Right: Fact Checking Claims about Our Third President* (Grove City, PA: Salem Grove Press, 2012). See also Warren Throckmorton's highly regarded blog, in which he frequently covers Barton: http://www.patheos.com/blogs/warrenthrockmorton/.

41. Dahlia Lithwick, "Read It and Weep: How the Tea Party's fetish for the Constitution as written may get it in trouble," *Slate,* January 4, 2011. http://www.slate.com/articles/news_and_politics/jurisprudence/2011/01/read_it_and_weep.html

42. I wasn't serious, but since you're here: https://www.thegreatcourses.com/courses/the-first-amendment-and-you-what-every-one-should-know.html, and https://www.thegreatcourses.com/courses/civil-liberties-and-the-bill-of-rights.html.

43. Pat Buchanan, "Judge Moore & God's Law," September 29, 2017, https://townhall.com/columnists/patbuchanan/2017/09/29/judge-moore--gods-law-n2388179.

44. The Constitution is "an invitation to a struggle for the privilege of directing American foreign policy," Edward S. Corwin, *The President: Office and Powers* 4th rev. ed. (New York: New York University Press, 1957), 171.

45. See David Neiwert, *Alt-America: The Rise of the Radical Right in the Age of Trump* (New York: Verso Books, 2017), 41–44.

46. See, e.g., Steven Calabresi and Christopher Yoo, *The Unitary Executive; Presidential Power from Washington to Bush* (New Haven: Yale University Press, 2008); John Yoo, *The Powers of War and Peace: The Constitution and Foreign Affairs after 9/11* (Chicago: University of Chicago Press, 2005). Criticisms are legion. For a nice overview, see Conor Friedersdorf, "My Debate with John Yoo, Who Misunderstands the Constitution," *The Atlantic Monthly,* December 7, 2011, https://www.theatlantic.com/politics/archive/2011/12/my-debate-with-john-yoo-who-misunderstands-the-constitution/249598/. See also, Helen Duffy, *The War on Terror and the Framework of International Law* (New York: Cambridge University Press, 2005).

47. See note 46.

48. See Jack Goldsmith, *The Terror Presidency: Law and Judgment Inside the Bush Administration* (New York: W. W. Norton, 2007). See also Jack Goldsmith and Eric A. Posner, *The Limits of International Law* (New York: Oxford University Press, 2005). For an extended criticism of such policies from a constitutional perspective, see John E. Finn, "Constitutions & the Judiciary," in *The Consequences of Counterterrorist Policies in Democracies*, ed. Martha Crenshaw (New York: Russell Sage, 2010).

49. Michael S. Schmidt and Michael D. Shear, "Trump Says Russian Inquiry Makes US 'Look Very Bad,'" *The New York Times,* December 29, 2017, https://www.nytimes.com/2017/12/28/us/politics/trump-interview-mueller-russia-china-north-korea.html?hp&action=click&pgtype=Homepage&clickSource=story-heading&module=first-column-region&region=top-news&WT.nav=top-news%5C. (Yes, I know the DOJ is part of the Executive Branch. It's independence of the President is more complicated than that suggests.)

50. On the other hand, John Yoo may have moderated his earlier position a little. See John Yoo, "Executive Power Run Amok," *New York Times,* February 2, 2017, https://www.nytimes.com/2017/02/06/opinion/executive-power-run-amok.html.

51. Chris Rodda, "Hey Glenn Beck, Our Constitution is Not Based on the Bible," July 9, 2010, https://www.alternet.org/story/147497/hey_glenn_beck,_our_constitution_is_not_based_on_the_bible.

52. John E. Finn, "Federalism in Perpetuity: West German and United States Federalism in Comparative Perspective," *New York University Journal of International Law and Policy* 22, no. 1 (1989-1990).

53. See John E. Finn, *Peopling the Constitution* (Lawrence: University Press of Kansas, 2014), especially Essay Two; Robert A. Schapiro, *Polyphonic Federalism: Toward the Protection of Fundamental Rights* (Chicago: University of Chicago Press, 2009); Heather K. Gerken, "A New Progressive Federalism," 24 *Democracy: A Journal of Ideas* 24 (Spring, 2012) https://democracy-journal.org/magazine/24/a-new-progressive-federalism/. For a less sanguine treatment, see Sotirios A. Barber, *The Fallacies of States' Rights* (Cambridge: Harvard University Press, 2013).

54. Letter from James Madison to Richard Peters (19 August 1789). Papers 12:346–48. http://press-pubs.uchicago.edu/founders/documents/v1ch14s53.html.

55. James Madison, *On the Adoption of the Federal Constitution, as Recommended by the General Convention at Philadelphia,* vol. 3, 1787 (Philadelphia: J.B. Lippincott, 1901), 438.

56. Clinton Rossiter, ed., *The Federalist Papers* (Signet: 2003). *Federalist* #44 (Madison).

57. James Madison, "To a Friend of the Union and States Rights," (1833) in *Letters and other Writings of James Madison,* eds. William C. Rives and Philip R. Fendall (Philadelphia: J.B. Lippincott, 1865), IV: 335.

58. Ilya Somin, "Nullification and secession in America," *Washington Post,* December 18, 2016, https://www.washingtonpost.com/news/volokh-conspiracy/wp/2016/12/18/rethinking-nullification-and-secession/?utm_term=.af7b3ef1ee9a; and Sanford Levinson, ed., *Nullification and Secession in Modern Constitutional Thought* (Lawrence: University Press of Kansas, 2016). See also Bradley D. Hays, "A Place for Interposition? What John Taylor of Caroline and the Embargo Crisis Have to Offer Regarding Resistance to the Bush Constitution," *Maryland Law Review* 67, no. 1 (2007): 200. Hays notes that many early uses of interposition involved challenges to executive authority.

59. Ron Chernow, *Alexander Hamilton* (New York: Penguin Press, 2004), 587.

60. Reacting to South Carolina's claims, President Andrew Jackson issued a proclamation calling such an argument (advanced by his Vice President John C. Calhoun), an "impracticable absurdity." https://memory.loc.gov/cgi-bin/ampage?collId=llsl&fileName=011/llsl011.db&recNum=818. Jackson said: "I consider then the power to annul a law of the United States, assumed by one

State, INCOMPATIBLE WITH THE EXISTENCE OF THE UNION, CONTRADICTED EXPRESSLY BY THE LETTER OF THE CONSTITUTION, UNAUTHORIZED BY ITS SPIRIT, INCONSISTENT WITH EVERY PRINCIPLE ON WHICH IT WAS FOUNDED, AND DESTRUCTIVE OF THE GREAT OBJECT FOR WHICH IT WAS FORMED. . . . " Congress subsequently passed the "Force Act," which authorized Jackson to use military force against a state that resisted the tariff acts.

61. http://www.Tenthamendmentcenter.com.

62. http://blog.tenthamendmentcenter.com/2017/08/defining-nullification/.

63. http://tenthamendmentcenter.com/2012/11/14/nullification-in-one-lesson/.

64. "Texas proposal looks to nullify federal law in between state lines," April 28, 2017, http://www.foxnews.com/politics/2017/04/28/texas-proposal-looks-to-nullify-federal-law-in-between-state-lines.html.

65. "Texas proposal looks to nullify federal law in between state lines."

66. Lois Beckett, "Nullification: How States Are Making It a Felony to Enforce Federal Gun Laws," May 2, 2013, https://www.propublica.org/article/nullification-how-states-are-making-it-a-felony-to-enforce-federal-gun-laws.

67. Joe St. George, "Worries over deportation prompt protests in Denver," November 16, 2016, http://kdvr.com/2016/11/16/worries-over-deportation-prompt-protests-in-denver/.

68. Ilya Solmin, "Nullification and secession in America," *Washington Post*, December 18, 2016, https://www.washingtonpost.com/news/volokh-conspiracy/wp/2016/12/18/rethinking-nullification-and-secession/?utm_term=.ce6c718c31e0.

69. Alexander Mooney, "7 years ago Texas governor says secession possible," April 16, 2009, http://politicalticker.blogs.cnn.com/2009/04/16/texas-governor-says-secession-possible/.

70. Evan McMurry, "5 far-right groups trying to secede from America," *Salon*, October 12, 2013, https://www.salon.com/2013/10/12/five_different_culturally_homogenous_secessionist_movements_partner/.

71. Annabelle Tinsit, "5 US Independence Movements Inspired by Brexit," *Politico*, July 4, 2016, https://www.politico.com/magazine/story/2016/07/5-us-independence-movements-inspired-by-brexit-214010.

72. James Poulos, "America's Slumbering Secession Obsession," September 23, 2014, https://www.thedailybeast.com/americas-slumbering-secession-obsession.

73. Scott Malone, "Exclusive: Angry with Washington, 1 in 4 Americans open to secession," September 19, 2014, https://www.reuters.com/article/us-usa-secession-exclusive/exclusive-angry-with-washington-1-in-4-americans-open-to-secession-idUSKBN0HE19U20140919.

74. Poulos, "America's Slumbering Secession Obsession," 2014.

75. Poulos, "America's Slumbering Secession Obsession," 2014.

76. David P. Currie, "Through the Looking Glass: The Confederate Constitution in Congress, 1861–1865," *University of Virginia Law Review* 90, no. 5 (2004): 1257, fn. 39.

77. Walter Williams, "Secession: It's Constitutional,"*American Renaissance,* November 27, 2012, https://www.amren.com/news/2012/11/secession-its-constitutional/.

78. Williams, "Secession: It's Constitutional," 2012.

79. Located here: http://sonoftheoccupiedsouth.blogspot.com/2010/10/declaration-of-southern-cultural.html?m=0. For an incisive discussion, see Paul V. Murphy, *The Rebuke of History: The Southern Agrarians and American Conservative Thought* (Chapel Hill: University of North Carolina Press, 2001), 247–249.

80. See *Hammer v. Dagenhart*, 247 US 251 (1918): "In interpreting the Constitution, it must never be forgotten that the Nation is made up of States to which are entrusted the powers of local government. And to them and to the people the powers not expressly delegated to the National Government are reserved."

81. Daniel Lessard Levin and Malcom W. Mitchell, "A Law Unto Themselves: The Ideology of the Common Law Court Movement," *South Dakota Law Review* 44, no. 9 (1999): 18.

CHAPTER 3. SPEECH FREAKS

1. Vincent Law, "Charlottesville Was A Turning Point For White People In America" (updated title): "The White Civil Rights movement began in Charlottesville," August 13, 2017, https://altright.com/2017/08/13/charlottesville-was-a-turning-point-for-white-people-in-america/.

2. Gwynn Guilford, "The complete story of what happened in Charlottesville, according to the alt-right," August 15, 2017, https:/qz.com/1053220/charlottesville-attack-how-the-violence-unfolded-through-the-eyes-of-the-alt-right.

3. Guilford, "What Happened in Charlottesville."

4. Matthew Sheffields, "Trolling for a race war: Neo-Nazis are trying to bait leftist 'Antifa' activists into violence—and radicalize white people," *Salon Magazine,* April 27, 2017, https://www.salon.com/2017/04/27/trolling-for-a-race-war-neo-nazis-are-trying-to-bait-leftist-antifa-activists-into-violence-and-radicalize-white-people/.

5. Keith E. Whittington, *Speak Freely: Why Universities Must Defend Free Speech* (Princeton: Princeton University Press, 2018).

6. Michael Williams, "3 Texas men who chanted 'Heil Hitler' charged in shooting after Spencer speech,"*Hartford Courant*, October 21, 2017, http://www.courant.com/breaking-news/os-three-arrested-spencer-shooting-20171020-story.html.

7. Sara Sidney and Mallory Simon, "Neo-Nazi site founder says 'troll storm' is protected speech, wants lawsuit dismissed," December 4, 2017, http://www.cnn.com/2017/12/03/us/daily-stormer-troll-storm-lawsuit/index.htm.l

8. Larry Kohler-Esses, "Group Tied to Accused Charlottesville Killer Purged from Internet," August 14, 2017, http://forward.com/news/breaking-news/379977/the-far-right-group-that-accused-killer-james-fields-rallied-with-has-been/.

9. Andrew Wyrich, "Neo-Nazi site Daily Stormer is back on the web as Punished Stormer," *The Daily Dot,* August 24, 2017, https://www.dailydot.com/layer8/daily-stormer-punished-stormer/.

10. For an overview, see Martin Bouchard, ed., *Social Networks, Terrorism and Counter-terrorism: Radical and Connected* (London: Routledge Press, 2015).

11. https://legiscan.com/LA/text/SB364/2018.

12. See Wayne Batchis, *The Right's First Amendment: The Politics of Free Speech and the Return of Conservative Libertarianism* (Stanford: Stanford University Press, 2016).

13. Batchis, *The Right's First Amendment*, 32–34. Batchis argues for a more nuanced set of distinctions with two additional approaches, which he calls "commonsense conservatism" and "free market conservatism."

14. Batchis, *The Right's First Amendment*, see especially Chapters 4–6. For a thoughtful review of the argument, see Ken I. Kersch, "Review," *Law and Politics Book Review* 26, no. 7(2016): 132, http://www.lpbr.net/2016/11/the-rights-first-amendment-politics-of.html.

15. For the argument that speech codes are a violation of the First Amendment, see Azhar Majeed, "Defying the Constitution: The Rise, Persistence, And Prevalence Of Campus Speech Codes," *Georgetown Journal of Law & Public Policy* 7, no. 2 (2009): 481.

16. See *Dambrot v. Central Michigan University*, 55 F.3d 1177 (6th Cir. 1995).

17. *Doe v. University of Michigan*, 721 F. Supp. 852 (E.D. Mich. 1989).

18. For one argument, see Whittington, *Speak Freely*.

19. See Eugene Volokh, "Freedom of Speech, Permissible Tailoring and Transcending Strict Scrutiny," *University of Pennsylvania Law Review* 144, no. 6 (1996): 2417.

20. *Miller v. California*, 413 U.S. 15, 36 (1973) (obscenity); *Chaplinsky v. New Hampshire*, 315 U.S. 568 (1942) (fighting words).

21. See *Williamson v. Lee Optical Co.*, 348 U.S. 483, 490–91 (1955).

22. Only sort of a hypothetical. See John E. Finn, *The Perfect Omelet: Essential Recipes for the Home Cook* (New York: Countryman Press, 2017).

23. Certain elements of the Alt-right, among them Andrew Anglin and *The Daily Stormer*, are famous for perfecting, if not for inventing, the practice of doxxing one's enemies.

24. For two excellent treatments, see Mari Matsuda and Charles Lawrence, *Words that Wound: Critical Race Theory, Assaultive Speech, And The First Amendment* (Boulder: Westview Press, 1993); Jeremy Waldron, *The Harm in Hate Speech* (Cambridge: Harvard University Press, 2014).

25. For examples, see *Chaplinsky, v. New Hampshire*, 315 U.S. 568 (1942) (marketplace of ideas); *Schenck v. United States*, 249 U.S. 47 (1919) (security).

26. See John T. Nockleby, "Hate Speech" in *Encyclopedia of the American Constitution*, eds. Leonard W. Levy and Kenneth L. Karst, vol. 3, 2nd ed. (Detroit: Macmillan Reference, 2000), 1277–79.

27. Nockleby, "Hate Speech," 1277–79.

28. For a different account of the facts, see Gary Blasi and Stephen Shiffrin, "The Real Story of West Virginia Board of Education v. Barnette," in *Constitutional Law Stories*, ed. Michael C. Dorf (Mineola: Foundation Press, 2004), 433.

29. See also *Snyder v. Phelps* (2011), and in particular Justice Alito's dissent, in which he argued that "In order to have a society in which public issues can be openly and vigorously debated, it is not necessary to allow the brutalization of innocent victims like petitioner." Justice Alito's position recalls the "moralistic conservative" approach to speech we considered earlier.

30. Nicholas Stix, "The Death of the First Amendment: More Legal Lynchings of White Men," *VDare*, October 13, 2015, http://www.vdare.com/articles/more-legal-lynchings-of-white-men-and-the-death-of-first-amendment.

31. Stix, "The Death of the First Amendment."

32. Nicholas Stix, "Hate Crimes: Washington's War Against White Working Class Dissent," *VDare*, May 26, 2012, http://www.vdare.com/articles/hate-crimes-washington-s-war-against-white-working-class-dissent.

33. Stix, "Hate Crimes."

34. Stix, "Hate Crimes."

35. Richard Spencer, "What it Means to be Alt-Right," *AltRight.com*, August 11, 2017, https://altright.com/2017/08/11/what-it-means-to-be-alt-right/.

36. Michael Harriot, "Apparently, Free Speech Is a White Privilege," *The Root*, June 6, 2017, https://www.theroot.com/apparently-free-speech-is-a-white-privilege-1795805767. Similar legislation has been proposed in Missouri, Tennessee, South Dakota, and Maryland.

37. Vincent Law, "If You Want Free Speech, Get Rid Of Democracy: But you'll have to surrender political power," *Altright.com*, July 28, 2017, https://altright.com/2017/07/28/if-you-want-free-speech-get-rid-of-democracy/.

38. Victor Ray, "Weaponizing Free Speech," *Inside Higher Education*, July 30, 2017, https://www.insidehighered.com/advice/2017/06/30/right-using-comments-left-wing-professors-delegitimize-higher-ed-essay.

39. Steven W. Thrasher, "Yes, there is a free speech crisis. But its victims are not white men," *The Guardian*, June 5, 2017, https://www.theguardian.com/commentisfree/2017/jun/05/free-speech-advocats-black-women-silenced.

40. See also Chris Quintana and Brock Read, "Signal Boost: How Conservative Media Outlets Turn Faculty Viewpoints Into National News," The Chronicle of Higher Education, June 22, 2017, https://www.chronicle.com/article/Signal-Boost-How-Conservative/240423?cid=wcontentlist_hp_latest.

41. Dan Lieberman, "Death threats are forcing professors off campus," CNN.com, December 21, 2017, http://www.cnn.com/2017/12/21/us/university-professors-free-speech-online-hate-threats/index.html.

42. Quoted in Janet L. Dolgin, "Physician Speech and State Control: Furthering Partisan Interests at the Cost of Good Health," *New England Law Review* 48, no. 2 (2013): 293–314. A federal court declared the statute unconstitutional in *Wollschanger v. Farmer*, 880 F. Supp. 2d 1251 (S.D. Fla. 2012).

43. See Michael J. Lambert, "A Gunman's Paradise: How Louisiana Shields Concealed Handgun Permit Holders While Targeting Free Speech and Why Other States Should Avoid the Same Misfire," *Louisiana Law Review* 75, no. 2 (2014): 544, http://digitalcommons.law.lsu.edu/lalrev/vol75/iss2/11.

44. Eli Rosenberg, "NRA host calls for legislation to limit reporting on mass shooters. Then he says he didn't mean it," *The Denver Post*, May 24, 2018, https://www.denverpost.com/2018/05/24/nra-mass-shooting-reports-media-legislation/.

45. https://wallbuilders.com/separation-church-state/.

46. Frank Guliuzza III, *Over the Wall: Protecting Religious Expression in the Public Square* (Albany: SUNY Press, 2000). For my review, see Finn, "Review," *Law and Politics Book Review* 10, no. 6 (2000): 355–357, http://www.lawcourts.org/LPBR/reviews/guliuzza.htm.

47. Rob Boston, "Hypocrite Alert!: ACLJ Decides Church-State Separation Isn't So Bad After All," September 28, 2007, https://www.au.org/blogs/wall-of-separation/hypocrite-alert-aclj-decides-church-state-separation-isnt-so-bad-after-all.

48. Bryan Fischer, "Islam and the First Amendment: privileges but not rights," *Renew America*, March 24, 2011, http://www.renewamerica.com/columns/fischer/110324.

49. Hemant Mehta, "Bryan Fischer: Muslims Can and Should Be Excluded from Congress," *Patheos,* October 30, 2017, http://www.patheos.com/blogs/friendlyatheist/2017/10/30/bryan-fischer-muslims-can-and-should-be-excluded-from-congress/.

50. In *Torasco v. Watkins* (1961), for example, the Court stated that the establishment clause prevents government from aiding "those religions based on a belief in the existence of God as against those religions founded on different beliefs." In a footnote, the Court clarified that this principle extended to "religions in this country which do not teach what would generally be considered a belief in the existence of God...Buddhism, Taoism, Ethical Culture, Secular Humanism and others." See Jesse H. Choper, "Defining Religion in the First Amendment," *University of Illinois Law Review* 579 (1982). See also Donald P. Kommers; John E. Finn; Gary J. Jacobsohn; George Thomas; and Justin Dyer, eds., *American Constitutional Law: Essays, Cases, Comparative Notes*, 4th ed., (St. Paul: West Academic Publishing, 2018), Chapter 13.

51. *Church of the Lukumi Babalu Aye, Inc. v. Hialeah*, 508 U.S. 520 (1993).

52. Katherine Stewart, "An After School Satan Club could be coming to your kid's elementary school," *Washington Post,* July 30, 2016, https://www.washingtonpost.com/local/education/an-after-school-satan-club-could-be-coming-to-your-kids-elementary-school/2016/07/30/63f485e6-5427-11e6-88eb-7dda4e2f2aec_story.html?utm_term=.08b6ca178d19.

53. Rowena Lindsay, "Should Satanists be allowed to run after-school clubs in public schools?" October 19, 2016, https://www.csmonitor.com/USA/2016/1019/Should-satanists-be-allowed-to-run-after-school-clubs-in-public-schools.

CHAPTER 4. GUN NUTS

1. Chuck Roots, "Roots in Ripon - Are Guns the Problem?" October 16. 2017, http://www.middletowninsider.com/2017/10/roots-in-ripon-are-guns-problem.html#more.

2. Quoted in *Gathering Storm: America's Militia Threat,* by Morris Dees (New York: HarperCollins, 1997), 87.

3. Alan Feuer and Jeremy W. Winters, "Fringe Groups Revel as Protests Turn Violent," *New York Times,* June 2, 2017, https://www.nytimes.com/2017/06/02/us/politics/white-nationalists-alt-knights-protests-colleges.html.

4. Quoted in "New fight club ready for street violence," by Bill Morlin, April 21, 2017, https://www.splcenter.org/hatewatch/2017/04/25/new-fight-club-ready-street-violence.

5. https://www.facebook.com/basedstickman/posts/419732191728122.

6. Amanda Marcotte, "Alt-right hopes to organize street-fighting goon squad: Is it more than macho posturing?" *Salon Magazine,* May 2, 2017, https://www.salon.com/2017/05/02/alt-right-hopes-to-organize-street-fighting-goon-squad-is-it-more-than-macho-posturing/.

7. See David C. Williams, "Constitutional Tales of Violence: Populists, Outgroups, and the Multicultural Landscape of the Second Amendment," *Tulane Law Review* 74, no. 2 (1999): 387–395.

8. B. Bruce-Briggs, "The Great American Gun War," reprinted in *The Gun Control Debate: You Decide*, edited by Lee Nisbet (Buffalo: Prometheus Books, 1990).

9. For an insightful discussion of these cultures, see Williams, "Constitutional Tales of Violence," 395–406.

10. https://townhall.com/columnists/michaelbrown/2017/10/26/since-when-did-jesus-get-connected-to-guns-n2400386.

11. Williams, "Constitutional Tales of Violence," 394.

12. See *United States v. Miller* (1939).

13. For a discussion, see Lawrence B. Solum, "District of Columbia v. Heller and Originalism," *Northwestern Law Review* 103, no. 2 (2009): 939.

14. See Jack Balkin, *Living Originalism* (Cambridge: Harvard University Press, 2011). What originalism means and what it requires is a complicated, contentious matter, sometimes among the justices, and certainly among professors. Randy Barnett, "News Flash: The Constitution Means What it Says," *The Wall Street Journal,* June 27, 2008, https://www.wsj.com/articles/SB121452412614009067.

15. Dennis A. Henigan, "How Justice Stevens May Have Saved Our Gun Laws," *Huffington Post,* June 14, 2010, https://www.huffingtonpost.com/dennis-a-henigan/how-justice-stevens-may-h_b_537412.html.

16. For an overview, see Veronica Rose, "OLR BACKGROUNDER: STATE GUN LAWS AFTER HELLER AND MCDONALD," December 6, 2010, https://www.cga.ct.gov/2010/rpt/2010-R-0455.htm.

17. Max Greenwood, "S.C. Republicans introduce bill to consider secession over gun rights," April 2, 2018, http://thehill.com/homenews/state-watch/382003-south-carolina-house-republicans-introduce-bill-to-consider-secession.

18. Sharon LaFraniere, Sarah Cohen, and Richard A. Oppel, Jr., "How often do Mass Shootings Occur? On Average, Every Day, Records Show," *New York Times,* December 2, 2015, https://www.nytimes.com/2015/12/03/us/how-often-do-mass-shootings-occur-on-average-every-day-records-show.html.

19. For a sample, see the Comments Section that accompanies Awr Hawkins, "Sen. Chris Murphy: Congress Must 'Get Off Its Ass' and Restrict 2nd Amendment," *Breitbart.com,* October 2, 2017, http://www.breitbart.com/big-government/2017/10/02/sen-chris-murphy-congress-restrict-2nd-amendment/.

20. John Paul Stevens, "Repeal the Second Amendment," *The New York Times,* March 22, 2018, https://www.nytimes.com/2018/03/27/opinion/john-paul-stevens-repeal-second-amendment.html.

21. Mike Maharrey, "The Right to Keep and Bear Arms is a Natural Right, not a Constitutional Right," May 4, 2016, https://gunowners.org/oped05042016.htm.

22. http://www.sheriffbrigadesofpenn.com/.

23. http://www.sheriffbrigadesofpenn.com/.

24. http://www.sheriffbrigadesofpenn.com/wp-content/uploads/2012/12/Our-Right-To-Bear-Arms-Is-A-God-Given-Right.pdf.

25. For a general discussion of unconstitutional constitutional amendments, see Yaniv Roznai, *Unconstitutional Constitutional Amendments: The Limits of Amendment Powers* (New York: Oxford University Press, 2017); Gary Jacobsohn, "An unconstitutional constitution? A comparative perspective," *International Journal of Constitutional Law* 4, no. 3 (2006): 460–487; John E. Finn, *Constitutions in Crisis: Political Violence and the Rule of Law* (New York: Oxford University Press, 1991).

26. David C. Williams, "The Militia Movement and the Second Amendment Revolution: Conjuring with the People," *Cornell Law Review* 81, no. 4 (1996): 879–947.

27. Kevin Sullivan, "Primed to Fight the Government," *Washington Post,* May 21, 2016, http://www.washingtonpost.com/sf/national/2016/05/21/armed-with-guns-and-constitutions-the-patriot-movement-sees-america-under-threat/?utm_term=.ef93215d2167

28. Sullivan, "Primed to Fight the Government."

29. Sullivan, "Primed to Fight the Government."

30. Sullivan, "Primed to Fight the Government."

31. Chip Berlet, "From Tea Parties to Militias," in *Right-Wing Radicalism Today: Perspectives from Europe and the US,* edited by Sabine von Mering and Timothy Wyman McCarty (London: Routledge, 2013), 150.

32. "Militia members arrested in alleged plot targeting Muslims," *CBS News,* October 14, 2016, https://www.cbsnews.com/news/militia-members-arrested-mosque-attack-plot/. For a detailed account, see Jessica Pressler, "The Plot to Bomb Garden City, Kansas," *New York Magazine,* December 12, 2017, http://nymag.com/daily/intelligencer/2017/12/a-militias-plot-to-bomb-somali-refugees-in-garden-city-ks.html.

33. Casey Michael, "How Militias Became the Private Police for White Supremacists," *Politico,* August 17, 2017, https://www.politico.com/magazine/story/2017/08/17/white-supremacists-militias-private-police-215498.

34. See "Oath Keepers Promise to Patrol the Polls on Election Day," *Hatewatch*, October 26, 2016, https://www.splcenter.org/hatewatch/2016/10/26/oath-keepers-promise-patrol-polls-election-day.

35. "Foreword," Richard Abanes, *American Militias: Rebellion, Racism, and Religion* (Downers Grove, Illinois: InterVarsity Press, 1996), ix.

36. Richard Abanes, *American Militias,* 2.

37. Richard Abanes, *American Militias,* 2.

38. Berlet, "From Tea Parties to Militias," 2013.

39. Berlet, "From Tea Parties to Militias," 12. (Emphasis in original.)

40. Berlet, "From Tea Parties to Militias," 62.

41. See Darren J. Mulloy, *American Extremism: History, Politics and the Militia Movement* (New York: Routledge, 2004), 2ff.

42. Jonathan Karl, *The Right to Bear Arms: The Rise of America's New Militias* (New York: Harpers, 1995).

43. In some ways this reflects the thinking of the anti-Federalists, who generally believed that state and local governments would be less disposed to violating rights or infringing upon the liberties of their citizens. David C. Williams, "Constitutional Tales of Violence: Populists, Outgroups, and the Multicultural Landscape of the Second Amendment," *Tulane Law Review* 74, no. 2 (1999): 387, 891.

44. Williams, "Constitutional Tales of Violence," 887–904.

45. Robert Brent Toplin, *Radical Conservatism: The Right's Political Religion* (Lawrenceville: University Press of Kansas, 2006), 38.

46. Berlet, "From Tea Parties to Militias," 129.

47. Lisa Ling, "What this American militia leader wants you to know," *CNN,* October 22, 2017, http://www.cnn.com/2017/10/19/us/lisa-ling-militia-member-interview-this-is-life/index.html.

48. David Neiwert, *Alt-America: The Rise of the Radical Right in the Age of Trump* (New York: Verso Books, 2017), 104-107.

49. Neiwert, *Alt-America,* 39.

50. Thomas Halpern, "The Militia Movement," in Thomas Halpern and Brian Levin, *The Limits of Dissent: The Constitutional Status of Armed Civilian Militias* (Amherst, Ma.: Aletheia Press, 1996), 12.

51. For a discussion of the connections between the Second and Fifth Amendments, see Francis X. Sullivan, "The Usurping Octopus of Jurisdictional Authority: The Legal Theories of the Sovereign Citizens Movement," *University of Wisconsin Law Review* (1999).

52. David Neiwert, "Antigovernment 'Patriots' Gather Near Scene of Nevada Rancher's Dispute Over Cattle Grazing Rights," Southern Poverty Law Center, April 10, 2014, https://www.splcenter.org/hatewatch/2014/04/10/anti-

government-patriots-gather-near-scene-nevada-ranchers-dispute-over-cattle-grazing

53. Alan W. Bock, "Ambush at Ruby Ridge How government agents set Randy Weaver up and took his family down," Reason.com, October 1, 1993, http://reason.com/archives/1993/10/01/ambush-at-ruby-ridge

54. Michael Barkun, *Religion and the Racist Right* rev. ed. (Chapel Hill: University of North Carolina Press, 1997), xi.

55. There are subtle but important differences among some of Identity's most influential advocates. For a nuanced discussion of these differences, see Barkun, *Religion and the Racist Right,* 200–209.

56. For an interesting discussion of conservative affinity for certain moral values, including sanctity, loyalty, and authority, see Jonathan Haidt, *The Righteous Mind: Why Good People Are Divided by Politics and Religion* (New York: Vintage, 2012).

57. Neil Gotunda, "A Critique of 'Our Constitution is Color-Blind,'" *Stanford Law Review* 44, no. 1 (1991). For a discussion of how color-blind constitutionalism is a part of color-blind ideology more generally, see Anita Tijerina Revilla, Amy Stuart Wells, and Jennifer Jellison Holme, "We Didn't See Color: The Salience of Color Blindness in Desegregated Schools," in *Off White: Readings on Power, Privilege, and Resistance*, 2nd ed., edited by Micelle Fine, Lois Weiss, Linda Powell Pruitt, and April Burns (New York: Routledge, 2004), 288–289.

58. Brian Levin, "Militias and the Constitution," in *The Limits of Dissent: The Constitutional Status of Armed Civilian Militias*, Thomas Halpern and Brian Levin, (Amherst, MA: Aletheia Press, 1996), 35.

59. Sullivan, "The Usurping Octopus of Jurisdictional Authority," 36.

60. Robert J. Spitzer, "Private militias are not a legitimate expression of Second Amendment rights," Syracuse.com, August 18, 2017, http://www.syracuse.com/opinion/index.ssf/2017/08/private_militias_are_not_a_legitimate_expression_of_second_amendment_rights_comm.html.

61. http://www.imdb.com/title/tt0088689/trivia.

62. Levin, "Militias and the Constitution," 88.

63. The most famous exposition of the difference between advocacy and incitement is *Brandenburg v. Ohio*, 395 U.S. 444 (1969).

64. Levin, "Militias and the Constitution," 91.

65. *Brandenburg v. Ohio*, 395 U.S. 444 (1969). In many cases, the distinction is a matter of judgment. For a discussion in the case of militias, see Isaac Molnar, "Resurrecting the Bad Tendency Test to Combat Instructional Speech: Militias Beware," *Ohio State Law Journal* 59, no. 4 (1998): 1333.

66. The true threats doctrine is an especially complicated area in First Amendment jurisprudence. See *Elonis v. United States*, 575 US___(2015).

67. Sara Rathod, "Why the Law Turns a Blind Eye to Militias," *Mother Jones*, October 25, 2016, http://www.motherjones.com/politics/2016/10/para-military-militia-laws-training./

68. Rathod, "Why the Law Turns a Blind Eye to Militias."

69. Rathod, "Why the Law Turns a Blind Eye to Militias."

70. Levin, "Militias and the Constitution," 82.

71. Williams, "Constitutional Tales of Violence," 887–904.

72. Williams, "Constitutional Tales of Violence," 904–924.

73. For one example, see https://www.oathkeepers.org/thinking-outside-de-bate-parameters-imposed-others/.

74. Tench Coxe, *The Pennsylvania Gazette* (February 20, 1788), http://thef-ederalistpapers.org/founders/others/tenche-coxe-the-pennsylvania-gazette-feb-20-1788.

75. It is dated, but still one of the best treatments is Melville B. Nimmer, "The Meaning of Symbolic Speech under the First Amendment," *University of California Los Angeles Law Review* 21, no. 1 (1973–1974): 29–62.

76. The leading case is *Employment Division v. Smith*, 494 U.S. 872 (1990), in which Justice Scalia, writing for a majority, held that "neutral" state laws that have a significant effect upon the free exercise of religion should be judged using the lowly rationality test.

77. See Neiwert, *Alt-America*, 137–160.

78. See Kevin Sullivan, "Primed to Fight the Government," *Washington Post*, May 21, 2016, http://www.washingtonpost.com/sf/national/2016/05/21/armed-with-guns-and-constitutions-the-patriot-movement-sees-america-under-threat/?utm_term=.ef93215d2167

CHAPTER 5. COMMON LAW COURTS AND SOVEREIGN CITIZENS

1. Bill Morlin, "Antigovernment Extremists in Oregon Now Plan Their Own Justice System," Southern Poverty Law Center, January 13, 2016, https://www.splcenter.org/hatewatch/2016/01/13/antigovernment-extremists-oregon-now-plan-their-own-justice-system.

2. Betsy Hammond, "Self-appointed 'judge' arrives in Burns to ask local residents to charge government officials with crimes," *The Oregonian*, January 12, 2016, http://www.oregonlive.com/oregon-standoff/2016/01/self-ap-pointed_judge_arrives_i.html#incart_river_index.

3. Staff, "Members of Fake Courts Are Facing Real Jail Time," April 12, 2017, https://www.splcenter.org/hatewatch/2017/04/12/members-fake-courts-are-facing-real-jail-time.

4. Staff, "Members of Fake Courts Are Facing Real Jail Time."

5. Morlin, "Antigovernment Extremists in Oregon."

6. Morlin, "Antigovernment Extremists in Oregon."

7. Daniel Lessard Levin and Michael W. Mitchell, "A Law unto Themselves: The Ideology of the Common Law Court Movement," *South Dakota Law Review* 44, no. 1 (1999): 9–15.

8. David H. Bennett, *The Party of Fear* (Chapel Hill: University of North Carolina Press, 1988), 353.

9. Catherine McNicol Stock, *Rural Radicals: Righteous Rage in the American Grain* (Ithaca: Cornell University Press, 1996), 171.

10. For a discussion of some of its constituent parts, see Michael Barkun, *Religion and the Racist Right: The Origins of the Christian Identity Movement,* 2nd ed. (Chapel Hill: University of North Carolina Press, 1997), 207 ff.

11. Levin and Mitchell, "A Law unto Themselves," 9–15.

12. James Corcoran, *Bitter Harvest: Gordon Kahl and the Posse Comitatus: Murder in the Heartland* (New York: Viking Press, 1990).

13. Corcoran, *Bitter Harvest*.

14. "New Yorker Claims National Network of Pseudo-Legal Grand Juries," https://www.splcenter.org/fighting-hate/intelligence-report/2014/new-yorker-claims-national-network-pseudo-legal-grand-juries

15. https://www.nationallibertyalliance.org/nla-plan

16. In the 1990s, the ADL "estimated that about one-half of all common law court members had strong ties to militias." See ADL Releases Report on Militia Activity, *U.S. Newswire*, April 17, 1997. See also Francis X. Sullivan, "The Usurping Octopus of Jurisdictional Authority: The Legal Theories of the Sovereign Citizen Movement," *Wisconsin Law Review* 43 (1999).

17. "27 States Act Against Antigovernment Movement's Common Law Courts," SPLC Center, June 15, 1998, https://www.splcenter.org/fighting-hate/intelligence-report/1998/27-states-act-against-antigovernment-movement%E2%80%99s-common-law-courts.

18. Brian Levin, "Militias and the Constitution," in *The Limits of Dissent: The Constitutional Status of Armed Civilian Militias,* Thomas Halpern and Brian Levin (Amherst, MA: Aletheia Press, 1996), 105. See also Sullivan, "The Usurping Octopus of Jurisdictional Authority."

19. "27 States Act Against Antigovernment Movement's Common Law Courts," SPLC Center, June 15, 1998.

20. Leonard Zeskind, "Basis of Freemen's Philosophy is Racism," June 15, 1998, https://www.splcenter.org/fighting-hate/intelligence-report/1998/basis-freemen%E2%80%99s-philosophy-racism.

21. Sullivan, "The Usurping Octopus of Jurisdictional Authority."

22. "Common-Law Victims," SPLC Center, June 15, 1998, https://www.splcenter.org/fighting-hate/intelligence-report/1998/common-law-victims.

23. Levin and Mitchell, "A Law unto Themselves," 32.

24. Levin and Mitchell, "A Law unto Themselves," 29.

25. "27 States Act Against Antigovernment Movement's Common Law Courts," SPLC Center, June 15, 1998.

26. "27 States Act Against Antigovernment Movement's Common Law Courts," SPLC Center, June 15, 1998.

27. Levin and Mitchell, "A Law unto Themselves," 33–34.

28. "Common-Law Victims," June 15, 1998, https://www.splcenter.org/fighting-hate/intelligence-report/1998/common-law-victims.

29. Lorelei Laird, "'Sovereign citizens' plaster courts with bogus legal filings—and some turn to violence," *American Bar Association Journal*, May 14, 2014, http://www.abajournal.com/magazine/article/sovereign_citizens_plaster_courts_with_bogus_legal_filings/.

30. Laird, "'Sovereign citizens' plaster courts with bogus legal filings."

31. "27 States Act Against Antigovernment Movement's Common Law Courts," SPLC Center, June 15, 1998.

32. "27 States Act Against Antigovernment Movement's Common Law Courts," SPLC Center, June 15, 1998.

33. Quoted in Levin and Mitchell, "A Law unto Themselves," 9.

34. Susan P. Koniak, "Review of Rural Radicals and Gathering Storm," *Michigan Law Review* 95 (1997).

35. See *Greenstreet v. Heiskell*, 940 S.W.2d 831 (Tx. Ct. App. 1997).

36. *Hilgeford v. Peoples Bank, Inc.*, 652 F. Supp. 230 (N.D. 1986).

37. *Vella v. McCammon*, 671 F. Supp. 1128, 1129 (S.D. Tex. 1987).

38. Daryl Johnson, "Hate in God's Name," September 25, 2017, https://www.splcenter.org/20170925/hate-god%E2%80%99s-name

39. Johnson, "Hate in God's Name."

40. Staff, "New Multi-Million Dollar Scam Takes off in Antigovernment Circles," (December 18, 2002.) https://www.splcenter.org/fighting-hate/intelligence-report/2002/new-multi-million-dollar-scam-takes-antigovernment-circles

41. "27 States Act Against Antigovernment Movement's Common Law Courts," SPLC Center, June 15, 1998.

42. "Common-Law Groups," June 13, 2002, https://www.splcenter.org/fighting-hate/intelligence-report/2000/common-law-groups.

43. Staff, "New Multi-Million Dollar Scam Takes off in Antigovernment Circles," December 18, 2002, https://www.splcenter.org/fighting-hate/intelligence-report/2002/new-multi-million-dollar-scam-takes-antigovernment-circles.

44. Wilson Huhn, "Political Alienation in America and the Legal Premises of the Patriot Movement," *Gonzaga Law Review* 34, no. 3 (1999): 417, 421–422.

45. See, for example, Robert W. Wangrud; Randy L. Geiszler; Gerald A. Koellermeier, Sr.; Edward J. Arlt; "PREAMBLE to the UNITED STATES CONSTITUTION: Who Are the Posterity?," Behold! Newsletter—1986, http://www.beholdonline.info/essays/preamble.html. For additional examples, see Leonard Zeskind, *Blood and Politics: The History of the White Nationalist Movement from the Margins to the Mainstream* (New York: Farrar, Strauss, and Giroux, 2012), 80–81.

46. Leonard Zeskind, "Basis of Freemen's Philosophy is Racism," June 15, 1998, https://www.splcenter.org/fighting-hate/intelligence-report/1998/basis-freemen%E2%80%99s-philosophy-racism.

47. Attributed to William Penn, but to my knowledge not verified. See James H. Billington, *Respectfully Quoted: A Dictionary of Quotations* (Mineola, NY: Dover Publications, 2010), 145.

48. *National Alliance Handbook*, 46.

49. For more detail, see Levin and Mitchell, "A Law unto Themselves," 15.

50. Wes Burnett, "This Court Is Different . . . It Is the Court of the People," *Republic of Texas Magazine,* June 1996, in "If at First You Don't Secede: Ten Reasons Why the 'Republic of Texas' Movement Is Wrong," James W. Paulsen, *South Texas Law Review* 38, no. 2 (1997): 801, 821.

51. For a useful overview, see Julia Melle, "Illogical Extremes: The Sovereign Citizens Movement and the First Amendment," *Temple Political and Civil Rights Law Review* 22, (2013): 554–556.

52. Melle, "Illogical Extremes," 583.

53. Max Weber, *Politics as a Vocation* (Munich: Duncker & Humboldt, 1919).

54. Laird, "'Sovereign citizens' plaster courts with bogus legal filings."

55. Sullivan, "The Usurping Octopus of Jurisdictional Authority," 162.

56. Maegan Vazquez, "Sessions invokes 'Anglo-American heritage' of sheriff's office," CNN.com, February 12, 2018, http://www.cnn.com/2018/02/12/politics/jeff-sessions-anglo-american-law-enforcement/index.html.

57. Levin and Mitchell, "A Law unto Themselves."

58. Levin and Mitchell, "A Law unto Themselves," 9.

59. Levin and Mitchell, "A Law unto Themselves," 20.

60. See Eugene Schroder and Micki Nellis, *Constitution: The Story of the Nation's Descent from a Constitutional Republic Through a Constitutional Dictatorship to an Unconstitutional Dictatorship: Fact Or Fiction* (Buffalo Creek Press, 2000), 68–69. Also cited in Levin and Mitchell, "A Law unto Themselves," 20–21, 85.

61. It predates the 2014 and 2016 incidents, but the point is made well in Lane Crothers, *Rage on the Right: The American Militia Movement from Ruby Ridge to Homeland Security* (Lanham, MD: Rowman & Littlefield, 2004).

62. Laird, "'Sovereign citizens' plaster courts with bogus legal filings."

63. Levin and Mitchell, "A Law unto Themselves," 35.

64. On magical thinking in general, see J. Eric Oliver and Thomas J. Wood, "Conspiracy Theories and the Paranoid Style(s) of Mass Opinion," *American Journal of Political Science* 58, no. 4 (2014): 952. On conspiratorial thinking, see Cass R. Sunstein and Adam Vermeule, "Conspiracy Theories," *Political Philosophy* 17, no. 2 (2009): 202.

65. "The Great IRS Hoax," https://famguardian.org/Publications/GreatIRSHoax/GreatIRSHoax.htm

66. "The Great IRS Hoax."

67. Irwin Schiff, "Pay no income tax—Home Page," 2007, http://www.paynoincometax.com/.

68. See Levin and Mitchell, "A Law unto Themselves," 37. See also *McLaughlin v. Commissioner*, 832 F.2d 986, 987 (7th Cir. 1987).

69. *United States v. Drefke*, 707 F.2d 978, 983 (8th Cir. 1983).

70. See, for example, *Parker v. Commissioner*, 724 F.2d 469, 471 (5th Cir. 1984).

71. As quoted in *United States v. Collins*, 920 F.2d 619, 621 (10th Cir. 1990).

72. Christopher S. Jackson, "The Inane Gospel of Tax Protest: Resist Rendering Unto Caesar--Whatever His Demands," *Gonzaga Law Review* 32, no. 391 (1996–97): 291–308.

73. Rob Nugent, "The Income Tax Violates the Thirteenth Amendment," https://steemit.com/taxation/@randr10/the-income-tax-violates-the-thirteenth-amendment.

74. *Porth v. Brodrick*, 214 F.2d 925 (10th Cir. 1954).

75. See the fascinating article by Jol A. Silversmith, "The Missing Thirteenth Amendment: Constitutional Nonsense and Titles of Nobility," *Southern California Interdisciplinary Law Review* 8 (1999): 577. See also Scott Bomboy, "The case of the missing 13th amendment to the Constitution," December 6, 2016, https://constitutioncenter.org/blog/the-case-of-the-missing-13th-amendment-to-the-constitution.

76. Scott Bomboy, "The case of the missing 13th amendment to the Constitution," December 6, 2016, https://constitutioncenter.org/blog/the-case-of-the-missing-13th-amendment-to-the-constitution.

77. For "taxpayer," see *United States v. Smith* 1991 WL 326647 (M.D. Ala., December 30, 1991). For "person," see *United States v. Singer*, 1990 WL 161258 (E.D. Pa., October18, 1990).

78. For an overview of the main legal tenets of SCM, see Michelle Theret, "Sovereign Citizens: A Homegrown Terrorist Threat and its Negative Impact on South Carolina," *South Carolina Law Review* 63 (2012): 853.

79. "Order Denying Motion to Correct Clear Error," *United States v. Jared S. Fogle* (US Dist. Crt, S.D. Indiana, November 11, 2017), https://www.courthousenews.com/wp-content/uploads/2017/11/JaredFogle.pdf.

80. "What is a 'Sovereign Citizen'?" November 11, 2008, https://www.splcenter.org/fighting-hate/intelligence-report/2015/what-sovereign-citizen.

81. Johnson, "Hate in God's Name."

82. Laird, "'Sovereign citizens' plaster courts with bogus legal filings."

83. Sarah Burge, "TEMECULA: 'Sovereign citizen' who reclaimed foreclosed home sentenced," *The Press Enterprise,* January 10, 2014, http://www.pe.com/2014/01/10/temecula-8216sovereign-citizen8217-who-reclaimed-foreclosed-home-sentenced.

84. https://www.splcenter.org/search?keyword=sovereign%20citizen&page=3.

85. Yereth Rosen, "Alaska couple admits to plot to kill federal judge and others," August 8, 2012, https://www.reuters.com/article/us-usa-militia-alaska/alaska-couple-admits-to-plot-to-kill-federal-judge-and-others-idUS-BRE87R03K20120828.

86. Johnson, "Hate in God's Name."

87. Johnson, "Hate in God's Name."

88. Spencer Dew and Jamie Wight, "God's Law: Universal Truth According to Religious Sovereign Citizens," October 15, 2015, https://divinity.uchicago.edu/sightings/gods-law-universal-truth-according-religious-sovereign-citizens.

89. "Sovereign Citizens Movement," https://www.splcenter.org/fighting-hate/extremist-files/ideology/sovereign-citizens-movement.

90. In addition to the Introduction and Chapter 2, see Richard Abanes, *American Militias: Rebellion, Racism, and Religion* (Downers Grove, IL: InterVarsity Press, 1996), 29–30.

91. J.M. Berger, "Without Prejudice: What Sovereign Citizens Believe," June, 2016, https://extremism.gwu.edu/sites/extremism.gwu.edu/files/downloads/JMB%20Sovereign%20Citizens.pdf

92. For examples taken from primary sources, see Richard Abanes, *American Militias: Rebellion, Racism, and Religion* (Downers Grove, IL: Inter-Varsity Press, 1996), 32-34.

93. "Sovereign Citizens Movement," https://www.splcenter.org/fighting-hate/extremist-files/ideology/sovereign-citizens-movement.

94. Levin and Mitchell, "A Law unto Themselves," 23–24.

95. Johnson, "Hate in God's Name."

96. http://www.embassyofheaven.org/vt_questions.htm.

97. http://www.embassyofheaven.org/vt_questions.htm.

98. "Sovereign Citizens Movement," https://www.splcenter.org/fighting-hate/extremist-files/ideology/sovereign-citizens-movement.

99. "Sovereign Citizens Movement."

100. The phrase is from Jeremy Bentham, talking about natural rights. Jeremy Bentham, *The Works of Jeremy Bentham*, vol. 2, *Judicial Procedure, Anarchical Fallacies*, works on *Taxation* (London: Simpkin, Marshall and CO., 1843).

101. Office of Associate Chief Counsel (Procedure and Administration), Administrative Provisions and Judicial Practice Division (2005-04-04). "Rev. Rul. 2005–21." Internal Revenue Service, https://www.irs.gov/irb/2005-14_IRB#RR-2005-21.

CHAPTER 6. INAUTHENTIC AND ILLEGITIMATE

1. For a discussion of the "authentic constitution" from an "originalist" perspective, see Arthur E. Palumbo, *The Authentic Constitution: An Originalist View of America's Legacy* (New York: Algora Press, 2009).

2. See John E. Finn, "Some Notes on Inclusive Constitution-Making, Citizenship, and Civic Constitutionalism," in *Comparative Constitutional Theory,* edited by Gary J. Jacobsohn and Miguel Schor (Cheltenham: Edward Elgar Publishing, 2018), 436–455.

3. For a discussion of cultural secession, see Paul V. Murphy, *The Rebuke of History: The Southern Agrarians and American Conservative Thought* (Chapel Hill: University of North Carolina, 2001), 248.

4. Southern Poverty Law Center, "Attacking the 14th Amendment," September 15, 2000, https://www.splcenter.org/fighting-hate/intelligence-report/2000/attacking-14th-amendment.

5. "A proposed Thirteenth Amendment to prevent secession, 1861," https://www.gilderlehrman.org/content/proposed-thirteenth-amendment-prevent-secession-1861.

6. Comment, "Unorthodox and Paradox: Revisiting the Ratification of the Fourteenth Amendment," *University of Alabama Law Review* 53 (2002): 555.

7. Andrew Kaczynski, "Roy Moore in 2011: Getting rid of amendments after 10th would 'eliminate many problems'," CNN.com, December 11, 2017, http://www.cnn.com/2017/12/10/politics/kfile-roy-moore-aroostook-watchmen/index.html.

8. Kaczynski, "Roy Moore in 2011."

9. Harold Holzer, ed., *The Lincoln-Douglas Debates: The First Complete, Unexpurgated Text* (New York: Harper Collins, 1993), 54; 252.

10. For an insightful decision, see Mark A. Graber, *Dred Scott and the Problem of Constitutional Evil* (New York: Cambridge University Press, 2008).

11. Eric Foner, "Birthright Citizenship Is the Good Kind of American Exceptionalism," *The Nation,* August 27, 2015, https://www.thenation.com/article/birthright-citizenship-is-the-good-kind-of-american-exceptionalism/.

12. Patrick J. Buchanan, "Is America Still a Nation,"? *Taki's Magazine,* July 4, 2017, http://takimag.com/article/is_america_still_a_nation_patrick_buchanan#axzz4s66tLeVX.

13. Jon Harrison Sims, "Racial Unity and the American Republic," *American Renaissance,* November, 2011, https://www.amren.com/features/2011/11/racial-unity-american-republic/.

14. Sam T. Francis, "Race and the American Identity," *American Renaissance,* December, 1998, https://www.amren.com/news/2017/07/race-american-identity/.

15. Vox Day and John Red Eagle, *Cuckservative: How "Conservatives" Betrayed America* (Kouvola, Finland: Castalia House, 2015).

16. Thomas Jefferson's concept of equality only ran so far, as evidenced not only by his ownership of slaves (and his stance regarding manumission), but also by his comments in "Notes on the State of Virginia," http://docsouth.unc.edu/southlit/jefferson/jefferson.html.

17. http://www.youtube.com/watch?v=CJ3B6L2fUA8.

18. See George M. Fredrickson, *White Supremacy: A Comparative Study in American and South African History* (New York: Oxford University Press, 1981), 145.

19. Quoted in Linda Qiu, "Donald Trump's campaign manager: 400,000 'anchor babies' born in US every year," August 23, 2015, http://www.politifact.com/truth-o-meter/statements/2015/aug/23/corey-lewandowski/donald-trumps-campaign-manager-says-there-are-4000/.

20. Seyward Darby, "The Rise of the Valkyries: In the alt-right, women are the future, and the problem," *Harper's Magazine,* September 17, 2017. https://harpers.org/archive/2017/09/the-rise-of-the-valkyries/.

21. See Paul Bedard, "Census: Whites become 'minority' in 2044, Hispanic population twice blacks," *Washington Examiner*, December 15, 2014, http://www.washingtonexaminer.com/census-whites-become-minority-in-2044-hispanic-population-twice-blacks/article/2557393. See also Doug G. Ware, "Census: White children to become minority by 2020," *UPI*, March 5, 2015, https://www.upi.com/Top_News/US/2015/03/05/Census-White-children-to-become-minority-by-2020/9751425612082/.

22. See, for example, Edwin S. Rubenstein, "The Economic Case for an Immigration Moratorium," *VDARE*, March 3, 2011, http://www.vdare.com/articles/the-economic-case-for-an-immigration-moratorium.

23. Edwin S. Rubenstein, "Ending Birthright Citizenship Would Halve GOP Drift to Demographic Disaster in California. What Are We Waiting For?" *VDARE*, March 24, 2011, http://www.vdare.com/articles/national-data-by-edwin-s-rubenstein-238.

24. For a discussion, see Jeffrey S. Passel and D'Vera Cohn, "Number of babies born in U.S. to unauthorized immigrants declines," *Fact Tank*, September 11, 2015, http://www.pewresearch.org/fact-tank/2015/09/11/number-of-babies-born-in-u-s-to-unauthorized-immigrants-declines/.

25. Lauren Carrol, "Trump: 'Many' scholars say 'anchor babies' aren't covered by Constitution," August 25, 2015, http://www.politifact.com/truth-o-meter/statements/2015/aug/25/donald-trump/trump-many-scholars-say-anchor-babies-arent-covere/.

26. See John Reid, "'Original Intent'? Anchor Baby Clause's Authors Explicitly Envisaged No Non-White Immigration," *VDARE*, September 3, 2015, http://www.vdare.com/articles/original-intent-anchor-baby-clauses-authors-explicitly-envisaged-no-non-white-immigration.

27. See, for example, Paul Finkelman, "Original Intent and the Fourteenth Amendment: Into the Black Hole of Constitutional Law," *Chicago Kent Law Review* 89 (2014): 1019, https://scholarship.kentlaw.iit.edu/cklawreview/vol89/iss3/7; and John Yoo, "On Citizenship, the 'Birthers' Are Right," August 22, 2015, http://www.nationalreview.com/article/422914/citizenship-birthers-are-right-john-yoo.

28. Finkelman, "Original Intent and the Fourteenth Amendment," and Yoo, "On Citizenship."

29. "PREAMBLE to the UNITED STATES CONSTITUTION: Who Are the Posterity?" Behold! Newsletter —1986, http://www.beholdonline.info/essays/preamble.html. See also https://www.facebook.com/notes/freeman-delusion-the-organized-pseudolegal-commercial-argument-in-australia/the-white-supremist-foundations-of-modern-opca-thought/529321887405412/.

30. Steve Sailer, "The Zeroth Amendment," *Taki's Magazine,* July 10, 2017, http://takimag.com/article/the_zeroth_amendment_steve_sailer/print#ixzz4yoRGbujR.

31. Francis X. Sullivan, "The Usurping Octopus of Jurisdictional Authority: The Legal Theories of the Sovereign Citizen Movement," *Wisconsin Law Review* (1999).

32. On magical thinking, see J. Eric Oliver and Thomas J. Wood, "Conspiracy Theories and the Paranoid Style(s) of Mass Opinion," *American Journal of Political Science* 58 (2014): 952. On conspiratorial thinking, see Cass R. Sunstein and Adam Vermeule, "Conspiracy Theories," *Political Philosophy* 17 (2009): 202.

33. Oliver and Wood, "Conspiracy Theories and the Paranoid Style(s) of Mass Opinion;" and Sunstein and Vermeule, "Conspiracy Theories." See also Michelle Theret, "Sovereign Citizens: A Homegrown Terrorist Threat and its Negative Impact on South Carolina," *South Carolina Law Review* 63 (2012): 853–868.

34. Leonard Zeskind, *Blood and Politics: The History of the White Nationalist Movement from the Margins to the Mainstream* (New York: Farrar, Straus and Giroux, 2012), 81.

35. See, for example, *United States v. Sullivan,* 274 U.S. 259 (1927).

36. Daniel Lessard Levin and Michael W. Mitchell, "A Law unto Themselves: The Ideology of the Common Law Court Movement," *South Dakota Law Review* 44 (1999): 9–36.

37. *United States v. Benson,* 561 F.3d 718 (7th Cir. 2009).

38. Levin and Mitchell, "A Law unto Themselves," 35.

39. Levin and Mitchell, "A Law unto Themselves," 35.

40. Joseph J. Thorndike, "Why Repealing the 16th Amendment Probably Wouldn't Matter," *Tax Notes,* May, 2013, http://jay.law.ou.edu/faculty/jforman/ABA/ABAMay2013ThorndikeArticle.pdf.

41. "Republican Platform 2016," Committee on Arrangements for the 2012 Republican National Convention, "We Believe in America," Doc 2012-18350, 2012 TNT 170-15, https://prod-cdn-static.gop.com/media/documents/DRAFT_12_FINAL%5b1%5d-ben_1468872234.pdf.

42. https://prod-cdn-static.gop.com/media/documents/DRAFT_12_FINAL[1]-ben_1468872234.pdf.

43. "Repeal the 16th Amendment," April 8, 2014, https://www.teapartypatriots.org/2014/04/08/repeal-the-16th-amendment/.

44. Kevin Drum, "Repealing the Sixteenth Amendment," August 22, 2011, http://www.motherjones.com/kevin-drum/2011/08/repealing-16th-amendment/.

45. Such as "Repeal the 16th Amendment Then Replace It with VAT," *Wall Street Journal,* November 26, 2015, https://www.wsj.com/articles/repeal-the-16th-amendment-then-replace-it-with-vat-1448572952. On the other hand, see J. Allen Tharp, "Time to repeal 16th Amendment," *San Antonio Press News,* May 31, 2013, http://www.mysanantonio.com/opinion/commentary/article/ -to-repeal-16th-Amendment-4566646.php.

46. David B. Levenstam, "Constitutional Challenge," *Reason,* January 1, 1999, http://reason.com/archives/1999/01/01/constitutional-challenge.

47. Rick Perry, *Fed Up! Our Fight to Save America from Washington* (New York: Little, Brown and Company, 2010), 38.

48. "Repeal the 17th Amendment," *The Campaign to Restore Federalism.com,* http://www.restorefederalism.org/.

49. Andrew Kaczynski, "Roy Moore in 2011: Getting rid of amendments after 10th would 'eliminate many problems'," CNN.com, December 11, 2017, http://www.cnn.com/2017/12/10/politics/kfile-roy-moore-aroostook-watchmen/index.html.

50. W. Cleon Skousen, *The Five Thousand Year Leap* (Malta, ID: National Center for Constitutional Studies, 2009), 163.

51. David Schleicher, "States' Wrongs," *Slate,* February 27, 2014, http://www.slate.com/articles/news_and_politics/jurisprudence/2014/02/conservatives_17th_amendment_repeal_effort_why_their_plan_will_backfire.html.

52. "Repeal the 17th Amendment," *The Campaign to Restore Federalism.com,* http://www.restorefederalism.org/.

53. For an overview, see Wendy J. Schiller, Charles Stewart III, and Benjamin Xiong, "U.S. Senate Elections Before the 17th Amendment: Political Party Cohesion and Conflict, 1871–1913," *Journal of Politics* 75, no. 835 (2013). Among other things, the authors conclude that Seventeenth Amendment has produced a Senate that is even less responsive to voters than it was under the indirect election system.

54. Schiller, Stewar, and Xiong, "U.S. Senate Elections Before the 17th Amendment."

55. Seyward Darby, "The Rise of the Valkyries: In the alt-right, women are the future, and the problem," *Harper's Magazine,* September 17, 2017. https://harpers.org/archive/2017/09/the-rise-of-the-valkyries/. See also Emma Bowman, "The Women Behind The 'Alt-Right,'" August 20, 2017, https://www.npr.org/2017/08/20/544134546/the-women-behind-the-alt-right.

56. https://twitter.com/richardbspencer/status/780590283675217920?lang=en

57. https://twitter.com/richardbspencer/status/780590283675217920?lang=en

58. Darby, "The Rise of the Valkyries."

59. Addy Baird, Zack Ford, Jack Jenkins, and Judd Legum, "Textbook co-authored by Roy Moore in 2011 says women shouldn't run for office," *Think Progress,* November 29, 2017, https://thinkprogress.org/moore-study-course-vison-forum-135402ed8816/.

60. Kim Lacapria, "Donald Trump Supporters are Calling to #Repealthe19th?" Snopes.com, October 13, 2016, https://www.snopes.com/2016/10/13/donald-trump-supporters-repealthe19th/.

CONCLUSION

1. Paul V. Murphy, *The Rebuke of History: The Southern Agrarians and American Conservative Thought* (Chapel Hill: University of North Carolina Press, 2001), 10.

2. John E. Finn, *Peopling the Constitution* (Lawrence: University Press of Kansas, 2014). See also Gary J. Jacobsohn, *Constitutional Identity* (Princeton: Princeton University Press, 2010); Michael Rosenfeld, "Constitutional Identity," in *The Oxford Handbook of Comparative Constitutional Law* edited by Michel Rosenfeld and András Sajó (New York: Oxford University Press, 2012).

3. David H. Bennett, *The Party of Fear: From Nativist Movements to the New Right in American History* (Chapel Hill: University of North Carolina Press, 1988), 3.

4. David Neiwert, "Ash on the Sills: the Patriot Movement," *Montana Law Review* 58, no. 1 (1997). See also Bennett, *The Party of Fear,* 3–4 and *passim.*

5. Michael Walzer, *What it Means to be an American: Essays on the American Experience* (New York: Marsilio Publishers, 1996), 111.

6. Thomas Jefferson to Samuel Kerchival, 1816, https://founders.archives.gov/documents/Jefferson/03-10-02-0255.

7. George Thomas, "Madison and the Perils of Populism," *National Affairs* 33 (Fall 2016), 155.

8. See, for example, Sanford Levinson, *Framed: America's 51 Constitutions and the Crisis of Governance* (New York: Oxford University Press, 2012); Jack M. Balkin, *Constitutional Redemption: Political Faith in an Unjust World* (Cambridge: Harvard University Press, 2011); Jeremy D. Bailey, "Should We Venerate That Which We Cannot Love? James Madison on Constitutional Imperfection," *Political Research Quarterly* 65, no. 732 (2012). See also Alexander Hamilton, James Madison, and John Jay; Clinton Rossiter, eds., *The Federalist Papers* (New York: Signet, 2003), #49 (Madison).

9. Theda Skocpol and Vanessa Williams, *The Tea Party and the Remaking of Republican Conservatism* (New York: Oxford University Press, 2016), 50–51.

10. Skocpol and Williams, *Remaking of Republican Conservatism*, 50–51.

11. See http://campconstitution.net/.

12. Christopher W. Schmidt, "Popular Constitutionalism on the Right: Lessons From the Tea Party," *Denver University Law Review* 88 (2011): 523–537.

13. For more information, or to enroll, see https://www.buildingblocksforliberty.org/constitution-boot-camp.html.

14. http://www.constitutionalbootcamp.com/.

15. For an especially interesting discussion of the Constitution in crisis, see this much praised work, surely the definitive treatment of such a fascinating and important subject: John E. Finn, *Constitutions in Crisis: Political Violence and the Rule of Law* (New York: Oxford University Press, 1991).

16. Laurie Cockerell, *Founders' Fables: Ten Tales for Future Patriots* (Fort Worth: Kinderfable Press, 2010).

17. A series of children's books designed to provide "a foundation of freedom for your child." https://tuttletwins.com/.

18. Kyle Smith, "Hey, hey, we're the rightees," *New York Post*, September 4, 2011. Also quoted in "Madison Rising," *Alchetron*, https://alchetron.com/Madison-Rising.

19. http://home.hiwaay.net/~becraft/INTRO.html.

20. Richard Abanes, *American Militias: Rebellion, Racism and Religion* (Downers Grove, IL: InterVarsity Press, 1996), 30.

21. John E. Finn, "On the Care and Maintenance of Constitutions," *Tulsa Law Review* 51: 301 (2016).

22. George Thomas, *The Founders and the Idea of National University: Constituting the American Mind* (New York: Cambridge University Press, 2014), 228–229.

23. Thomas, *Idea of National University*, 229–30.

24. Garrett Epps, "Stealing the Constitution: Inside the right's campaign to hijack our country's founding text—and how to fight back," *The Nation*, January 20, 2011, https://www.thenation.com/article/stealing-constitution/. As if to underscore the point, the Christian right agrees. See Paul B. Skousen, *How to Read the Constitution and the Declaration of Independence Audiobook* (Salt Lake City: Izzard Ink Publishing, 2016).

25. See, for example, this report: Maureen Costello, "Teaching Hard History," *Southern Poverty Law Center*, January 31, 2018, https://www.splcenter.org/20180131/teaching-hard-history.

26. My usage is similar to Francis Fukuyama's reference to the social virtues, by which he means the habits and dispositions that contribute to econom-

ic prosperity. Francis Fukuyama, *Trust: The Social Virtues and* the *Creation of Prosperity* (New York: The Free Press, 1995), 43–48. The claim is also similar to Tom R. Tyler's observation that "trust is an important facilitator of democratic government." Tyler, "Trust and Democratic Governance," in *Trust and Governance,* edited by Valerie Braithwaite and Margaret Levi (New York: Russel Sage Foundation, 2003), 269.

27. This conception of civic trust rests on the proposition that there is an important connection between some forms of interpersonal trust (and in particular what some have termed "generalized trust"), social capital, and political stability. Fukuyama includes as social virtues "honesty, reliability, cooperativeness, and a sense of duty to others." Fukuyama, *Trust: The Social Virtues,* 47. I have argued elsewhere that civility and tending are essential to maintaining the Civic Constitution. Finn, *Peopling the Constitution,* 1–31.

28. On friendship as a civic virtue see Aristotle, *Nicomachean Ethics,* trans. H. Rackham, (1926; repr. Cambridge, Mass., 1975); and also Danielle S. Allen, *Talking with Strangers: Anxieties of Citizenship since Brown v. Board of Education* (Chicago: University of Chicago Press, 2004), especially Chapter 9; Sibyl A. Schwarzenbach, "On Civic Friendship," *Ethics* 1, no. 107 (1996): 97–128.

29. Fukuyama, *Trust: The Social Virtues,* 48; and Danielle S. Allen, *Talking with Strangers: Anxieties of Citizenship since Brown v. Board of Education* (Chicago: University of Chicago Press, 2004).

30. Finn, *Peopling the Constitution,* 16–26.

31. As I argued in *Peopling the Constitution,* constitutional civility is a predisposition to reflect upon the meaning of the consitutional as a way of constituting the good life and as what can be constitutionally defended as the good society. Finn, *Peopling the Constitution* (Lawrence: University Press of Kansas, 2014), Essay One.

32. As I argued in *Peopling the Constitution,* constitutional civility is a predisposition to reflect upon the meaning of the constitution as a way of constituting the good life and as what can be constitutionally defended as the good society. Finn, *Peopling the Constitution* (Lawrence: University Press of Kansas, 2014), Essay One. David Neiwert, *Alt-America: The Rise of the Radical Right in the Age of Trump* (New York: Verso, 2017), 374.

33. Neiwert, *Alt-America,* 374–375.

34. Allen, note 28 *supra* at p. xiii. See also Schwarzenbach, "On Civic Friendship," *Ethics* 1, no. 107 (1996): 97.

35. Allen, *Talking with Strangers,* xiii.

36. Robert D. Putnam, *Bowling Alone: The Collapse and Revival of American Community* (New York: Simon and Shuster, 2001).

37. Ray Oldenburg, *The Great Good Place: Cafes, Coffee Shops, Bookstores, Bars, Hair Salons, and Other Hangouts at the Heart of a Community* (Boston: Marlowe and Company, 1999).

38. For a concise overview, see Christopher Beem, "Civic Virtue and Civil Society," *Los Angeles Times,* May 27, 1996, http://articles.latimes.com/1996-05-27/local/me-8978_1_civil-society.

39. Alexander Hamilton, James Madison, and John Jay; *The Federalist Papers,* ed. Clinton Rossiter (New York: Signet, 2003), #49 (Madison).

40. Robert Brent Toplin, *Radical Conservatism: The Right's Political Religion* (Lawrence: University Press of Kansas, 2006), 266.

41. Max Lerner, "Constitution and Court as Symbols," *Yale Law Journal* 46, no. 8 (1937) 1290–1291, http://digitalcommons.law.yale.edu/ylj/vol46/iss8/3.

42. Sotirios A Barber, *Constitutional Failure* (Lawrence: University Press of Kansas, 2014), 20.

43. Barber, *Constitutional Failure*, 20.

44. Alexander Hamilton, James Madison, and John Jay; *The Federalist Papers,* ed. Clinton Rossiter, (New York: Signet, 2003), #2 (Jay).

INDEX

absolutist approach, 82
accommodationist understanding, 98–99
Adams, John Quincy, 131
admiralty law, 9
Alien and Sedition Acts of 1798, 60
Alito, Justice, 109, 225n29
Alt-America, 3, 4; conservatives
    populating, 15; as white, 3, 4
Alt-common law, 145, 146, 149, 151
Alt-constitution, 3, 4–5, 8–11, 11, 209n31,
    237n90; alternative constitutional
    history as, 161; Amendments not
    included in, 169; antebellum
    constitution for, 50–51; Bible and
    Declaration of Independence with,
    167; Christian bent to, 72; citizenship
    and Constitution versus, 169; civic
    virtues undermined by, 200–201; Civil
    War, Reconstruction and, 5–6, 170;
    common law courts for, 11, 141;
    compact theory built into, 71;
    constitutional fundamentalism in, 9;
    Constitution and, 13, 195; Corwin
    amendment and, 172–173; education
    efforts by, 197–198; executive branch
    favored by, 52; far right faith items of,
    8; Founders and, 36, 200; Fourteenth
    rejected by, 6, 11, 170; on freedom of
    religion, 99; freedom of speech
    provision in, 10; free exercise clause as
    Christian in, 101; government

legitimacy and role in, 35; identity as
    thread of, 195; militias and, 130;
    missionary zeal for, 5; principles of,
    8–9; racism, bigotry, sexism concealed
    in, 13; rigidity of, 103; for states' rights,
    50–51, 53; Tenth Amendment,
    federalism and, 56; tenth amendment
    of, 57; Thomas opinion as cornerstone
    for, 99; TONA included in, 171;
    unalienable rights in, 43–44, 111;
    unitary executive embraced for, 52–53
AlternativeRight.com (website), 27–28
Alt-establishment clause, 96
Alt-fifth amendment, 121
Alt-first amendment, 95, 96, 102; First
    Amendment disagreeing with, 82–83;
    as full speech protection, 83; hate
    speech and, 85–86; line between
    speech and conduct in, 132; minorities
    and persons of color not protected by,
    99–100, 133; no protection offered by,
    131–132; no speech limitations in, 79,
    83, 84; paramilitary training protected
    by, 130; on state favoring equality, 52;
    whites and, 52, 75, 76, 77, 83, 89, 91,
    100
Alt-freedom of speech, 35, 89, 91, 93–94;
    Alt-first amendment and, 79, 84, 95,
    132
Alt-free exercise clause, 96, 100